Grand Strategy

'Grand Strategy' confuses many. It sounds grandiose but really it's just a way to solve certain kinds of problems. Grand strategy's big idea – and its big attraction - is that it offers the possibility of shaping events rather than being shaped by them. Some grand strategies succeed, some fail dismally. America's Cold War grand strategy triumphed but then the nation's Iraq grand strategy proved at best ineffective. How can we avoid future grand strategy catastrophes and instead make success more likely?

Grand strategies begin in the minds of people. They are simply problem-solving ideas. Drawing on recent studies in cognition, and integrating contemporary international relations theories, this book develops a lucid and structured way for us to make better grand strategy. The penalties for failure are too high, the promise of better tomorrows too important to turn a blind eye to grand strategy. We all need to get better at it whether for devising new grand strategies or critiquing those our country – or organisation - want us to be part of.

Peter Layton is a Visiting Fellow at the Griffith Asia Institute, Griffith University. He has a doctorate from the University of New South Wales on grand strategy and has taught on the topic at the Eisenhower College, US National Defence University. He has extensive defence experience, and for his work at the Pentagon on force structure matters was awarded the US Secretary of Defense's Exceptional Public Service Medal. For his academic work he was awarded a Fellowship to the European University Institute, Italy. He contributes regularly to the public policy debate on defence and foreign affairs issues and is widely published.

Grand Strategy

Peter Layton

Contents

Figures

Tables

1

Introduction: Present Failings, New Approaches

In 1934 the British Government adopted a sophisticated grand strategy of deterrence and engagement to try to avoid fighting a major war with Germany. In 1965 the Soviet government embarked on a grand strategy that sought to make it an accepted equal partner with America in the management of global affairs. In 2002 the American government announced a grand strategy to try to bring democracy to many Middle Eastern countries with Iraq being the first.

All three grand strategies produced dismal results. The British grand strategy ended in global conflict, the end of the British Empire and the demise of Britain as a first-rate power, exactly the outcomes the grand strategy was designed to avoid. The Soviet grand strategy was not only unsuccessful but arguably set in train events that led to the downfall of the USSR. The American occupation of Iraq partly succeeded but the costs in unintended consequences, blood, treasure and prestige were so high that the grand strategy was hurriedly abandoned.

These grand strategies spanned different kinds of government - a great colonial empire, a communist authoritarian regime and an extended commercial republic - but the policies these states implemented were all alike in not achieving their intended outcomes. The people that devised these grand strategies did not intend this. Failure was not their goal, but these were massive failures. How can we make better grand strategies and try to avoid catastrophes?

The first step is to appreciate what 'grand strategy' is. While, a strategy generally focuses on immediate concerns, a grand strategy looks well beyond this to a desired future and how to reach it. It is a conceptual roadmap that imagines a series of successive actions that could potentially improve - if only from the activist state's viewpoint - the political relations existing between the different states involved.

States mainly use grand strategies to improve their relations with a particular state or group of states, although some occasionally also boldly try to change aspects of the whole international system. There are other approaches (discussed in Chapter 8) that can be used to respond to events but a grand strategy is a methodology for purposefully shaping tomorrow.

There is a second important aspect often overlooked. A grand strategy applies the full array of the instruments of national power (the 'means') including diplomatic, informational, military and economic measures. In contrast, a strategy focuses on applying a single type of instrument. Moreover unlike strategy, a grand strategy also involves building the material and non-material resources needed for implementation. These resources once developed are allocated to the subordinate strategies that individually direct each instrument of national power in accordance with the overarching grand strategy. Without this guidance, these lower-level strategies would be uncoordinated, work at odds with each other and be unlikely to succeed. Reflecting this essential function, Colin Gray declares: "all strategy is grand strategy."[1]

The most common way for governmental policymakers to formulate new grand strategies seems to be through applying historical analogies to current problems. People look backwards, choose an historical event and the responses made to address it, and then bring forward this understanding and impose it onto current problems and emerging issues. This approach is particularly useful for busy people as the need for deep, time-consuming analysis is avoided with preprocessed solutions quickly mapped onto new dilemmas. Moreover, this approach works with well-known human cognitive biases towards readily perceiving matches and easily disregarding differences. Unfortunately, numerous significant strategic failures can be traced to the use of historical analogies.[2]

---

1. Colin S. Gray, *The Strategy Bridge: Theory for Practice*; Oxford: Oxford University Press, 2010, p. 28.
2. Yuen Foong Khong, *Analogies at War: Korea, Munich, Dien Bien Phu, and the Vietnam Decisions of 1965;* Princeton: Princeton University Press, 1992, p. 9.

A recent example was their use by the George W. Bush administration in planning the 2003 American invasion of Iraq. For this administration the collapse of communism in Eastern Europe at the end of the Cold War showed that for democracy to arise only the removal of an authoritarian regime was needed; the breakup of Yugoslavia in the 1990s showed that allies would readily help with stabilization and reconstruction; the recent Afghanistan war showed how easy regime change could be; Nazi Germany showed that unaddressed threats worsen so Saddam's Iraq needed near-term action and lastly as Al-Qaeda had used terrorism against the American homeland therefore so would Saddam Hussein.[3]

Crucially, such misuse should not be disregarded as only being limited to those with a limited knowledge of history or a rigorous academic education in the discipline. Some of the 'best and brightest' academics served as advisers during the Kennedy and Johnson administrations but it seemed "the temptation of careless use of historical knowledge overpowers acquired... methodological skills."[4] The principal problem is that looking backwards at history a comprehensive understanding of the problem extending over time can be seen. In looking at an emerging problem its specific nature and key characteristics are literally unknown as they are still evolving. Choosing a historical analogy as being an appropriate guide to the future is akin to gambling on the results of a future sporting event. Success in either is serendipitous at best.

Given the well-known failures of historical analogies, think tanks and scholars have embraced an alternative approach. There is now a plethora of books, papers and articles that propose

Richard E. Neustadt and Ernest R. May, *Thinking in Time: The Uses of History for Decisionmakers* New York: The Free Press, 1986, p. xiii.
3. Steven Metz, *Decisionmaking in Operation Iraqi Freedom: Removing Saddam Hussein by Force*, ed. John R. Martin, Operation Iraqi Freedom Key Decisions Monograph Series; Carlisle: Strategic Studies Institute, U.S. Army War College, 2010, p. 44-46. See also: David B. Macdonald, *Thinking History, Fighting Evil: Neoconservatives and the Perils of Analogy in American Politics*; Lanham: Rowman & Littlefield Publishers, 2009.
4. Yaacov Y. I. Vertzberger, 'Foreign Policy Decisionmakers as Practical-Intuitive Historians: Applied History and Its Shortcomings ', *International Studies Quarterly* Vol. 30, No. 2, June 1986, pp. 223-47, p. 241.

policymakers across various states adopt a particular grand strategy to address some specific contemporary challenge.[5] This approach has several serious shortcomings.

Firstly, the policymakers may hold important information about the problem not available to the proposed grand strategy's author, which invalidates the solution offered. Secondly, there could be political aspects concerning the problem that the author is unaware of, or considers differently to the policymakers involved. Thirdly, in aiming to convince rather than educate, the prescribed solutions offered are generally derived from a particular view of how the world functions.[6] The policymakers considering grand strategy alternatives however may not necessarily hold the same worldview or be convinced that it is the only one to examine the issue against. Fourthly, the authors mostly advocate solutions based on a worldview appropriate to a single specific circumstance. The solutions are then unlikely to be useful when people encounter other situations, especially when the author's worldview merges theoretical perspectives in an eclectic, idiosyncratic manner.[7] Lastly, most of these prescriptive publications consider only how the grand strategy advocated will induce change; the development of the resources needed to implement the grand strategy is generally

5. Examples include: Robert J. Art, *A Grand Strategy for America*; Ithaca: Cornell University Press, 2003. G. John Ikenberry, 'An Agenda for Liberal International Renewal', in Michèle A. Flournoy and Shawn Brimley (eds.), *Finding Our Way: Debating American Grand Strategy*; Washington: Center for a New American Security, 2008, pp. 43-60. Christopher Layne, *The Peace of Illusions: American Grand Strategy from 1940 to the Present*; Ithaca: Cornell University Press, 2006. Robert J. Lieber, *The American Era: Power and Strategy for the 21st Century*; New York: Cambridge University Press, 2005.
6. There are multiple examples of this in Michael E. Brown et al. (eds.), *America's Strategic Choices: Revised Edition*; Cambridge: The MIT Press; 2000.
7. Posen's grand strategy of restraint proposal in Michèle Flournoy's and Shawn Brimley's *Finding Our Way* is an example of this. The proposal while built around state-centric realism carefully integrates identity politics that in being 'first image' would not normally be considered Posen's proposal arguably fits only the unique worldview he has devised. Barry R. Posen, 'A Grand Strategy of Restraint', in Michèle A Flournoy and Shawn Brimley (eds.), *Finding Our Way: Debating American Grand Strategy*; Washington: Center for a New American Security, June 2008, pp. 81-102, pp. 84-86.

assumed.[8]   This approach aids conciseness but is a notable shortcoming especially in times of economic and financial turbulence.

Both the historical analogies and the advocacy approach share a fundamental failing. They each propose a take-it-or-leave solution, not a way for people to better understand and apply the information they themselves possess about a problem. Historical analogies and advocacy works offer pre-processed unique solutions not a problem-solving method useable in many situations. And yet, support with problem solving is what people actually need when developing strategies.   After examining such high-level policymaking across several decades, Alexander George found people could be best assisted by giving them a means to methodically investigate complex problems: "a correct diagnosis of a policy problem should precede and - as in much of medical practice - is usually a prerequisite for making the best choice from among policy options."[9]

Accordingly, to address 'how can we make better grand strategies', this book develops an optimized grand strategy diagnostic process. The aim of this process is to assist busy people make sound judgments about complex strategy problems. Such a process:

> "is not itself a strategy but...the starting point for constructing a strategy. The usefulness of an abstract model for policy-making is limited to providing the basic framework for understanding the general requirements for designing and implementing a strategy. The abstract model identifies...the general logic...needed for the strategy to be successful."[10]

8. Examples of this are found Barry R. Posen and Andrew L. Ross, 'Competing Visions of U.S. Grand Strategy', *International Security,* Vol. 21, No. 3, Winter 1996/97, pp. 3-51; and Pascal Vennesson, 'Competing Visions for the European Union Grand Strategy ', *European Foreign Affairs Review,* Vol. 15, No. 1, 2010, pp. 57-75.
9. Alexander L. George, *Bridging the Gap: Theory and Practice in Foreign Policy*; Washington: United States Institute of Peace, 1993, p. 17-18.
10. Ibid., p. 118.

The process is designed to help people structure their initial thinking about a grand strategy problem and provide a useful starting point for developing alternative courses of action. Using the process, people can ascertain what is relevant amongst the typically large amount of information presented about the problem, how all this fits together and what further confirmatory information should be sought.

The envisaged diagnostic process offers a new way to better structure our thinking about grand strategy but in so doing draws attention to another area George was deeply influential in. Much of his early work on decision-making was on cognition, particularly the mental biases that influence how policymakers interpret information and develop policy solutions.[11] Each individual has a unique set of beliefs that leads to information being screened and processed in different ways. A nation's international policies may best be seen as being addressed to the "image of the external world" as perceived by the policymakers concerned, not necessarily simply in response to the objectively real world.[12] George's work indicates that for a diagnostic process to be effective it needs to be designed to take into account that the thinking of policymakers is impacted by their beliefs and cognitive biases. The cognitive processes of policymakers will influence the use they make - and can make - of the diagnostic process. *How* policymakers think about issues is as important as *what* they think about.

There is though considerably more to strategic-level decision-making than just the initial thinking of the people involved, including small group dynamics, organizational processes, bureaucratic politics, culture, national identity and domestic politics. The interplay of these other various aspects determine which ideas are eventually selected for implementation, but they do not in

11. Alexander L. George, 'The "Operational Code": A Neglected Approach to the Study of Political Leaders and Decision-Making', *International Studies Quarterly*, Vol. 13, No. 2, 1969, pp. 190-222.
12. Alexander L. George, *Presidential Decisionmaking in Foreign Policy: The Effective Use of Information and Advice* Boulder: Westview Press, 1980, p. 55.

themselves generate the preliminary ideas.[13] These ideas spring from the thinking of individuals, not from the group and organizational processes that decide which particular ideas live or die. The UNESCO Constitution observes that: " wars begin in the minds of men...."[14] Arguably, so do grand strategies: they originate in people's minds.

To devise an optimized diagnostic process, this book uses a design methodology focused on the principal function of grand strategy from a policymaking perspective: inducing purposeful change in the political relations existing between the different states involved.[15] This function is subjected to deductive reasoning to develop two typologies: one that relates types of grand strategy to specific change methods and a second that addresses developing the power needed to implement a grand strategy.

Chapter Two deeply examines the meaning of grand strategy from a policymaking viewpoint. The Chapter develops the definition of grand strategy as: *the art of developing and applying diverse forms of power in an effective and efficient way to try to purposefully change the order existing between two or more intelligent and adaptive entities.* Chapter Three combines this understanding with

---

13. A seminal work in Foreign Policy Analysis, Graham Allison's book explaining why specific policies were chosen to address the 1962 Cuba Missile Crisis, well illustrates this matter. Individuals initially determined a range of alternative courses of action. These several potential courses of action were then debated and analysed in groups of varying sizes with the final decisions taken on which to adopt being influenced, so the book determined, by numerous interacting organizational processes and the impact of bureaucratic politics. Graham T. Allison, *Essence of Decision: Explaining the Cuban Missile Crisis*; Boston: Little Brown and Company, 1971.
14. 'Unesco Constitution', viewed 24 June 2013 portal.unesco.org/en/ev.php-URL_ID=15244&URL_DO=DO_TOPIC&URL_SECTION=201.html.
15. A design methodology is conceptually different to that used in many International Relations studies focused on explaining why past events occurred. It focuses on approaches to intentionally creating change, synthesizes diverse knowledge, integrates empirical and normative thought, assumes people have bounded cognition, employs heuristics, and uses flexible placements to orient thinking rather than fixed-meaning categories. Gerry Stoker, 'Blockages on the Road to Relevance: Why Has Political Science Failed to Deliver?', *European Political Science,* Vol. 9, No. 1, 2010, pp. S72-S84, p. S80-S82.

specific International Relations theoretical perspectives to develop the grand strategy diagnostic process. The process is then critiqued to determine if there are other potential alternatives that could be more efficacious. This chapter provides the confidence that the diagnostic process while simple is not simplistic. For busy policymakers with limited time, a grand strategy diagnostic process framework that is easy to apply is essential but it must also not mislead. Chapter Four then sets out the grand strategy diagnostic process and includes an easy-to-apply diagrammatic form.

Chapters Five, Six and Seven examine practical examples of each of the three different types of grand strategy: denial, engagement and reform. Each chapter applies the diagnostic process to historical case studies to make clear the particular grand strategy's design and operating logic. Some unsuccessful grand strategies are included as these bring out some particularly important design aspects. Chapter Eight concludes in discussing grand strategy as a practical problem-solving method when compared with some alternative approaches that in certain circumstances may be more suitable.

2

The Idea Of Grand Strategy

Grand strategies have been used for a very long time. Historical studies have analysed the grand strategies by the Romans 1st-3rd Century AD, during Phillip II's reign in Spain 1554-1598, in the Russian Empire during 1650-1831 and by the English in the War of the Spanish Succession 1702-1712.[1] The modern understanding of grand strategy though is derived from the more recent experiences of World War One, World War Two and the Cold War.[2] These major events shaped how we think about grand strategy today and how it's now used to solve problems.

Grand strategy is a term whose meaning has progressively evolved across time and through use. It might initially be introduced by breaking it down into firstly 'strategy' and then as modified by the adjective 'grand'. Strategy is a word that causes great confusion. There are countless numbers of books that try to reveal its secrets and complexities through applying it to specific issues but many of these simply complicate matters. If we shift to thinking instead about the fundamental concepts involved, the term can become much clearer.

---

1. Kimberly Kagan, 'Redefining Roman Grand Strategy', *The Journal of Military History,* Vol. 70, No. 2, April 2006, pp. 333-62. Geoffrey Parker, *The Grand Strategy of Philip II*; New Haven: Yale University Press, 2000. John P. Ledonne, *The Grand Strategy of the Russian Empire, 1650-1831*; Oxford: Oxford University Press, 2004. John B. Hattendorf, *England in the War of the Spanish Succession: A Study of the English View and Conduct of Grand Strategy, 1702-1712*; New York: Garland, 1987.
2. The expression was used in the 19th century, principally in the sense of military strategy in the Jominian tradition with its emphasis on lines of operation and the taking of territory. Examples include: James H. Ward, *A Manual of Naval Tactics: Together with a Brief Critical Analysis of the Principal Modern Naval Battles*; New York: D. Appleton & Company, 1859, p. 153. George Ward Nichols, *The Story of the Great March: From the Diary of a Staff Officer*; New York: Harper & Brothers 1865, p. 17. W.T.Sherman, 'The Grand Strategy of the War of the Rebellion', *The Century Illustrated Monthly Magazine,* Vol. 36, 1888, pp. 597-98.

The crucial issue that defines a 'strategy' is that it involves interacting with intelligent and adaptive others, whether friends, neutrals or adversaries. This social interaction though is of a particular kind. Each party involved continuously modifies their position, intent and actions based on the perceptions and actions of the others participating. Here the arcane world of game theory has something useful to say. These interactions "...are *essentially bargaining situations*...in which the ability of one participant to gain his ends is dependent...on the choices or decisions the other participant will make."[3]

In operation a strategy constantly evolves in response to the other actors implementing their own countervailing or supportive strategies. Edward Luttwak termed this "the paradoxical logic of strategy" where successful actions cannot be repeated as the other party adapts in response to ensure the same outcome cannot be gained in this way again.[4] Strategy is simply a particular form of interactive social activity where victory comes from bargaining with those involved.

If this is what strategy is, its scope is encompassed in a simple oft-used model. Art Lykke deconstructed the art of strategy into ends, ways and means where the 'ends' are the objectives, the 'ways' are the courses of actions and the 'means' are the instruments of national power.[5] The 'means' are used in certain 'ways' to achieve specific 'ends'. All three parts are important however some confuse matters in trying to simplify this even further.

Some try to think of strategy as being a balance between ends and means. Christopher Layne for example writes that "grand strategy is simple: it is the process by which a state matches ends to

3. Thomas C. Schelling, *The Strategy of Conflict*; New York: A Galaxy Book, Oxford University Press 1963, p. 5.
4. Edward N. Luttwak, *Strategy: The Logic of War and Peace*; Cambridge: Belknap Press, 1987, p. 7-65.
5. Jr. Arthur F. Lykke, *Military Strategy: Theory and Application*; Carlisle: U.S. Army War College, 1989, p. 3-9. Harry R. Yarger, 'Toward a Theory of Strategy: Art Lykke and the Army War College Strategy Model', in Jr. J. Boone Bartholomees (ed.), *U.S. Army War College Guide to National Security Policy and Strategy*; Carlisle Barracks: Strategic Studies Institute, June 2006.

means."[6] Historically however, nations with great means have often found it surprisingly difficult to convert these into achieving their desired ends.[7] Given its great means, the U.S. should have readily been able to achieve its objectives in Iraq after the country was occupied in 2003 or indeed in the 1960s in South Vietnam. The outcomes actually achieved though suggest that strategy is more than the simple balancing of ends and means. The ways also need consideration.

Sir Lawrence Freedman incorporates this viewpoint in observing that strategy is "about getting more out of a situation than the starting balance of power would suggest."[8] Good strategy then involves an astute course of action, a shrewd 'way', that is additive to the available power; the impact of the means is magnified. In contrast, poor strategy subtracts from the available means; it destroys the power you have. This might all be simplified into Ends = Ways + Means albeit it is essential to recall the inherent impossibility of actually summing unlike objects. Nevertheless, the formula highlights that if a strategy fails it may not be solely due to inadequate means; there could be shortcomings in the way the means are used as well. If the means are meagre, the ends may still be achievable through using the means in more clever ways without needing to adjust the ends downwards to be bought into balance. Freedman writes that such:

> "…underdog strategies, in situations where the starting balance of power would predict defeat, provide the real tests of creativity. Such strategies often look to the possibility of success through the application of a superior intelligence which takes advantage of the boring, ponderous, muscle-

6. Christopher Layne, 'Rethinking American Grand Strategy: Hegemony or Balance of Power in the Twenty-First Century?', *World Policy Journal,* Vol. 15, No. 2, Summer 1998, pp. 8-28, p. 8.
7. Critics of this power-as-resources model decry this as a 'vehicle fallacy'. David Macdonald, 'The Power of Ideas in International Relations', in Nadine Godehardt and Dirk Nabers (eds.), *Regional Powers and Regional Orders*; Abingdon: Routledge, 2011, pp. 33-48, p. 34.
8. Lawrence Freedman, *Strategy: A History*; Oxford: Oxford University Press, 2013, p. xii.

bound approach by those who take their superior resources for granted."[9]

The word 'strategy' is ultimately derived from ancient Greek and in originally concerning the art or skills of the general is directly related to the 'ways' in Lykke's simple model. Importantly however, the addition of the adjective 'grand' to 'strategy' does not in some manner amplify the 'ways' used. Instead, adding 'grand' to 'strategy' enlarges the term mainly as concerns ends and means. The reason for this lies in the origins of the term.

In the early years of the 20th Century strategic thinkers began to consider that the word 'strategy' alone was becoming increasingly inadequate. Grand strategy was implied in the works of Alfred Thayer Mahan in the late 19th Century however, the modern meaning of the term was first made explicit by fellow navalist Sir Julian Stafford Corbett in 1906.[10] In his "Strategical Terms and Definitions Used in Lectures on Naval History" Corbett divided strategy into two parts: major or grand strategy dealing with the "whole resources of the nation for war" including military, economic, diplomatic and political matters, and minor strategy focused on operational plans.[11]

Corbett's perceptiveness was not fully appreciated until the First World War. The war ushered in a new style of conflict that was not just between armies but rather between whole nations and which necessitated the mobilization, organization and control of the societies and economies involved. After the conflict it seemed likely that all future such wars would be 'total' and draw on the full potentialities of societies and economies to the point of exhaustion.[12] Given this, earlier conceptions of strategy were now considered seriously out of step with the demands of the times.[13] In 1929

---

9. Ibid.
10. Lukas Milevski, *The Modern Evolution of Grand Strategic Thought*; Oxford: Oxford University Press, 2016, p. 27-44.
11. Julian S. Corbett, *Some Principles of Maritime Strategy* Classics of Sea Power Series; Annapolis: United States Naval Institute, 1911 (reprinted 1988), p. 308.
12. Maurice Pearton, *The Knowledgeable State: Diplomacy, War and Technology since 1830*; London: Burnett Books, 1982, p. 155-76.
13. H. De Watteville, 'The Conduct of Modern War', *The RUSI Journal,* Vol. 75, No. 497, 1930, pp. 70-81, p. 70-73.

British General Sir Frederick Maurice wrote that strategy needed to be: "defined anew to meet our broadened views of what the conduct of war entails...."[14] Strategy as a term was in need of some elaboration in order to give the abstract thinking of policymakers, military staffs and officials more precision, clarity and sophistication

In his 1923 book "The Reformation of War", Colonel, later Major General, Fuller introduced three different types of strategy: grand, major and minor. His grand strategy directed a nation's "...military aspects, the moral [sic] of the civil population, the commercial and industrial resources...[and] the element of spirit".[15] This was an expansive vision that extended the notion of strategy well beyond military matters deep into the nation's civil fabric. Fuller's articulation of "the first duty of a grand strategist" well illustrates this; it was to "appreciate the commercial and financial position of his country; to discover what its resources and liabilities are..."[16]

For Fuller, grand strategy was to be undertaken at the highest level of the Government and involved coordinating the material and social forces of the Empire in peacetime so as to be well prepared for any future conflict. In this Fuller drew upon the seminal thinking of the 19th Century German strategist Carl von Clausewitz who saw war as an instrument of policy; war for Clausewitz had its own grammar "but not its own logic."[17] Fuller agreed with the underlying judgment, conceiving grand strategy similarly as an instrument of government policy.[18]

Basil Liddell-Hart made Fuller's innovative concept more coherent in his 1929 book "Decisive Wars of History". In so doing,

---

14. Sir Frederick Maurice, *British Strategy: A Study of the Application of the Principles of War*; London Constable and Co, 1929, p. 62.
15. Col. J.F.C. Fuller, *The Reformation of War (2nd Edition)*; London: Hutchinson and Co, 1923 p. 214.
16. Ibid., p. 218.
17. Carl Von Clausewitz, *On War: Edited and Translated by Michael Howard and Peter Paret*; Princeton: Princeton University Press, 1984, p. 605.
18. Jay Luvaas, 'Clausewitz, Fuller and Liddell Hart', *Journal of Strategic Studies*, Vol. 9, No. 2-3, 1986, pp. 197-212, pp. 200-01.

he provided what has proved to be a seminal description of grand strategy:

> "...the term 'grand strategy' serves to bring out the sense of 'policy in execution.' For the role of 'grand strategy' is to co-ordinate and direct all the resources of a nation towards the attainment of the political object...defined by national policy. Grand strategy should both calculate and develop the economic resources and manpower of the nation.... So also with the moral resources, for to foster and fortify the will to win and to endure is as important as to possess the more concrete forms of power. And it should regulate the distribution of power between the several Services and between the Services and industry. Nor is this all, for fighting power is but one of the instruments of grand strategy. It should take account of and apply the power of financial pressure, diplomatic pressure, commercial pressure, and, not least, ethical pressure to weaken the opponent's will. A good cause is a sword as well as a buckler. Furthermore, while the horizon of strategy is bounded by the war, grand strategy looks beyond the war to the subsequent peace. It should not only combine the various instruments, but so regulate their use so as to avoid damage to the future state of peacefulness."[19]

Grand strategy accordingly has come to be envisioned as being more expansive than strategy principally in terms of the ends sought, the diversity of means used and in considering how these means are developed. Importantly, the core of what strategy is, the 'ways' seem overlooked.

The Ends of Grand Strategy

Liddell-Hart's formulation brings out that grand strategy has grand ambitions in trying to purposefully construct a preferred future

19. B.H. Liddell-Hart, *The Decisive Wars of History: A Study in Strategy*; London: G.Bell & Sons, 1929, p. 150. This description would be repeated with a few minor word changes in his later, more famous work: B.H. Liddell-Hart, *Strategy*, 2nd Revised edn.; New York: Penguin, 1991, pp. 321-22.

order beyond the current problems. Grand strategy involves undertaking a planned series of successive actions to create a preferred world at some defined future time. It is "a conceptual road map" that leads to a favored destination.[20]

Steven Metz neatly combines this roadmap image with grand strategy's interactive nature in declaring it: "...entails [creating] order extended in time, space, and milieus. [It] attempts to impose coherence and predictability on an inherently disorderly environment composed of thinking, reacting, competing, and conflicting entities."[21] A grand strategy accordingly attempts to bring an improvement to the international order existing between the various states involved, even if this improvement is only from the activist state's viewpoint.

International order is a somewhat vexed term, used in many different ways and sometimes conceived very expansively. For the practical business of grand strategy making though, it can be used very precisely. John Ikenberry in examining potential American grand strategies defined international order as "a political formation in which settled rules and arrangements exist between states to guide their interaction."[22] This definition usefully sets the boundaries of international order in terms of what policymakers can practically use grand strategies for. Grand strategy's primary purpose is to attempt to change the current 'political formation' into a more desirable one from the implementing state's perspective. Grand strategy is fundamentally about inducing change.

There are further nuances that may be discerned. Ikenberry looks outward from the state as policymakers do. His international orders are 'political formations' that each state creates with others, individually or in some larger grouping. This approach helpfully focuses attention on the importance of defining the object of a grand strategy. The ends of a grand strategy need to be quite clear on who

20. Colin Dueck, *Reluctant Crusaders: Power, Culture, and Change in American Grand Strategy*; Princeton: Princeton University Press, 2006, p. 11.
21. Steven Metz, *Iraq and the Evolution of American Strategy*; Washington: Potomac Books, Inc., 2008, p. xviii.
22. G. John Ikenberry, *Liberal Leviathan: The Origins, Crisis, and Transformation of the American World Order*; Princeton: Princeton University Press, 2011, p. 36.

the target is, in terms of sub-state actors, single states, alliance partners, regional groupings or the complete international system.

Ikenberry's definition considers order as the 'settled rules and arrangements between states.' The use of 'settled' suggests that the rules and arrangements are at least tacitly agreed to between the parties involved and have some degree of durability. This introduces the notion of time. Grand strategies are sometimes described as being long-term albeit there is little discussion concerning how long their outcomes should be sustained to be considered successful. This has echoes in the somewhat narrower debate about the decisiveness of battles and war; in such circumstances achieving finality over the longer term is rare.[23]

Success, in terms of changing international order to that which is desired, needs to focus on being 'settled' in a qualitative not quantitative sense. If the new order created is both acknowledged by those involved and becomes the basis on which their future actions are undertaken, then the original grand strategy may be considered successful. This measure of success, while usefully generic, has some shortcomings in that a 'settled' order might still be actively revised at some indeterminate time. This problem seems inherent, as policymaking involves future actions and what these may be is ultimately unknowable.

Delving more deeply into the notion that grand strategy aims to change the present order into a more desirable one however raises some concerns. Firstly, the focus on changing the extant international order between those states involved may imply that grand strategy as a methodology is ill-suited to *status quo* powers. The counter is that the *status quo* does not just happen, rather it must be maintained and sustained. The international system contains some two hundred states and innumerable sub-state groups all jostling for their place in the sun and to advance their objectives. In such a complex and dynamic system, trying to stop change requires applying power in a measured and focused way rather than avoiding

23.   Brian Bond, *The Pursuit of Victory: From Napoleon to Saddam Hussein*; Oxford: Oxford University Press, 1996, pp. 199-204. Russell F. Weigley, *The Age of Battles: The Quest for Decisive Warfare from Breitenfeld to Waterloo*; London: Pimlico, 1991, pp. 537-40.

using power. Grand strategy accordingly is useful for *status quo* powers that simply want the current order to remain unchanged for as Donald Kagan remarks: "A persistent and repeated error through the ages has been the failure to understand that preservation of peace requires active effort, planning and the expenditure of resources, and sacrifice...."[24]

Secondly, the idea of a grand strategy being directly determined by the future international order sought may seem at odds with notions of a grand strategy instead being directly determined by the 'national interest.' Anne-Marie Slaughter for example sees the "initial step in developing any grand strategy is to identify vital national interests that the [grand] strategy must protect and advance."[25] In being used in such a manner, 'national interest' is intended to denote a policy that is beneficial to the nation as a whole not solely to individuals or groups within it, to other nations or to some greater ideological good. The term has however long been criticized as somewhat meaningless.

In 1952 Arnold Wolfers in a seminal article complained that: "...when political formulas such as "national interest"...gain popularity they need to be scrutinized with particular care. They may not mean the same things to different people. They may not have any precise meaning at all. ...they may be permitting everyone to label whatever policy [they] favour with an attractive and possibly deceptive name."[26] Echoing this, in a detailed examination of the grand strategy used by the UK to change the international order between it and the states of Western Europe in 1945-1963, Alan Milward found that the concept of national interest was of no

24. Donald Kagan, *On the Origins of War: And the Preservation of Peace*; New York: Anchor Books, 1996, p. 567.
25. Anne-Marie Slaughter, 'America's Path: Grand Strategy for the Next Administration', in Richard Fontaine and Kristin M. Lord (eds.), *America's Path: Grand Strategy for the Next Administration*; Washington: Center for a New American Security, May 2012, pp. 43-56, p. 46.
26. Arnold Wolfers, '"National Security" as an Ambiguous Symbol', *Political Science Quarterly,* Vol. 67, No. 4, December 1952, pp. 481-502, p. 481.

practical use to the policymakers of the time.[27] As declarations of 'national interest' included no causal path by which they were realised, he considered such pronouncements more akin to expressing a national aspiration. These criticisms aside, declarations of national interests may still be of some use in indirectly informing the international order objectives set for a grand strategy. In so doing though, national interest declarations have only a secondary role in grand strategy, not a determinant one.

Thirdly, in a similar manner to that made for national interests, some hold that perceived threats should directly drive grand strategy. An example is Barry Posen's oft-used description of grand strategy as: "... a state's theory about how it can best 'cause' security for itself. ...A grand strategy must identify likely threats to the state's security.... Priorities must be established among both threats and remedies because...the number of possible threats is great, and given the inescapable limits of a national economy, resources are scarce."[28] Countering this, today the logic of threat seems replaced by the logic of risk as there are no major threats, only possibilities of some developing. Threats may then be better-handled using risk management approaches that seek to limit the damage that may be inflicted if the feared threat eventuates (discussed further in Chapter 8). More fundamentally, labeling something as a threat, like articulating a national interest, does not in itself explain how that threat will be countered. Defining a threat can provide policy guidance that informs choosing an approach to address the threat but in itself is simply a declaration.

Fourthly, in further discussing the ends of grand strategy there has been some debate about whether grand strategy is only applicable to making war. The initial 20th Century usage of the term arose from the experiences of World War One and thus the grand strategy process may at first seem most appropriate for such circumstances. Some remain strongly attracted to grand strategy

---

27. Alan S. Milward, *The Rise and Fall of a National Strategy 1945-1963: The United Kingdom and the European Community Volume 1*; Abingdon: Routledge, 2012, pp. 6-7.
28. Barry R. Posen, *The Sources of Military Doctrine: France, Britain, and Germany between the World Wars*; Ithaca: Cornell University Press, 1984, p. 13.

staying closely related to military threats and making war.[29] This position though confuses threats and means with ends; policy ends not armed threats or military means should drive grand strategy.

War is an instrument of policy, and as a means may be used by a grand strategy to achieve an objective set by policy. War, however, is not the totality of grand strategy, nor should it drive it. If grand strategy serves policy, that policy does not necessarily have to be only concerned with wars, military matters or armed threats. Grand strategy is ends-oriented not threat-centred and is, as grand strategy historian John Gaddis observes, a type of strategy rather than being tied to any particular means:

> "…grand strategy is …about how one uses whatever one has to get to wherever it is one wants to go. Our knowledge of it derives chiefly from the realm of war and statecraft, because the fighting of wars and the management of states have demanded the calculation of relationships between means and ends for a longer stretch of time than any other documented area of collective human activity. But grand strategy need not apply only to war and statecraft: it's potentially applicable to any endeavour in which means must be deployed in the pursuit of important ends".[30]

The Means of Grand Strategy

The other important aspect of grand strategy highlighted in the term's historical origins is the 'means' in terms of both their diversity and development. In terms of diversity, Liddell-Hart's seminal description asserted that grand strategy involved more than simply using governmental means to achieve objectives, rather it was much more expansive in embracing whole-of-nation means. These

---

29. For examples see: Dueck, p. 10. Parker, p. 1. Layne, 'Rethinking American Grand Strategy: Hegemony or Balance of Power in the Twenty-First Century?', p.8. Posen, *The Sources of Military Doctrine: France, Britain, and Germany between the World Wars*, p. 13.
30. John Lewis Gaddis, 'What Is Grand Strategy? Karl Von Der Heyden Distinguished Lecture ', *American Grand Strategy after War*; Triangle Institute for Security Studies and the Duke University Program in American Grand Strategy: Duke University 26 February 2009, p. 7.

can be many and varied but can be readily classified in four basic types. Harold Lasswell determined that a: "...fourfold division of policy instruments is particularly convenient when the external relations of a group are being considered: information, diplomacy, economics and military (words, deals, goods and weapons.)"[31] This is the basis of the DIME acronym oft-used at defence and military staff colleges throughout the world.

These four separate categories may be briefly expanded upon to allude to their individual breadth and depth albeit this elaboration here is indicative not exhaustive and there are always new forms of policy instruments arising. The information instruments grand strategies can use include strategic communication, public diplomacy, psychological operations and information warfare. The main instruments of diplomacy include negotiated agreements, international organizations, international law and alliances. In considering economics when used as an external instrument of national power, the principal elements include foreign aid, financial regulations, trade policy and sanctions. Military instruments primarily employ the threat of, or the use, of violence. There are however some activities difficult to easily place into a single category. Civil police provided for a peacekeeping operation may be considered as a military instrument or related to diplomacy but could be essential to a state restoring its economy.

Importantly, the classification scheme does not imply any linkage to any particular ends sought; economic instruments for example can be used for many different purposes not just those associated with economic matters. As an illustration, economic sanctions applied against Iraq in the 1990s were intended to constrain the nation's military potential, aid diplomatic initiatives and reinforce strategic communication, not simply cause economic damage. Dividing national power into various categories though suggests that no single instrument is sufficient, that consideration should be given to all and that the relative effectiveness and efficiency of each should be compared when assessing grand strategic options.

31. Harold D. Lasswell, *Politics: Who Gets What, When, How*; New York: McGraw-Hill, 1958, pp. 204-05.

In general, grand strategies typically employ an integrated blend of the various instruments, with different emphasis placed depending on the policy ends sought. The timing of when these instruments are applied, and for how long, similarly varies. The same generic instruments of national power may then be used in any type of grand strategy but the way they are used varies depending on the specific grand strategy employed. Different grand strategies seek different effects by using the same instruments in different ways.

Importantly, grand strategy looks beyond the means being simply diverse and also includes their building and mobilization. Fuller observed that: "While strategy is more particularly concerned with the movement of armed masses, grand strategy...embraces the motive forces which lie behind...."[32] The instruments of national power are constructed from the material resources of manpower, money and materiel, and the non-material resources of legitimacy and soft power, both properly considered as " constitutive of power, [and] not merely a veil."[33] In accessing the necessary resources for a grand strategy to use, the domestic and the international can both be exploited. The international system is as much a potential source of grand strategic resources for states and organizations as their parent societies are.

When considering in such a generic manner the development of a grand strategy's means, the importance of the type of state may be unhelpfully concealed. In this, the interactions between the grand strategy process and the state are complex, significant and of concern. Strong states, those with greater institutional capacities and greater control over their societies, have some decided advantages as the following example illustrates.

One of the material resources grand strategies extract from their societies is money. There are however, significant extraction differences in terms of tax collection and tax structures between states with strong or weak institutional capacities. For weak states,

---

32. Fuller, p. 219.
33. Christian Reus-Smit, 'International Crises of Legitimacy', *International Politics,* Vol. 44, No. 2-3, 2007, pp. 157-74, p. 161. Joseph S. Nye, *The Future of Power*; New York: PublicAffairs 2011, p. 82.

the proportion of taxes collected in relation to their GDP is around 13-14% compared to some 30% for strong states. For weak states there are few tax collection options for their: "...tax structures are based far more heavily on trade taxes as a percentage of total revenue than domestic taxes on goods and services or direct taxes on income and profits. ....Such revenues are easy to extract...a government does not have to be very effective in establishing its authority throughout the realm...in order to collect them "[34]

By comparison, institutionally strong states are able to make greater use of direct taxation and can extract considerably more money with much greater efficiency, flexibility and responsiveness from their domestic societies. The more sophisticated extraction mechanisms of strong states, and their broader revenue bases, allows these states to adjust more rapidly than weak states to changes in the international environment, to be less vulnerable or sensitive to external shocks, to take better advantage of opportunities and to respond more effectively to threats. Strong states accordingly have a considerably more diverse range of practical grand strategic alternatives available to them than weak states.

In this, the ambitions of the state and its desire for ever-more expansive grand strategies have often positively interacted. Reflecting Charles Tilly's famous maxim 'that war made the state and the state made war', the evolution of the state has been paralleled in grand strategy.[35] Strong states have made stronger grand strategies and strong grand strategies have made states stronger. This ratcheting up effect has been particularly noticeable since the 16th Century, as states have gradually become the dominant political grouping in the international system. The demands of the absolutist 'total war' grand strategies employed during the two World Wars of the 20th Century continued this; by 1945 the state had gained significantly more control over its society than ever before.

---

34. Lewis W. Snider, 'Identifying the Elements of State Power: "Where Do We Begin"?', *Comparative Political Studies,* Vol. 20, No. 3, October 1987 pp. 314-56, p. 326.
35. Charles Tilly, *Coercion, Capital, and European States, Ad 990-1990*; Cambridge: Basil Blackwell, 1990, pp. 67-95.

Since the Second World War however the situation has somewhat changed. The development of a comprehensive global marketplace has potentially allowed all states access to the considerable manpower, money and materiel resources external to them. They now have the option of using the global marketplace to overcome their resource shortcomings, even if so doing may introduce certain dependencies on external entities.

In earlier times, states needed a certain scale to allow them to develop their own advanced technology. In the contemporary globalised marketplace however, technology of any type is almost immediately available to anyone. Today, states of any size, type and sophistication can readily obtain the latest technology as needed to support their grand strategies. More deeply, the competitive nature of the globalised marketplace has had an impact on grand strategy beyond simply improving access to greater resources. Even in the traditionally state-centric function of weapons production: "…the scales have decisively shifted against [autarky]: no state, including the great powers, can now effectively remain on the cutting edge in military technology if it does not pursue significant internationalization in the production of weaponry."[36] The grand strategies of all must now take into account the globalised marketplace within which they reside.

Similar considerations apply to finance. States can potentially access almost limitless funding for their grand strategies from the global market, thereby making domestic extraction less important or even necessary. In the 'new wars' within weak and failing states non-state actors have taken this to its logic extremes; the financing of these conflicts flows from the outside inwards rather than the traditional reverse. Mary Kaldor, originator of the term, notes that in countries beset by intrastate 'new wars':

"…there is no [state] production and no taxation. Instead external support to ordinary people, in the form of remittances and humanitarian assistance, is recycled via

36. Stephen G. Brooks, *Producing Security: Multinational Corporations, Globalization, and the Changing Calculus of Conflict*; Princeton: Princeton University Press, 2005, p. 6.

various forms of asset transfer and black-market trading into military resources. Direct assistance from foreign governments, protection money from the producers of commodities and assistance from the diaspora enhance the capacity of the various fighting units to extract further resources from ordinary people and thus sustain their military efforts."[37]

Globalisation has adjusted the balance between strong and weak states in their respective abilities to undertake more expansive grand strategies. This change is even more marked in the case of non-state actors as the 'new wars' example indicates. Non-state actors can now conceivably undertake grand strategies that were previously impractical.

The material means of a grand strategy may attract the most obvious attention however the non-tangible means are also important. Grand strategies are undertaken within a particular all-enveloping social context that "can be thought of as constituting a field in which the (interdependent) strategies of actors are pursued. This terrain consists of the inter-subjective norms and rules that constitute meaning…. ".[38]

A state's grand strategy can be more effectively and efficiently advanced when it is compatible and well matched with the social context (also called social structure) it operates within. Other states and non-state actors will be innately supportive of the grand strategy because of the power applied to them by the favourable background social structures. Conversely a grand strategy that acts in contradiction to the social structure's norms and rules may experience friction with other actors and encounter difficulties in implementation. A grand strategy in this situation would need to attempt to overcome this structural drag through building and using

37. Mary Kaldor, *New and Old Wars: Organized Violence in a Global Era, 3rd Edition*; Stanford: Stanford University Press, 2012, p. 104.
38. Edward Lock, 'Soft Power and Strategy: Developing a 'Strategic' Concept of Power', in Inderjeet Parmar and Michael Cox (eds.), *Soft Power and US Foreign Policy: Theoretical, Historical and Contemporary Perspectives* Abingdon: Routledge, 2010, pp. 32-50, p. 44.

greater material resources. A grand strategy aims to exploit and if need be build a supportive social structure within which to operate.

In this, the two important social rules for a grand strategy are legitimacy and soft power. Legitimacy concerns foreground judgments made by others about a state's actions and behaviours, whereas soft power involves influencing others' background perceptions of a state's international image. Building legitimacy calls for asserting: that the actions of the grand strategy being undertaken meet current best practice; that the group has commendable values and suitable expertise; that the actions are effective; and persuasively articulating that implementing this grand strategy is the correct course of action. Building soft power for a grand strategy involves exploiting popular culture, using public diplomacy and place branding and involving groups such as businesses, NGOs and civil society.

Integrating Ends, Ways and Means

Ends, ways and means may be understood as individual elements but the essence of grand strategy is their integration into a coherent, cohesive whole. In a conceptual sense, a grand strategy is a system, a set of interdependent elements where change in some elements or their relations induces change across the system, and the entire system exhibits properties and behaviours different from the constituent parts. In systems, as Robert Jervis observes: "...outcomes cannot be understood by adding together the units or their relations, and many of the results of actions are unintended."[39] Being a system, a grand strategy can only be understood in its totality and not as a set of disaggregated elements or units.

Alan Milward determined that not only did the grand strategies of World War Two's major combatants impact their domestic societies but that the grand strategies adopted were also influenced and shaped by their respective domestic foundations. He developed a useful concept termed 'strategic synthesis' that involved states purposefully striking a balance between the demands of their

---

39. Robert Jervis, *Systems Effects: Complexity in Political and Social Life*; Princeton: Princeton University Press, 1997, p. 6.

chosen grand strategies and the ability of their domestic resource base to meet these demands.[40] In this the development of the means and their application were not simply opposite sides of the same coin but were instead mutually determining elements. The domestic base and a state's application of a grand strategy were interdependent therefore a successful synthesis must: "...take into account, political, military, social and psychological [factors]. The more factors which are correctly assessed and incorporated into this synthesis the greater the chance of success."[41]

Aaron Friedberg argued that during the Cold War America progressively developed a suitable grand strategic synthesis, while the Soviet Union did not. The Soviet Union with a strong statist political culture choose a grand strategy that made it into a "garrison state", where primacy was given to military preparation at significant detriment to society and the ultimate collapse of the USSR. Conversely, the U.S. with an anti-statist ideology was more prudent and struck a better balance between military preparedness, long-term economic growth and societal prosperity. The U.S. became a "contract state", limiting extraction and mobilization to very specific areas of the economy and becoming reliant upon private enterprise for the necessary research, development and manufacture of armaments.[42] The American grand strategy as it evolved progressively imposed less of a burden on its society and this gave the U.S. greater resilience and robustness than the increasingly brittle Soviet Union. The Soviet Union's strategic synthesis was fatally flawed while America's better balanced grand strategy in due course prevailed.

The concept of a grand strategic synthesis cleverly captures the notion of the integration of ends, ways and means in a material sense. The Second World War and the Cold War though were contests of ideologies making the integration of material aspects with

40. Alan S. Milward, *War, Economy and Society 1939-1945*; Berkeley: University of California Press, 1979, pp. 19-23.
41. Ibid., p. 19.
42. Aaron L. Friedberg, *In the Shadow of the Garrison State: America's Anti-Statism and Its Cold War Grand Strategy*; Princeton: Princeton University Press, 2000, pp. 75-80, 341-51.

ideas an important step in the development of coherent grand strategies. A compelling vision that integrates the ends, ways and means in the minds of people "is as important as to possess the more concrete forms of power." [43]

Across the long, difficult, costly Cold War, America continued to implement a grand strategy of containment originally suggested by George Kennan in 1946. Daniel Drezner writes: "containment's [lasting] appeal was that it offered a coherent *vision* for how to deal with the Soviet Union, as well as concrete policy steps that flowed from that vision."[44] Kennan's vision was not just compelling but also durable in remaining potent across decades and numerous changes in government and within the broader society.

A compelling vision that plausibly integrates ends, ways and means is now seen as an important element when formulating a grand strategy. A recent American Deputy Secretary of Defense Michèle Flournoy writing with others about the need for a new American grand strategy observed that: " Even as the specifics of how to best implement a grand strategy may be hotly debated, the broad contours of the vision, if shared, can help set a direction for the country that can be sustained over time and across administrations."[45]

Articulating a vision does not necessarily prevent a grand strategy evolving as may be necessary. Kennan's vision remained powerful and compelling but the actual implementation of the containment grand strategy varied considerably over the time, both in taking advantage of new opportunities and responding to Soviet initiatives. The appeal of the visionary construct has deepened in recent years with interest in developing a so-called national strategic narrative. This approach seeks to overcome criticisms that grand strategies like

---

43. Liddell-Hart, *Strategy*, pp. 321-22.
44. Emphasis added. Daniel W. Drezner, 'The Grandest Strategy of Them All', *The Washington Post,* 17 December 2006 pp. B03.
45. Michèle A. Flournoy et al., 'Making America Grand Again', in Michèle A. Flournoy and Shawn Brimley (eds.), *Finding Our Way: Debating American Grand Strategy*; Washington: Center for a New American Security, 2008, pp. 123-50, p. 126.

the US National Security Strategy are "written by specialists for specialists."[46]   National strategic narratives are effectively grand strategies written in a manner able to be clearly understood by all.

Such narratives tell a story about the proposed grand strategy in a way that frames issues and policies in a consistent conceptual framework.   The narrative provides an interpretive structure that people can use to make sense of historical facts, current problems and emerging issues.   In this, a strategic narrative is intended to have a strong sense of time and of our deliberate progress through it, while including a consistent logic chain that appeals to both the rational and emotional components of human cognition.   Including this emotional 'hook' engages audiences and brings life, meaning and legitimacy to an otherwise abstract logic chain.   The visionary nature is thus accentuated in the search for achieving greater coherence of actions and behaviours across the targeted audience.

Crucially the audience is greater than simply the group for which the grand strategy is developed. Such visionary grand strategic narratives also aim to frame issues and policies for the international audiences beyond, including neutrals, undecided groups and those against the grand strategy is aimed at. The narrative is ostensibly to garner the support of domestic and foreign audiences however, this process has a darker side. It can also be used as a discursive device that tries to convince others to internalize the visionary narrative in a manner that they then self-regulate their behaviour.

Making Grand Strategy

The scope and nature of grand strategy may now be apparent but who can use this problem-solving methodology? Some hold that only great powers can make grand strategy but there is however, nothing inherent in grand strategy's nature that restricts its use only to certain kinds of state.[47]   Indeed, smaller states with more

---

46. Wayne Porter and Mark Mykleby, *A National Strategic Narrative by Mr.Y*; Washington: Woodrow Wilson Center, 2011, p. 2.
47. Paul Kennedy, 'Grand Strategy in War and Peace: Toward a Broader Definition', in Paul Kennedy (ed.), *Grand Strategies in War and Peace*; New Haven: Yale University Press, 1991, pp. 1-7, p. 6, Footnote 18.

constrained resources may have a greater need for a grand strategy than great powers.

Some others hold only states can make strategy although with states varying so much in scale, capabilities and capacities it may seem unusual to group them all as equals in this field.[48] There seems no compelling logic that only states can undertake the functions related to making grand strategy. Instead any organization or agency that can meet the criteria of developing and applying diverse means can choose to make grand strategy. In this, the implementation can be expected to differ greatly from that of most states because of the much more limited power and dissimilar environmental context of many non-state actors. Even so, as noted earlier "underdog strategies…provide the real tests of creativity" and are admired for it.

Strategic studies academic Matthew Connelly convincingly writes of the grand strategy employed by the Algerian insurgents in the 1950s that successfully developed, coordinated and employed military, diplomatic, economic and informational instruments to achieve major political objectives.[49] Mary Habeck does similarly with non-state actor Al Qaeda.[50] As could be expected, the concept of grand strategy has also permeated business studies thinking in particular to guide corporate-level strategic management of multiple subordinate business firms.[51] The integration of power development

48. Art, p. 1-2. Dueck, p. 11.   Kevin Narizny, *The Political Economy of Grand Strategy*; Ithaca: Cornell University Press, 2007, p. 9. Sherle R. Schwenninger, 'Revamping American Grand Strategy', *World Policy Journal,* Vol. 20, No. 3, Fall 2003, pp. 25-44, p. 25.
49. Matthew Connelly, 'Rethinking the Cold War and Decolonization: The Grand Strategy of the Algerian War of Independence', *International Journal of Middle East Studies*, No. 33, 2001, pp. 221-45.
50. Mary Habeck, 'Attacking America: Al-Qaida's Grand Strategy in Its War with the World', *Templeton Lecture on Religion and World Affairs* Philadelphia: Foreign Policy Research Institute 3 October 2013.
51. For example see: Michael J. Ward et al., *Driving Your Company's Value: Strategic Benchmarking for Value* Hoboken: John Wiley & Sons, Inc., 2004, pp.122-27. Gary R. Heerkens, *The Business-Savvy Project Manager: Indispensable Knowledge and Skills for Success* New York: McGraw-Hill, 2006, pp. 49-53. David H. Fater, *Essentials of Corporate and Capital Formation*; Hoboken: John Wiley & Sons, Inc, 2010, pp. 271-75. William G. Forgang,

with the instruments of power and the careful balancing of resources with goals seems important to all, perhaps even more so for businesses and small organizations with limited resources.

While states or non-state actors may be able to make grand strategy, this leaves undetermined where in a government or organisation is the appropriate place. Edward Luttwak insightfully talks of a grand strategy 'level', as it is only at a particular level of a government or organization that the appropriate knowledge and capacity to determine and direct grand strategy is located.[52]   John Gaddis similarly observes that making grand strategy "requires the ability to see how all of the parts of a problem relate to one another, and therefore to the whole thing" and this is only possible at the highest levels of a government or organization. [53] At such levels the management capabilities that a grand strategy needs are located: these are the ability to determine the 'ends' that motivate a grand strategy and the ability to direct the development and application of the 'means' being employed. From this high level, the grand strategy then flows downward through the organization informing, directing and guiding actions undertaken by more subordinate levels.

The Life Cycle of a Grand Strategy

There is sometimes a perception that grand strategies are set-and-forget methodologies that once started continue unchanged for an indefinite but protracted period.   This is a serious misunderstanding for grand strategies should instead remain dynamic throughout their life. A grand strategy fundamentally involves interacting with intelligent others, all seeking their own objectives. A grand strategy as initially conceived will inevitably decline in effectiveness and efficiency over time as others take actions that oppose it, either deliberately or unintentionally. Moreover, the complex environment within which the grand strategy

Strategy-Specific Decision Making: A Guide for Executing Competitive Strategy; Armonk: M.E.Sharpe, Inc, 2004, pp. 132-35.
52. Luttwak, pp. 177-78.
53. Gaddis, 26 February 2009, p. 9.

operates remains continually evolving and changing; they "are not, and should not be, static."[54]

The crucial need to continually develop longer-term strategies throughout their lives was firmly grasped by business management planners as the long post-Second World War economic boom was succeeded in the 1970s by a series of rolling financial crises and economic shocks. In this newly complex, volatile and uncertain environment the earlier systemized, formal strategic planning approach proved inadequate. Accordingly, there was a shift from a strategy-as-a-design approach to a strategy-as-an-emergent-process approach.[55] In the later bottom-up approach, new high-level strategies were envisaged arising from those successful initiatives undertaken by middle-level managers more cognizant of market conditions and customer needs than distant strategic planners. With experience, the deliberate design approach and the emergent approach were combined to try to get the best from both techniques. The deliberate strategy was now intended and designed to learn from the positive and negative results of being implemented. Strategists were enjoined to be "open, flexible and responsive, in other words, willing to learn."[56]

This concept goes some way to addressing difficulties fully comprehending the continually changing relationships between ends, ways and means in a functioning grand strategy. This relationship may only become known progressively as the grand strategy is implemented. If a grand strategy starts to incur costs at variance with the initial thinking and beyond that justified by the ends sought, the grand strategy should be altered. Policymakers should be continually refining the grand strategy through integrating the deliberate design and emergent approach processes. Grand strategy is properly

---

54. Richard Fontaine and Kristin M. Lord, 'Debating America's Future', in Richard Fontaine and Kristin M. Lord (eds.), *America's Path: Grand Strategy for the Next Administration*; Washington: Center for a New American Security, May 2012, pp. 3-12, p. 6.
55. Robert M. Grant, 'Strategic Planning in a Turbulent Environment: Evidence from the Oil Majors', *Strategic Management Journal,* Vol. 24, 2003, pp. 491-517.
56. Henry Mintzberg and James A. Waters, 'Of Strategies, Deliberate and Emergent', *Strategic Management Journal,* Vol. 6, 1985, pp. 257-72, p. 271.

conceived as: "...a process of...developing clear objectives, understanding available resources...and then putting resources against tasks in an iterative fashion, adjusting objectives, approaches, and resource allocation as appropriate to the changing situation."[57]

Seeing grand strategies as a process means they have a distinct life cycle: they arise, evolve through learning and then at some point finish. The grand strategy in use would then transition to another grand strategy or to a plan of some type (as discussed in Chapter 8).

A grand strategy may finish when it reaches its desired objective although an earlier termination may be as likely given a grand strategy is characterised by interaction with intelligent and adaptive others. Minor adjustments may only go so far in addressing steadily changing situations and eventually the extant grand strategy may reach a point at which its utility is less than its costs.[58] Clausewitz's notion of a culminating point captures this idea.

For Clausewitz an offensive strategy continued until it could no longer advance and then the strategy needed to transition to the defensive.[59] Applying this to the mater of grand strategy, at some time in its life cycle a grand strategy will reach a culminating point where it has achieved the greatest effect for the effort expended. Beyond this point greater efforts will yield diminishing effects and bring only marginally greater benefits. The culminating point may then be thought of as a point of diminishing marginal utility. There are two broad alternatives that may be considered when a grand strategy reaches its culminating point. The grand strategy may be terminated, with a careful transition to a replacement new grand strategy or some other methodology. Conversely, the grand strategy may be continued if there are reasonable expectations it will still achieve the desired objectives. The focus may then shift to

---

57. Frederick W. Kagan, 'Grand Strategy for the United States', in Michèle A. Flournoy and Shawn Brimley (eds.), *Finding Our Way: Debating American Grand Strategy*; Washington: Center for a New American Security, 2008, pp. 61-80, p.63.
58. A grand strategy may also reach such a point of diminishing returns because of poor implementation, not just due to the original conception losing effectiveness.
59. Clausewitz, p. 528.

optimising the grand strategy's effectiveness and efficiency to shift its culminating point further into the future.

Such a perspective though, means that grand strategies may work in sequence, one following another, but not in parallel, that is two or more simultaneously seeking the same goal. Inherent in the idea of grand strategy is that there is only one grand strategy coordinating a series of subordinate strategies. More than one grand strategy trying to seek the same goal at the same time can lead to incoherence and confusion.

The concept of grand strategies having a life cycle further suggests they will be progressively implemented over the longer-term. As such it may be reasonably expected that crises will arise during this period and should be prepared for. The options available to grand strategy policymakers include exploiting any new opportunities that may have arisen to help advance the grand strategy, ignoring the crisis if it has no particular impacts on the issue at hand or ending the extant grand strategy if the situation has now significantly changed.

In discussing the issue of the life cycle of a grand strategy, the question may arise as to the length of this life cycle. In terms of some precise temporal measurement – a month, six months, a decade – no extant definition of grand strategy provides advice. This may be because defining a specific time period would immediately raise the question of what if the grand strategy being considered is a fraction shorter or longer, is it not then a grand strategy? Instead definitions of grand strategy have sensibly classified grand strategy on the functions it performs albeit this has implications. Using functionality as the basis for understanding means grand strategies are not 'grand' because of some measureable characteristic whether in terms of magnitude, time or size of entity using it. Grand strategy is instead a particular type of problem-solving methodology unrelated to some quantitative measure.

Multiple Grand Strategies

An attraction in using the grand strategy methodology is that it brings a useful coherence in the use of the diverse instruments of power. With a grand strategy, the means will be focused on achieving a defined objective rather than them unintentionally working at cross-purposes to each other. This can be a "…double-edged sword. The fact that grand strategy provides a focus is usually a good thing, but the flip side of the focus can be distortion or myopia."[60]   There may be too much attention on a single issue leaving others unaddressed or overlooked. In the contemporary international system however there are many different problems, concerns and issues that trouble policymakers. It is unlikely one approach, one grand strategy, can satisfactorily address them all, or even manage the most important. Countering this however, states can have the capacity to undertake numerous tasks simultaneously, suggesting more than simply a single grand strategy may be able to be undertaken when managing the complexities evident in the modern international system. The implication is that a state can implement several grand strategies simultaneously, each with different objectives and addressing different matters.

As was discussed earlier, the primary function of a grand strategy is changing the order existing between two or more entities. The object of a grand strategy can therefore vary from only another single entity to the entire international system. A state may then have a grand strategy to try to shape the wider international system to its advantage, and several more grand strategies specifically focused on particular states or group of states deemed important whether based on geographic proximity, alliance relationships, economic importance, threat posed or cultural linkages. In such a case, the overarching grand strategy would inform the objectives set for the nested less-expansive grand strategies and would not have the same objectives as them. Such a concept is an extension of classification by Ikenberry of grand strategies as either milieu or

---

60. Hal Brands, *What Good Is Grand Strategy? Power and Purpose in American Statecraft from Harry S. Truman to George W. Bush*; Ithaca: Cornell University Press, 2014, p. 192.

positional: a milieu grand strategy focuses on shaping the general international environment while positional grand strategies aim to address a specific state or group of states.[61]

Crucially, this notion of multiple grand strategies rests on the understanding that a grand strategy is a problem solving methodology. It is not a form of strategy that only applies in a particular environment or context but rather is a device policymakers may choose to use to tackle specific issues of concern. These issues may be multiple and various, and need addressing using several grand strategies. The Malayan Emergency grand strategy 1948-1960 examined as a case study later is an example of the nesting of a less-expansive grand strategy addressing the problems of a specific colonial state within a broader overarching grand strategy concerned with global order.

This top down approach while having a certain logic and 'tidiness' may not necessarily be found in the somewhat confused and messy arena of real-world, time-compressed policymaking. As two other case studies examine, the U.S. grand strategy to revitalize Western Europe 1947-1952 and the U.S. Iraq Regime Change grand strategy 2001-2003, were devised before an overarching 'milieu' type grand strategy was fully set in place. Indeed, the two earlier 'positional' grand strategies provided insights useful later in the development of the overarching grand strategy which was, in conceptual terms, above them. While perhaps ad hoc, this pragmatic approach achieved the desired coherence.

This chapter has examined the idea of grand strategy in some depth and perhaps given an impression of completeness. The understanding developed across the chapter explains the definition: *grand strategy is the art of developing and applying diverse forms of power in an effective and efficient way to try to purposefully change the order existing between two or more intelligent and adaptive entities.* There are however two crucially important aspects yet to be discussed and which are surprisingly often overlooked.

---

61. Ikenberry, *Liberal Leviathan: The Origins, Crisis, and Transformation of the American World Order*, p. 164, pp. 349-50.

Firstly there is little discussion about the 'ways' and yet this is actually the essence of a grand strategy. Grand strategy is all about the course of action taken; it is the *way* the means are used to achieve the ends. What possible ways are there? How do you choose the right one? Secondly, if grand strategy is all about achieving ends, there is little debate about what they may be. What possible ends are there? And again, how do you know which one to choose?

3

Making Better Grand Strategies: Theoretical Foundations

Grand strategies begin in the minds of men and women. It is this thinking that is the foundation of all that follows. The process of thinking about grand strategy though involves both *how* policymakers think about complex issues and *what* they should think about. Form and content are both important.

Rational choice models are often conceived of as how we should think about problems. Such models assume actors have extensive knowledge of the situation, have well-defined objectives and can readily calculate the optimal choice.[1] These models though have not been validated in practice, being unsupported by human psychology studies and recent work in neuroscience. Instead of being demonstrably 'rational', people in reality attempt to simplify complex issues, have difficulty coping with ambiguous situations, prefer consistency, are poor estimators and are more reluctant to accept loss than seek gain.[2] Further research into how we actually think has divided the issue into information processing architectures (the form) and knowledge structures (the content).

The information processing architecture stream is built around 'bounded rationality': the idea that rational actors will only consider a limited range of alternatives that they have chosen

---

1. Kristen Renwick Monroe, 'Paradigm Shift: From Rational Choice to Perspective', *International Political Science Review,* Vol. 22, No. 2, 2001, pp. 151-72, p. 153.
2. Janice Gross Stein, 'Foreign Policy Decision Making: Rational, Psychological, and Neurological Models', in Steve Smith (ed.), *Foreign Policy: Theories, Actors and Cases* Oxford: Oxford University Press, 2007, pp. 101-16, p. 102-04. Rose Mcdermott, *Political Psychology in International Relations*; Ann Arbor: The University of Michigan Press, 2004, p. 14.

subjectively.[3] People are selective in the information they base their actions upon and generally select a satisfactory rather than an optimal solution to a problem. Several types of bounded rationality have been identified. Of these the cybernetic model is too simplistic in disregarding most aspects and recommending simply choosing an immediately intuitive solution.[4] The satisficing model seems rudimentary because in choosing the first satisfactory option, a much more effective and efficient solution may be disregarded.[5] Prospect theory constrains the consideration of options to those favouring defending the status quo rather than exploiting opportunities.[6] The preferred information processing approach instead is the poliheuristic model that usefully comprises two parts: "The first stage…uses decision heuristics and primarily corresponds to the cognitive school of decision making. The second stage involves analytic processing of surviving alternatives. It corresponds to rational choice theory."[7] Compared to the other options, the poliheuristic model is more methodical while still allowing people to quickly eliminate unsuitable alternatives and can be specifically tailored for the purpose envisaged. Information processing architectures are however incomplete without knowledge structures.

Knowledge structures are "a mental template that individuals impose on an informational environment to give it form and meaning."[8] These simplifying mechanisms match new

3. Herbert A. Simon, 'Human Nature in Politics: The Dialogue of Psychology with Political Science', *The American Political Review,* Vol. 79, No. 2, 1985, pp. 293-304, p. 294.
4. Alex Mintz and Karl Derouen, *Understanding Foreign Policy Decision Making*; New York: Cambridge University Press 2010, p. 69.
5. Barry Schwartz et al., 'Maximizing Versus Satisficing: Happiness Is a Matter of Choice', *Journal of Personality and Social Psychology,* Vol. 83, No. 5, 2002, pp. 1178-97, p. 1178.
6. Daniel Kahneman and Amos Tversky, 'Prospect Theory: An Analysis of Decision under Risk', *Econometrica,* Vol. 47, No. 2, March 1979, pp. 263-91.
7. The term poliheuristic can be understood as many (poly) shortcuts (heuristics). Alex Mintz, 'How Do Leaders Make Decisions? A Poliheuristic Perspective', *The Journal of Conflict Resolution,* Vol. 48, No. 1, 2004, pp. 3-13, p. 4.
8. James P. Walsh, 'Managerial and Organizational Cognition: Notes from a Trip Down Memory Lane', *Organization Science,* Vol. 6, No. 3, May-June 1995, pp. 280-321, p. 281.

circumstances against stored, memorized information rather than be considered anew each time a similar situation arises. New information is interpreted in ways that reduces the inconsistencies between these constructs and reality. The world is then perceived by an individual through their knowledge structures, not necessarily as it materially is. In this, knowledge structures are mainly influential before a decision is taken.[9] An analysis of Vietnam War grand strategy observes they play their greatest role "during the selection and rejection of policy options …by influencing the assessments and evaluations that policymakers must make in order to chose between alternative options."[10]

There are three broad types of knowledge structures: beliefs, schemas and analogies. Beliefs are that which we hold to be true and are used to perceive and make sense of the external world. Being general in content, they form the background against which people view the world but are less suitable for use as a problem-solving device.[11] Schemas are inclusive in being the product of an active reconstruction of experiences, values and stereotypes into a general, abstracted representation.[12] They facilitate problem solving by helping the mind organize a complex situation in a way that quickly aids comprehension. Schemas structure new situations through imposing a "known" cast of actors and their relationships onto events, filling in gaps in information with default knowledge while

9. Joanna Spear and Phil Williams, 'Belief Systems and Foreign Policy: The Cases of Carter and Reagan', in Richard Little and Steve Smith (eds.), *Belief Systems and the Study of International Relations*; New York: Basil Blackwell, 1988, pp. 190-208, p. 192.
10. Khong, p. 253.
11. Yaacov Y. I. Vertzberger, *The World in Their Minds: Information Processing, Cognition and Perception in Foreign Decision-Making* Stanford: Stanford University Press, 1990, p. 115. George, 'The "Operational Code": A Neglected Approach to the Study of Political Leaders and Decision-Making'.
12. S. T. Fiske and S. E. Taylor, *Social Cognition*; Reading: Addison-Wesley, 1984, p. 140.

allowing the mind to make additional inferences using pre-existing knowledge and concepts.[13].

In contrast, analogies while functioning like schemas, are particular and concrete rather than conceptual and nonspecific as schemas are. Historical analogies are based on the "inference that if two or more events separated in time agree in some aspect, then they may also agree in others."[14] While having great utility, people generally use historical analogies poorly with numerous significant policy failures traced to this.[15] Crucially, such problems are not limited to people without a rigorous academic education.[16]

There have been several proposals intended to counter human cognitive processes and minimize the problems beliefs, schemas and analogies can cause policy-making including multiple advocacy, devil's advocacy, organizational solutions and murder boards.[17] These various methods all lessen the negative impacts of the various cognitive biases although not reliably or consistently. Such approaches moreover add to the complexity of policy-making placing additional, unwanted demands on organizational resources and time.

A simpler and arguably better solution is to accept and work with the cognitive strengths and weakness of the human mind. This approach suggests using the most sophisticated available information processing architecture (poliheuristic choice) and then populating this with the most suitable knowledge structure (schemas) specifically tailored for the problem being examined. A poliheuristic choice architecture with grand strategy optimized schemas would generally provide people formulating grand strategies with a better

13. Deborah Welch Larson, 'The Role of Belief Systems and Schemas in Foreign Policy Decision-Making', Political Psychology', *Political Psychology,* Vol. 15, No. 1, 1994, pp. 17-33, p. 19-22.
14. Khong, p. 7.
15. Ibid., p. 9.
16. Vertzberger, p. 241.
17. George, *Presidential Decisionmaking in Foreign Policy: The Effective Use of Information and Advice* pp. 191-208, 169-74, and 75-89. Jonathan Renshon and Standley A. Renshon, 'The Theory and Practice of Foreign Policy Decision Making', *Political Psychology,* Vol. 29, No. 2, 2008, pp. 509-36, p. 530.

way of thinking than the present alternative of gambling on making the correct choice of a specific historical analogy. Using a formal approach rather than relying on serendipity would improve the probability of formulating successful grand strategies.

Freedman in approaching the problem from a historical perspective rather than an International Relations theory direction reached a similar conclusion. He proposed strategic scripts that would be generically optimised for various types of strategies (effectively through knowledge structures) and combine what he termed System 1 and 2 thinking processes, broadly the poliheuristic choice approach.[18] However, there is a missing dimension to all this. The approach may be useful in determining *how* people should think about grand strategy but *what* should they think about?

Applying Power

Grand strategy's purpose is to try to change the current international order into a more desirable one through bargaining with "thinking, reacting, competing, and conflicting entities" each with their own agendas and intentions. This notion of inducing desired change in a complex social relationship is at the core of all grand strategy thinking but needs developing further to be useful. Considering inducing purposeful change, there are only a limited number of possible ways:

a.   **Denial**: trying to stop another state or entity achieving a desired objective,

b.   **Engagement**: trying to work with another state or entity to achieve a jointly desired objective, or

c.   **Reform**: trying to transform the thinking of another state or entity.[19]

---

18. Freedman, pp. 600-05, 18-22.
19. While this discussion has concentrated on states, as has been discussed earlier there is nothing to prevent grand strategies being both implemented by non-state actors or being directed against non-state actors. The discussion in this section has

Undertaking these actions involves the application of power. Conceptually, power may be considered as both a resource and as an ability to create effects.[20] This dual nature is comparable with that of grand strategy that seeks both to develop and apply the instruments of power. Power as a resource is considered later; here we concentrate on the use of power to achieve effects.

Michael Barnett and Raymond Duvall usefully - if in a somewhat complicated manner - define power in international politics as "...the production, in and through social relations, of effects on actors that shape their capacity to control their fate."[21] Their two-dimensional taxonomy conceives different types of power that vary based on aspects of the social relationships between the actors involved. In the first dimension, the use of power can be direct where the actors involved are "in physical, historical, or social positional proximity", or indirect where the relationship between the actors involved is "detached and mediated, or operates at a physical, temporal, or social distance." In the second dimension, the use of power can be to exercise control over others, or to define and constitute who actors are in an ideational sense. These two dimensions break the concept of power as an effect into four types:

"Compulsory power exists in the direct control of one actor over the conditions of existence and/or the actions of another. Institutional power exists in actors' indirect control over the conditions of action of socially distant others. Structural power operates as the constitutive relations of a direct and specific—hence, mutually constituting—kind. Productive power works through diffuse constitutive relations to produce the situated social capacities of actors."[22]

---

been limited to states to avoid overly complicating the presentation of the argument.
20. Felix Berenskoetter, 'Thinking About Power', in Felix Berenskoetter and Michael J. Williams (eds.), *Power in World Politics* Abingdon: Routledge, 2007, pp. 1-22, p. 6. Nye, p. 7-10.
21. Michael Barnett and Raymond Duvall, 'Power in International Politics', *International Organization,* Vol. 59, No. 1, Winter 2005, pp. 39-75, p. 45.
22. Ibid., p. 48.

Of these four, three - compulsory, institutional and productive - are agent-centred, that is concerning the use of power by one actor over another and directly relate to the application of power. However, structural power is subject-centred and is examined from a resource perspective later.

The three types of agent-centred power may be extended and incorporated into the abstract ways of inducing change discussed earlier. Compulsory power involving an actor imposing its will on others over their resistance and objections can be related to a state seeking to stop others achieving their desired objectives. Institutional power in being collective and working through socially extended, diffuse relations can be associated with a state working with others to achieve jointly desired objectives. Lastly, productive power involving the shaping and fixing of norms, customs and social identities of others can be connected to a state seeking to reform another.[23] Importantly, the compulsory, institutional and productive forms of power also have broad conceptual linkages respectively with the international relations theories of realism, liberalism and constructivism.[24]

Extending these associations suggests that the three ways of inducing change - denial, engagement and reform - can be broadly and cautiously related to realism, liberalism and constructivism. However, these theoretical schools are 'broad churches' with many

---

23. Lipschutz elaborates further that: "Productive power is...that power rooted in the language and practices that construct and organise social life, individual and collective identities and membership in a political community." Ronnie D. Lipschutz, 'On the Transformational Potential of Global Civil Society', in Felix Berenskoetter and Michael J. Williams (eds.), *Power in World Politics* Abingdon: Routledge, 2007, pp. 225-43, p. 230.
24. The forms of power do not map precisely onto the different theories but "...each theoretical tradition does favour an understanding of power that corresponds to one or another of the concepts distinguished by our taxonomy." Barnett and Duval relate compulsory power to realism and institutional power to liberalism however, they are more circumspect with constructivist thinking being associated by them with both structural and productive power. Barnett and Duvall, p. 49-57. Others concur with this approach see: Robert Jackson and Georg Sorensen, *Introduction to International Relations: Theories and Approaches: 4th Edition*; Oxford: Oxford University Press, 2010, pp. 165-66.

different positions, beliefs and opinions; for the moment the linkage identified simply suggests a general relationship.

The denial course of action involves taking action to stop another achieving a desired objective and this is broadly attuned to realism. Realism considers that actors have an inherently competitive and conflictual nature and that this drives them to instinctively try to thwart the ambitions of other states. Given the first concern of states under realism is to maintain their relative position in the international system, there is a predisposition to resist change.[25] Realism has a "status quo bias" with continuity emphasized over change.[26] Modern realist paradigms are best at describing how the *status quo* is maintained and change is actively prevented.[27]

The denial course of action how ever can apply to circumstances more expansive than simply preventing change. This course of action can also apply to more extreme cases such as stopping another achieving their objective of survival, of retaining control of territory or of political independence. Realism reflects this, encompassing in its theoretical perspective states that seek to revise the *status quo* against others opposition and make "at a maximum, [a] drive for universal domination."[28] The key criterion is that of actively stopping others achieving their objectives.

Conversely, liberalism's notion of the operation of the international system being fundamentally cooperative is compatible with the course of action of working with another to achieve desired common objectives.[29] This is not to deny that realism does allow for

---

25. Kenneth N. Waltz, *Theory of International Politics*, First Edition edn.; New York: McGraw-Hill, Inc, 1979, p. 162.
26. John J. Mearsheimer, *The Tragedy of Great Power Politics*; New York: W.W. Norton and Company, Inc 2001, p. 20.
27. Barry Buzan et al., *The Logic of Anarchy: Neorealism to Structural Realism*; New York: Columbia University Press, 1993, p. 26.
28. Waltz, p. 116.
29. Mark W. Zacher and Richard A. Matthew, 'Liberal International Theory: Common Threads, Divergent Strands ', in Charles W. Kegley (ed.), *Controversies in International Relations Theory: Realism and the Neoliberal Challenge*; New York: St Martin's Press, 1995, pp. 107-50, p. 117-20.

cooperation particularly in alliances, but realism is fundamentally built upon conflictual relations. Liberalism is based instead on the possibilities of, and the opportunities for, cooperation.

Similarly, the constructivist concept of the state as being malleable and subject to being altered through changes in societal norms and identities is broadly compatible with the reform change objective of transforming another state in a particularly desirable way. Unlike realism and liberalism, constructivism includes the possibility of rapid, radical change and that national identity in being socially constructed can be remade, altered or reinforced. There is across the different types of constructivist thinking "a shared commitment to a transformational logic…"[30]

The broad relationships built between the three International Relations schools and the three change courses of action with their associated types of grand strategy simply reflects that each school has differences in the way they understand how-the-world-works. Importantly: "These differences do not merely represent competing empirical claims. They reveal also differences in problem focus and in the capacity to solve particular kinds of problems."[31] Building specific relationships between the identified ways of inducing change and the three major theoretical perspectives therefore attempts to match each school's focus to the particular grand strategic 'way' they are most suited to.

The required detail is however still lacking and for this realism, liberalism and constructivism need operationalizing into schemas. These schemas are not theories or models in the sense of explaining outcomes or predicting events but are word pictures able to stimulate and provoke individuals' thinking about grand strategy. Such word pictures are not meant to be comprehensive, nuanced or

---

30. Jennifer Sterling-Folker, 'Constructivist Approaches', in Jennifer Sterling-Folker (ed.), *Making Sense of International Relations Theory*; Boulder: Lynne Rienner Publishers, 2006, pp. 115-22, p. 120.
31. Peter J. Katzenstein and Rudra Sil, 'Rethinking Asian Security: A Case for Analytical Eclecticism', in Peter J. Katzenstein (ed.), *Rethinking Japanese Security: Internal and External Dimensions*; Oxon: Routledge, 2008, pp. 249-85, p. 266.

well rounded but rather to draw attention to certain important aspects while excluding less significant others.

In this, each of the three theories has numerous sub-schools and theoretical positions, some of which conflict or are inconsistent. Indeed, none of the three paradigms makes coherent claims about how states do or should act. Instead, deciding which sub-schools to operationalize is influenced by their intended use as word pictures for people to employ when examining grand strategic issues. Such a function means avoiding overlapping theoretical perspectives and a concentration on each viewpoint's unique attributes in a parsimonious manner that shuns vagueness and ambiguities. In so doing, the schemas developed are distinctly reductionist.

The principal realist theoretical perspective used to develop a denial grand strategy schema is John Mearsheimer's offensive realism.[32] In significantly extending neo-realism, Mearsheimer offers distinct, sharp-edged policy advice that details which instruments of national power are most important and how they should be employed in the future, including in future grand strategies.[33] Mearsheimer only addresses change in the international system in a limited indirect manner and for this aspect Robert Gilpin's perspectives are preferred.[34]

An alternative would be the other major strand of contemporary realist thought, neoclassical realism that also includes

32. Mearsheimer, *The Tragedy of Great Power Politics*.
33. Peter Toft, "John J. Mearsheimer: An Offensive Realist between Geopolitics and Power," *Journal of International Relations and Development*, Vol. 8, No. 4 (December 2005). Brian C. Schmidt, "Realism as Tragedy," *Review of International Studies,* Vol. 30, No. 3 (July 2004). Glenn H. Snyder, "Mearsheimer's World-Offensive Realism and the Struggle for Security: A Review Essay," *International Security,* Vol. 27, No. 1 (Summer 2002).
34. Robert Gilpin, *War and Change in World Politics* (Cambridge, Mass.: Cambridge University Press, 1981). William C. Wohlforth, "Gilpinian Realism and International Relations," *International Relations* Vol. 25, No. 4 (December 2011), pp. 504-506.

structure but introduces additional domestic and ideational factors.[35] Given the stress placed here on developing schemas that are distinct and sharp-edged, and with liberalism and constructivism having at their core domestic and ideational factors respectively, neoclassical realism is not considered a good fit for schema development.

The principal liberal theoretical perspective operationalized into an engagement grand strategy schema is Andrew Moravcsik's new liberalism that stresses the role of sub-state groups and domestic factors in international relations.[36] Liberalism at its core is a political theory rather than an international relations theory and has a strongly normative position defined by the centrality of individual human rights, private property and representative government. For the function envisaged though, Moravcsik's work usefully recasts liberal theory in positivist terms, emphasizes strategic interaction, has heuristic utility, develops causal generalizations and addresses international politics.[37]

Crucially, the engagement grand strategy is not a liberal grand strategy. A liberal grand strategy would incorporate the normative positions of liberal philosophers whereas the engagement grand strategy does not. The engagement grand strategy proposed here uses Moravcsik's work as the basis for how different groups within democratic or authoritarian states shape an entity's social purpose through preference formation. He holds this is more than simply 'second image' domestic politics being instead focused on the importance of state-society relations and the ultimate primacy of the societal context.[38] Moravcsik concentrates on explaining state

35. Brian Rathbun, 'A Rose by Any Other Name: Neoclassical Realism as the Logical and Necessary Extension of Structural Realism', *Security Studies,* Vol. 17, No. 2, 2008, pp. 294-321.
36. Andrew Moravcsik, "Taking Preferences Seriously: A Liberal Theory of International Politics," *International Organization,* Vol. 51, No. 4 (Autumn 1997).
37. Adam R. C. Humphreys, "What Should We Expect of a Liberal Explanatory Theory?" *Journal of International Political Theory*, Vol. 8, No. 1-2 (April 2012). Christian Reus-Smit, "The Strange Death of Liberal International Theory " *European Journal of International Law,* Vol. 12, No. 3 (June 2001).
38. See Note 55 at: Andrew Moravcsik, 'Liberal International Relations Theory: A Social Scientific Assessment', *Weatherhead Center for International Affairs Working Papers*; Cambridge, MA: Harvard University, 2001, pp., p. 55.

preferences and behaviors rather than defining types of international orders and so for this Keohane, Ikenberry, Russett and Oneal are used.[39] Moravcsik's insights inform how these orders may be achieved using an engagement grand strategy but the characterization of the particular international orders is derived from the work of the other scholars noted.

An alternative to using new liberalism could be to develop a schema based on institutionalist liberalism however in this book institutions are conceived as both an end and a means of grand strategy. Institutions are considered as an end, in the sense of being a type of international order in the engagement grand strategy schema and as a means by which grand strategy is implemented, and thus included in all three schemas. Accordingly this variant of liberalism does not form the basis of a schema.

The principal constructivist theoretical perspectives operationalized for the reform grand strategy schema are those of Jeffrey Legro, Martha Finnemore and Kathryn Sikkink that take an instrumental, strategic approach to changing social rules.[40] Such agentic constructivism is "concerned with how agents – that is real people and organizations – promote new ideas and practices."[41] Using constructivism may appear problematic as it is not a substantive theory of politics like realism and liberalism however, in offering a framework for thinking about social interaction and

---

39. Robert O. Keohane and Joseph S. Nye, *Power and Interdependence*, 2nd edn. (Glenview, Ill: Scott, Foresman and Company, 1989). G. John Ikenberry, *After Victory: Institutions, Strategic Restraint, and the Rebuilding of Order after Major Wars* (Princeton, NJ: Princeton University Press, 2001). Bruce Russett and John Oneal, *Triangulating Peace: Democracy, Interdependence, and International Organizations* (New York, NY: W.W. Norton and Company, 2001).
40. Legro, *Rethinking the World*. Martha Finnemore and Kathryn Sikkink, "International Norm Dynamics and Political Change," *International Organization*, Vol. 52, No. 4 (Autumn 1998).
41. Kathryn Sikkink, *The Justice Cascade: How Human Rights Prosecutions Are Changing World Politics* (New York: W. W. Norton & Company, 2011), pp. 236-237.

change, constructivism is appropriate for a process in which the user adds the context.[42]

An alternative could be to develop schemas based on critical theory, to use Ted Hopf's division of constructivism into conventional or critical.[43] Critical social theory though often uses inductive techniques and deconstructive methodologies, and questions how social structures arise rather than why.[44] Conventional constructivism by contrast has a positivist epistemological orientation and appears better suited to devising grand strategy schemas. Accordingly, it is used, although in its agentic form rather than the more customary social constructivist variety.

The operationalization of the three selected theories into specific grand strategy schemas is given in the following chapter. The approach taken is shaped by the purpose of a grand strategy being to induce change from the present towards a preferred future order. This notion is deeply embedded in international relations. In a seminal work, E. H. Carr, declared that international relations "…is the science not only of what is, but of what ought to be."[45]

The optimised grand strategy schemas developed by operationalizing realism, liberalism and constructivism are now integrated into the poliheuristic choice architecture. The grand strategy selection process is illustrated diagrammatically in the simple flow diagram below.

---

42.   Martha Finnemore and Kathryn Sikkink, "Taking Stock: The Constructivist Research Program in International Relations and Comparative Politics," *Annual Review of Political Science,* Vol. 4, No. 1 (June 2001), pp. 393.

43.   Ted Hopf, 'The Promise of Constructivism in International Relations Theory', *International Security,* Vol. 23, No. 1, Summer 1998, pp. 171-200, p. 172.

44.   Jeffrey T. Checkel, *Social Constructivisms in Global and European Politics (a Review Essay)*; Oslo, Norway: ARENA Working Papers 15, University of Oslo, 2003, pp. 2-3.

45.   Edward Hallett Carr, *The Twenty Years' Crisis, 1919-1939: An Introduction to the Study of International Relations*, 2nd edn.; New York: Harper & Row, 1939, p. 5.

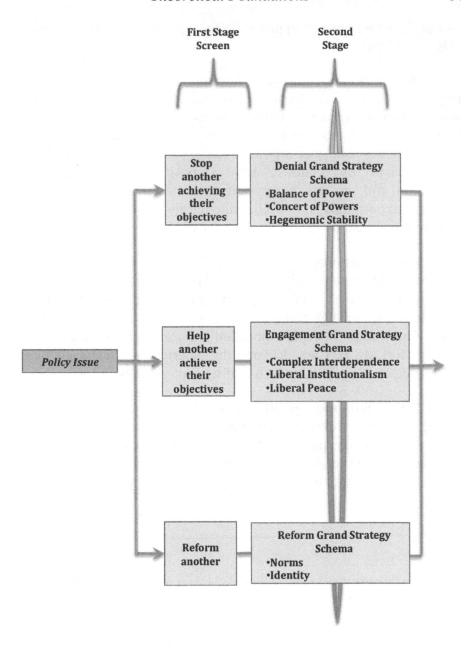

First Stage Screen

Second Stage

Policy Issue

Stop another achieving their objectives

Denial Grand Strategy Schema
•Balance of Power
•Concert of Powers
•Hegemonic Stability

Help another achieve their objectives

Engagement Grand Strategy Schema
•Complex Interdependence
•Liberal Institutionalism
•Liberal Peace

Reform another

Reform Grand Strategy Schema
•Norms
•Identity

Figure 1. Applying Power Framework

In linking 'ways' with the schemas within the poliheuristic choice information processing architecture, the 'how' and the 'what' of policymakers thinking about grand strategy is encompassed. The second stage in the diagram includes the alternative grand strategic objectives, the ends, to reinforce that the ambition of a grand strategy is to create a particular desired international order and that these outcomes are tied to specific courses of actions. This reflects that ends and the ways are interdependent. (Each 'end' is examined in more detail in the next chapter.)

Figure 2 below relates the three general types of grand strategies to some context-specific grand strategy examples in common usage, even if sometimes contested and confused.

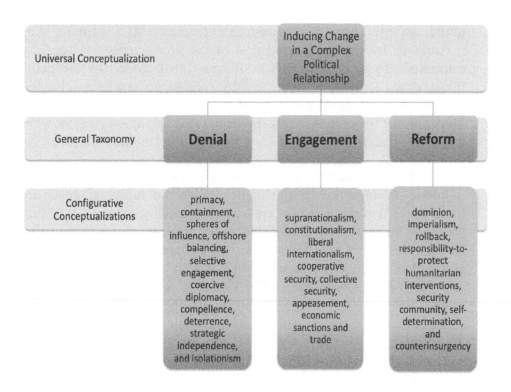

Figure 2: Types of Grand Strategies

Building Power

Change is induced through the shrewd use of power but where does this power come from? Manpower, money and materials must be extracted and mobilized, and people convinced that the ends are both necessary and just, for without such resources a grand strategy cannot be implemented. This is an area often overlooked.

The limited consideration of the need to build power was a major deficiency of the Bush Doctrine grand strategy of the first decade of the 21st Century. At the time many works advocating expansive American grand strategies simply assumed the easy availability of any level of power required and the Bush grand strategy did also. This was a shortcoming for in implementing the grand strategy there were undesired outcomes: "U.S. primacy was ...damaged by the unexpected cost of the protracted wars, recently estimated...to be $1.3 trillion.... It was [also] eroded by the debts that accrued... the U.S. debt held by foreign governments climbed steadily, from about 13 percent at the end of the Cold War to close to 30 percent at the end of the Bush years. ... Washington [was now] at a growing disadvantage vis-à-vis its rivals, most notably Beijing."[46]

There are costs - monetary and otherwise - involved in trying to induce change but benign neglect does not mean no costs are incurred or that there are no undesired secondary effects. Building power is an important matter and needs examination although this has mostly been left to historians with perhaps the most influential and widely quoted work being Paul Kennedy's magisterial *The Rise and Fall of the Great Powers.*[47] Kennedy argued that while great powers generally actively sought to change the world in their favour, success both initially and in preserving their achievements, hinged on building the requisite power and sustaining it. A state's ability to induce and maintain change in international order rested on the power it built.

---

46. Melvyn P. Leffler, '9/11 in Retrospect: George W. Bush's Grand Strategy, Reconsidered', *Foreign Affairs,* Vol. 90, No. 5, September/ October 2011, pp. 33-44, p. 38.
47. Paul Kennedy, *The Rise and Fall of the Great Powers: Economic Change and Military Conflict from 1500 to 2000*; New York: Vintage Books, 1989.

In considering building power, it quickly becomes apparent that grand strategies operate through time. The resources needed to support and implement a grand strategy need to be available when required but not before, or indeed after: "One must know *when* power needs to be maximized.... Policies attempting to maximize power for a specific point well in the future do not resemble policies maximizing power for today. The former policies demand economic investment, while the later require forgoing investments to achieve greater expenditures at the present time."[48]

In this regard, a grand strategy may be considered as having multiple elements that ideally will each be ready at the correct time and in the correct sequence. Some elements will need to work in conjunction and so will need to be developed in parallel; other elements may be required individually and so can be developed in series. Some elements may inherently be able to be developed quickly while others may take decades. Furthermore, the elements of a grand strategy each start from a different baseline and thus need varying amounts of time to reach the requisite capability and capacity. Throughout all of this there are differential rates of change.

A national economy may take decades to offer the capabilities and capacities a grand strategy may need, a new alliance may be several years in the making while a diplomatic initiative could be realized in months. A grand strategy has distinct ends though and, if the required means will not be available at the correct time for the necessary duration, a different grand strategy will need to be devised. Moreover, the international system is inherently dynamic. As the state is building its grand strategic means, the original situation is evolving in both a relative and absolute sense. Some of this evolution will be helpful, some will not. In this sense grand strategies are always forward looking; current circumstances are relevant only as a departure point.

In considering grand strategies addressing near-term

---

48. Mark R. Brawley, *Political Economy and Grand Strategy: A Neoclassical Realist View*; Abingdon: Routledge, 2010, p. 4, 2.

situations, there are circumstances where policymakers feel compelled to act and those where they perceive there are other alternatives.[49] Importantly, the distinction is a perception of the people concerned rather than based on some absolute criteria. Situations of necessity are those believed of vital importance, time-urgent and which definitely need high priority action. In contrast, situations of choice are those viewed as of lesser import and without pressing time imperatives, allowing a real choice to be made between taking action or not. Situations of choice are discretionary and there is no strategic imperative, but that does not mean that left ignored the eventual consequences will necessarily be favourable. There can be costs in inaction including in opening up the situation to a wider range of potential futures. Taking action in a situation of choice may constrain the future to being one of only a few possible more desirable outcomes. The shadow of the future can influence grand strategic thinking even if the issue is not pressing.

In considering grand strategies addressing longer-term situations, the major constraint when thinking about building power is that the future is ultimately unknowable. In some circumstances though broad trends may be able to be discerned and provide some basis for logical, rational planning as the four levels of uncertainty construct reveals: Level 1 is a "clear-enough future" with a single expected outcome, Level 2 envisages a future of only a few possible alternatives, Level 3 perceives that a range of non-discrete futures are possible but that this range is bounded, and in Level 4 any future is possible as any outcome may occur.[50]

In thinking specifically about building power, the four levels of uncertainty can be simplified to two distinct kinds. There are situations where the future appears sufficiently discernible to form a reasonable basis for long-term planning. This would broadly equate to Level 1 and 2 types of uncertainty where one or a small number of alternative futures are anticipated. In contrast, there are also

---

49.   Lawrence Freedman, 'On War and Choice', *The National Interest*, No. 107, May-June, 2010 pp. 9-16.   Richard N Haass, *War of Necessity, War of Choice: A Memoir of Two Iraq Wars*; New York: Simon & Schuste, 2009.
50.   Hugh Courtney et al., 'Strategy under Uncertainty', *Harvard Business Review*, Vol. 75, No. 6, November-December 1997, pp. 66-79, p. 69-71.

situations where the longer-term future is unclear and, while the relevant variables are known, a range of alternative outcomes appears possible making undertaking detailed long-term planning problematic. This approximates to the Level 3 uncertainty of a bounded future. Beyond this though, is Level 4 that envisages a limitless range of possible futures where even the variables cannot be identified; in such high uncertainty where policy ends are difficult to define, grand strategy processes seem inappropriate. In such conditions opportunistic or risk management approaches are favored (these alternative problem-solving methodologies are discussed in Chapter 8). Accordingly, in considering building power for a grand strategy aiming to address a longer-term situation, the crucial issue is whether the future is conceived of as being relatively certain (Level 1 and 2 uncertainty) or is instead uncertain but bounded (Level 3 uncertainty).

In combining these various factors, urgency and uncertainty can be related to the initial division into near-term or longer-term grand strategy issues. Near-term issues involve using the power at hand; this is further influenced depending on whether the situation is a compelling matter of necessity or a situation of choice. Longer-term issues involve building power for a particular use at some specific future time; this is further influenced depending on whether the future is conceived as a small number of discrete alternative possibilities or is uncertain although bounded.

These considerations inform the first stage of the building power framework (illustrated in Figure 3 later). As in the earlier applying power framework, the second stage involves schemas. To develop these schemas, the first step is to examine the foundational concepts underpinning them.

The building of the material means of a grand strategy, as with all public policies, concerns the development and allocation of the finite resources of a society.[51] Grand strategy involves making choices under material, social or political constraints, characteristics

---

51. Michael Moran et al., 'The Public and Its Policies', in Michael Moran, Martin Rein, and Robert E. Goodin (eds.), *The Oxford Handbook of Public Policy*; New York: Oxford University Press, 2006, pp. 3-35, p. 21.

broadly shared with the economics discipline, which is often described as "the science of allocating scarce resources."[52] In being about harvesting and harnessing a society's material resources, it is not surprising that some consider devising a grand strategy a "fundamentally economic question."[53]

Robert Gilpin in a seminal work of political economy noted that modern thinking could be encompassed in the general, abstracted representations of economic nationalism and economic liberalism.[54] These approaches underpin International Political Economy (IPE) however Open Economy Politics (OEP) is now seen as the dominant paradigm and the 'new IPE'. While offering an improved explanation of how the world political economy works, OEP has been criticized in being weak on how interests are constructed, the impact of structure and on how change occurs.[55] OEP may be stronger in explaining the mechanisms of economic policy-making but the nationalist-liberalist typology in focusing on two distinct and competing types of state policies is better when formulating grand strategies.

The central difference between economic nationalism and economic liberalism is the manner in which society's resources are allocated. Under economic nationalism the state actively manages the distribution of resources; economic liberalism by contrast involves the state manipulating market forces to distribute resources. This difference may be broadly re-titled as a managerial approach and a market approach respectively to allow the typology to have utility to more groups than only states and to remove any ideological bias implicit in the economic nationalism, economic liberalism

---

52. John Quiggin, 'Economic Constraints on Public Policy', in Michael Moran, Martin Rein, and Robert E. Goodin (eds.), *The Oxford Handbook of Public Policy*; New York: Oxford University Press, 2006, pp. 529-42, p. 529.

53. Jonathan Kirshner, 'Political Economy in Security Studies after the Cold War', *Peace Studies Program*; Ithaca, NY: Cornell University, April 1997, p. 8.

54. Robert Gilpin, *The Political Economy of International Relations*; Princeton: Princeton University Press International, 1987, p. 26-33. Gilpin included Marxism but with the USSR's collapse this became discredited and irrelevant. Robert Gilpin, *Global Political Economy: Understanding the International Economic Order*; Princeton: Princeton University Press, 2001, p. 13.

55. Robert O. Keohane, 'The Old Ipe and the New', *Review of International Political Economy*, Vol. 16, No. 1, February 2009, pp. 34-46, p. 36-40.

terms.[56]   Managerial or market then relates to the approach used in building power for a grand strategy not to any particular form of political organization. In terms of building power, in the managerial approach the entity concerned becomes deeply involved in developing the necessary resources and in actively directing its society. In the market approach the entity concerned manipulates and exploits local and global market forces by using inducements, incentives, regulations and rules to develop the resources the grand strategy needs

Within these two approaches, the ways that material resources can be accessed varies between extraction and mobilization.[57]   Extraction aims to create today's power to shape the international environment and encompasses taxing, recruiting, requisitioning, seizing or expropriating money, material and manpower resources. Conversely mobilization creates future power. States mobilize resources and intervene in the economy to stimulate national economic growth and enhance societal prosperity that can later be extracted.   Mobilization involves areas such as industry, technology, research and development, and education.

While economic matters are fundamental, a grand strategy can be more efficacious if supported by the non-material resources of legitimacy and soft power. Legitimacy is a quality others grant; building it involves determining the social grouping from which legitimacy is sought.[58] This group can then be influenced through a series of claims: that the action being undertaken accords with extant social rules, that the institution involved is built on core principles justifiable by these social rules, that this institution has suitable expertise, that the actions are demonstrably effective in addressing the issue and that the reasons for claiming legitimacy are

---

56. Gilpin noted that in economic nationalism and economic liberalism "...each position entails a total belief system...they provide scientific descriptions of how the world does work while they also constitute normative positions regarding how the world should work." Gilpin, *The Political Economy of International Relations*, p. 26.
57. Michael Mastanduno et al., 'Toward a Realist Theory of State Action ', *International Studies Quarterly* Vol. 33, No. 4, December 1989, pp. 457-74, p. 463.
58. Reus-Smit, p. 164.

persuasive.[59] This last dimension is key for at its core "...legitimacy requires consent, and consent requires persuasion."[60] The principal exception to this is securitization, a particular kind of rhetorical device that seeks legitimacy through claiming specific policies and actions are security issues.[61] It involves labelling an entity as a security threat through a speech act by an acknowledged actor to a relevant and accepting audience. Securitization does not operate through providing persuasive reasons but rather through the legitimacy accorded the acknowledged actor.

Building soft power is inherently different in that it involves uploading norms and rules to the social structure, which then indirectly influences other nations' elites and public. The specific norms and rules that are sought is to have the uploading state viewed favourably, seen as important to work cooperatively with, and be allowed to set the agenda of the relationship between the states concerned, overtly or surreptitiously.[62] The ultimate intent is to annex others' imagination, so they can only conceive of certain, desirable ways of relating to the state employing soft power.[63] Those being successfully influenced by soft power are positively attracted to the other state and its agenda because they cannot conceive of alternative courses of action.

Shaping soft power may involve using culture, public diplomacy and place branding. Culture is the main arena of soft power as this permeates all social relationships, institutions, discourses and media and generally operates unobtrusively in

---

59. Andrew Hurrell, 'Legitimacy and the Use of Force: Can the Circle Be Squared?', *Review of International Studies,* Vol. 31, No. Supplement S1, 2005, pp. 15-31, p. 23.

60. Mlada Bukovansky, 'Liberal States, International Order, and Legitimacy: An Appeal for Persuasion over Prescription', *International Politics,* Vol. 44, No. 2-3, 2007, pp. 175-93, p. 178.

61. Juha A. Vuori, 'Illocutionary Logic and Strands of Securitization: Applying the Theory of Securitization to the Study of Non-Democratic Political Orders', *European Journal of International Relations,* Vol. 14, No. 1, 2008, pp. 65-99, p. 71.

62. Nye, pp. 20-21.

63. Graham Murdock, 'Notes from the Number One Country: Herbert Schiller on Culture, Commerce and American Power', *International Journal of Cultural Policy,* Vol. 12, No. 2, 2006, pp. 209-27, p. 210.

establishing "…frames that shape the way we see the world, telling us what is important, and informing us about options and solutions."[64] Popular culture is particularly effective in communicating to others what constitutes success and the good life, but can be two-edged in providing symbols able to be recast by others for their own purposes. Public diplomacy involves governments engaging foreign publics and their leaders through regularly explaining the context of domestic and foreign policy decisions, undertaking strategic communications, and developing lasting relationships with key foreign elites through education, training and conference programs.[65] Public diplomacy extends beyond simply telling people news using modern media techniques to being more about creating a wider foreign community predisposed to a desired way of thinking. Place branding seeks to shape the image and perception others hold of the state employing it. States use place branding to manipulate their external reputation using techniques similar to that used by commercial brands.[66]

While an appealing concept, soft power is not as readily wielded as other forms of power. In a manner different to material power, the building of nonmaterial soft power relies at least partly on the target group for "…the efficacy of soft power…turns on the receptivity of others to the values and goals espoused."[67] More pithily, Joseph Nye remarks that: "Soft power is a dance that requires partners."[68] Further difficulties can arise because building soft power is time-consuming, demanding, and not fully under the control of the governments devising grand strategies. Building soft power mainly involves commercial companies, non-governmental organizations, private groups and civil society. All can be reticent and resistant to state direction while being able to damage existing soft power reserves intentionally or unintentionally relatively easily and quickly.

---

64. Peter Van-Ham, *Social Power in International Politics*; Abingdon: Routledge, 2010, p. 48.
65. Nye, pp. 105-06.
66. Van-Ham, pp. 117, 36-41.
67. Terence Casey, 'Of Power and Plenty? Europe, Soft Power, and 'Genteel Stagnation'', *Comparative European Politics,* Vol. 4, No. 4, 2006, pp. 399-422, p. 417.
68. Nye, p. 84.

Soft power has the potential to be an important instrument of national power within a grand strategy but the difficulties of wielding it and focusing its' power suggests that it is best considered supportive rather than central. Soft power's main purpose may then be simply to actively "...tilt the playing field of international politics" in a favourable direction.[69]

Soft power and legitimacy are incorporated in the building power schemas along with the type of economic approach – managerial or market – and the grand strategy's time imperatives expressed in terms of being a near or long term issue. Combining these aspects develops four alternative schemas for building power that are detailed in the next Chapter. [70] The overall building power framework is illustrated diagrammatically below:

---

69. Van-Ham, p. 167.
70. Historical works that illustrate these four schema include: Friedberg. Robert D. Hormats, *The Price of Liberty: Paying for America's Wars*; New York: Times Books, 2007. Michael Mandelbaum, *The Fate of Nations: The Search for National Security in the Nineteenth and Twentieth Centuries* Cambridge Cambridge University Press, 1988. Milward, *War, Economy and Society 1939-1945.*

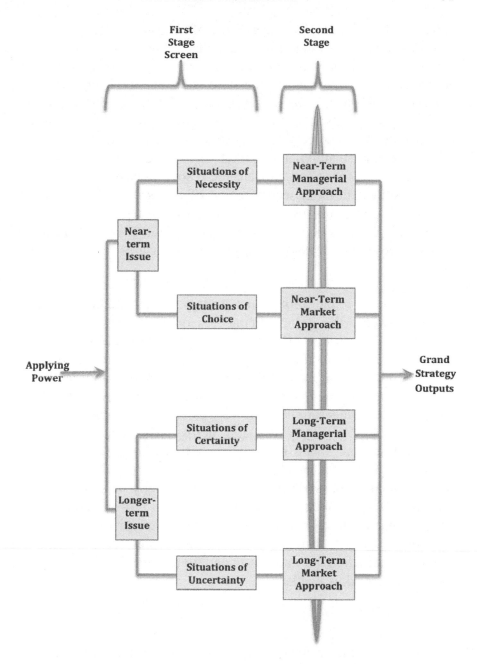

Figure 3. Building Power Framework

In using the framework to structure thinking about how to build the power a grand strategy needs policymakers initially consider if the matter is a near-term of long-term issue. If it is a short-term issue the alternatives vary depending on if the problem is a matter of necessity or choice. If it is a necessity a managerial approach is suggested where the state takes charge, becomes deeply involved itself in developing resources and actively directs society; legitimacy may be sought through motivating people through fear. If it is a matter of choice the suggested option is a market approach where the state manipulates market forces and uses incentives and regulations to access and allocate the resources it needs; legitimacy may be sought through securitization of the issue as a threat. The extant soft power resources will have to be accepted, as time does not permit these to be further developed; if these are unhelpful and impede the grand strategy compensatory measures may need to be taken.

If it is a longer-term grand strategic issue a distinction can be made between the future being reasonably certain or instead moderately uncertain. If the future is reasonably certain, a managerial approach allows the state to plan, mobilize and build the society and economy needed to meet the known demand; legitimacy may be sought through appeals to a centralist ideology. If the future has some real uncertainties, the suggested market approach would allow the state to vary demand across particular societal and industrial sectors, shape market forces to reallocate resources and attempt to grow a balanced society and economy capable of handling the full range of possible futures; legitimacy may be sought through appeals to the self-interest of individuals. Soft power resources may be developed although when the future is reasonably certain, the enveloping social structure can be more precisely targeted for modification; when the future is uncertain a more broadly based, less focused approach is needed.

Crucially, grand strategy involves a strategic synthesis where the ends and the means are interdependent. If in using the building power part of the framework the policymaker determines that the resources are not available for the grand strategy envisaged, the complete process should begin again. A grand strategy that cannot be resourced is one of hope not of practicality. In such a case, the ends, ways or means will need adjusting.

In this examination so far there has been a statist focus on building material and non-material power. This suggests that the type of state involved might be an important factor. Indeed, the modern idea of grand strategy arose as result of the large-scale mobilization of societies to meet the demands of the total wars in the first half of the 20th Century as discussed earlier. This process gave even liberal democratic governments much greater power and control over their societies and suggests that the more authoritarian the government the better a state can resource a grand strategy.[71]

Considered in terms of grand strategy policymaking the different types of government may be usefully considered as relating to agential power. John Hobson sees states as possessing varying degrees of domestic agential power, defined as the ability of "the state to determine policy and shape the domestic realm free of domestic structural constraints or non-state interference".[72] Hobson's conceptual framework suggests that a state with strong agential power would have more grand strategic power building options open to it than a state with weak agential power. Simplistically an authoritarian state might then be considered to have stronger agential power than a democratic one.

However, to implement a grand strategy the state requires the support of its parent society if only as a passive resource base. Rather than the type of the government, it is the state-society relationship that is the key to resourcing a grand strategy. Importantly, this relationship is not static but can vary as the grand strategy resource requirements demand.

Michael Barnett determined that states have three broad options in developing and guiding their societies resources: an

---

71. In Chapter 2 there was a short discussion of building power as related to strong and weak states. These states were so labeled depending on their institutional capabilities and capacities to extract personnel, money or material from their parent societies. For examples, strong states had effective, diverse tax collection regimes; conversely weak states had grave difficulties collecting tax. This is conceptually different to the distinction between authoritarian and democratic forms of government.
72. John M. Hobson, *The State and International Relations*; Cambridge: Cambridge University Press, 2000, p. 6.

accommodational strategy that utilizes the existing extraction and mobilization policies albeit these may be broadened or extended; a restructural strategy that changes the state-society relationship to increase the society's contribution; and an international strategy that instead relies on foreign sources. Only in the restructural strategy case, does the state become stronger or weaker in a domestic agential sense. In this circumstance, the state can choose to centralize or liberalize its control over society as a way of resourcing its desired grand strategy. Consequently, "…the government's adoption of an accommodational, a restructural, or an international strategy carries important implications for the trajectory of state power."[73]

Barnett 'three strategies' approach is useful in thinking about the manner in which the domestic agential power of a state may evolve as the state seeks to resource its chosen grand strategy. Barnett considers that states generally start with an accommodational strategy adjusting their state grand strategies and actions to the level of extraction and mobilization supportable by existing societal arrangements. If these arrangements prove insufficient, an international strategy can become attractive as being less disruptive to state-society relations however, willing external sources are not always available and even if they are the conditions and constraints on a state's grand strategy these sources may impose could be unacceptable. The final alternative involves the state being forced into adopting a problematical restructural strategy that will be the most difficult to accomplish.

A restructural strategy should not necessarily been seen as always meaning an increase in a state's domestic agential power. The democratic Israeli state after 1967 purposefully chose to weaken its domestic agential power though liberalization as this was considered necessary to adequately resource its desired grand strategy.[74] In 1973, Egypt governed by a military dictatorship similarly liberalized and relaxed its domestic agential power to allow the state to better resource its grand strategies. Communist China's

73. Michael N. Barnett, *Confronting the Costs of War: Military Power, State, and Society in Egypt and Israel*; Princeton: Princeton University Press, 1992, p. 37.
74. Ibid., pp. 259-60.

progressive adoption of liberal economic policies in the 1980s is another example of a state deliberately lessening its domestic agential power to increase its overall national power as part of its grand strategy. For these states with varying types of government, greater agential power was less important than building a larger economy and more sophisticated society.

This suggests that a balance needs to be struck between the degree of agential power and improving the scale and sophistication of societal resources. The North Korean state may have great agential power but has little ability to resource grand strategies whereas Taiwan with a similar population may have weaker state agential power but a much greater grand strategy resourcing ability. The type of government in itself is less important than the idea of grand strategy might imply.

In extending this argument further, the discussion so far has concerned states but non-state actors can also use the grand strategy methodology. In terms of resourcing a grand strategy, non-state actors in conceptual terms can modify the building power approaches as appropriate for their scale, abilities and circumstances. The same fundamentals apply in terms of manpower, money, materiel, legitimacy and soft power as the later case studies of the Liberation Tigers of Tamil Eeelam (LTTE), Hezbollah and the International Campaign to Ban Landmines (ICBL) reveal. Even so, non-state actors have much more limited capabilities and capacities than states and can have some real difficulties resourcing grand strategies.

The case studies suggest that to overcome these intrinsic resourcing difficulties, non-state actors more than states will seek to exploit international sources, mainly for money and materiel. The LTTE made extensive use of the Tamil Diaspora for funding and the global marketplace for acquiring military equipment. Hezbollah relied heavily, especially in its initial formative stages, on Iranian funding for Hezbollah-operated welfare and social programs, and on Iranian supply of military equipment, supplies and training. Lastly, the ICBL as its grand strategy progressed and resource demands rose sought and received funding from several states. The problem in such external resourcing is that the external sources may then have some undesired influence and control.

The resourcing difficulties of non-state actors suggest that their grand strategies will be shaped by resource considerations more than states. This means that non-state actor grand strategies are likely to be less robust and less able to recover from internal and external shocks than those of states. For non-state actors devising an effective and efficient strategic synthesis that integrates and balances the demands of the grand strategy and its required resourcing will be critical.

Critique

The applying power and building power frameworks when combined form a complete grand strategy conceptual framework able to provide a well-structured approach when formulating grand strategies. This framework is detailed in the next chapter together with the applying power and building power schemas. The framework however has several limitations that arise because of the way the frameworks were devised and the specific understanding of grand strategy used.

The main limitation is that the grand strategies have been classified according to a typology, but this is not a typological theory. The typology used differentiates amongst grand strategies based on a single independent variable: the goal of the grand strategy. A typology, unlike a typological theory, does not link independent and dependent variables in a causal relationship.[75]

There are further limitations inherent in the linking of realism, liberalism and constructivism to particular change goals. This approach is deliberately designed to ensure policymakers do not create incoherent grand strategies through adopting a worldview incompatible with their objectives. This overcomes a potential problem that: "…assumptions deemed valuable for solving the kinds

---

75. Alexander L. George and Andrew Bennett, *Case Studies and Theory Development in the Social Sciences*, Bcsia Studies in International Security; Cambridge: MIT Press, 2005, p. 237-39.

of problems favoured by a given research tradition will be hoisted upon the analysis of other kinds of problems for which these assumptions may not be well suited."[76] However, this intentional constraint also means that the other worldviews are deliberately disregarded in the particular problem being considered. There is a risk that the particular international relations theory used may focus the policymaker's gaze strongly on one aspect at the expense of other aspects that may be more or equally important in a particular situation.

In this, the absolute success of a theoretical position is less significant. To meet the needs of policy-makers in providing useful insights for grand strategy formulation it is not necessarily important that these international relations theoretical perspectives be fully coherent, consistent or comprehensive. Rather the critical information the three theories need to provide are concepts about ways to induce change albeit this is an area where realism, liberalism and constructivism each have some deficiencies, none having "a strong ability to explain change...."[77] This shortcoming does not though remove the value to be gained from providing policymakers with a better way to think about grand strategy. The content of the solution may not be as absolutely robust as ideally sought but the utility of the solution remains relative to traditional practices such as using historical analogies.

Additionally, in the framework's use of International Relations theoretical sub-schools there is an undeniable American bias. The international relations discipline has itself been criticized as being dominated by American thinking with the international relations thinking of other nations only peripheral.[78] In having such a bias however, there is a danger of unhelpfully narrowing the perspectives offered policymakers, particularly including in the diagnoses of grand strategic issues that involve non-Western

---

76. Katzenstein and Sil, in Katzenstein (ed.), *Rethinking Japanese Security: Internal and External Dimensions*; Oxon: Routledge, 2008, pp. 249-85, p. 268.
77. Jack Snyder, 'One World, Rival Theories', *Foreign Policy*, No. 145, November/ December 2004, pp. 52-62, p. 61.
78. Stanley Hoffman, 'An American Social Science: International Relations', *Daedalus,* Vol. 106, No. 3, Summer 1977, pp. 41-60.

cultures. Countering this concern, there do not seem to be any significant non-Western International Relations theories. There are some non-Western contributions but these do not, at least at the moment, meet the criteria of a theory. Instead contemporary work by non-Western scholars appears to mostly involve testing Western theories in non-Western settings.[79] Moreover, Alastair Johnston's seminal study of Chinese Ming dynasty strategic culture suggests - but does not prove - that potentially form may follow function and that contemporary international relation thinking may be more applicable to other cultures than first thought.[80] Amitav Acharya and Barry Buzan have also tacitly accepted this position in seeing no compelling need for Western International Relations theory to be replaced or substantially supplemented. Instead they consider the answer lies in International Relations theory becoming more inclusive, more firmly situated within world history, and more balanced in priorities, perspectives and interests.[81] Jayashree Vivekanandan has taken just such an approach in a recent work using realism, liberalism and constructivism that successfully examined the implementation of Mughal grand strategy in Northern India.[82] Western International Relations theory may be broadly suitable universally, suggesting the conceptual framework may be similarly useful across a wide array of circumstances.

There is a potentially important exception to this judgment. Scholars in China are devoting considerable effort to developing a Chinese theory of International Relations. This may be as result of China's recent geopolitical rise or individuals carving out a distinct

---

79. Amitav Acharya and Barry Buzan, 'Why Is There No Non-Western International Relations Theory? An Introduction', in Amitav Acharya and Barry Buzan (eds.), *Non-Western International Relations Theory: Perspectives on and Beyond Asia*; Abingdon: Routledge, 2010b, pp. 1-25, p. 10-15.
80. Alastair Iain Johnston, *Cultural Realism: Strategic Culture and Grand Strategy in Chinese History*; Princeton: Princeton University Press, 1995, pp. 259-66.
81. Acharya and Buzan, 'On the Possibility of a Non-Western International Relations Theory', in Acharya and Buzan (eds.), Non-Western International Relations Theory: Perspectives on and Beyond Asia; Abingdon: Routledge, 2010a, pp. 221-39, p. 229-39.
82. Jayashree Vivekanandan, *Interrogating International Relations: India's Strategic Practice and the Return of History* New Delhi: Routledge, 2011.

intellectual niche to advance their personal ambitions.[83] Either way, a so-called Chinese School is developing, even if there is on-going debate about whether this should be a China-specific 'International Relations theory with Chinese characteristics' or a more universally applicable 'Chinese School of International Relations theories'.[84] Whichever prevails, the new Chinese School may offer an alternative to the current American theoretical dominance or be able to be combined with these schools to provide a differently balanced foundation.

Considered more broadly, these limitations might suggest a completely different line of attack could be more effective. There has been strong interest recently in solving International Relations problems using analytic eclecticism, where different theoretical schools are combined in a blend most appropriate for the issue being examined.[85] Indeed, analytic eclecticism seems to have characteristics well suited to grand strategy making which is a concrete issue of policy and practice, is situated in the messy real world and involves multiple complex interactions. If a single grand strategy schema could be devised using analytic eclecticism, this approach would potentially be more accessible to policymakers than the one proposed in this book of using three separate schemas that compartmentalize realism, liberalism and constructivism.

The key difficulty with analytic eclecticism is the problem of incommensurability. Paul Feyerabend held that if two theoretical perspectives were incommensurable they were conceptually incompatible.[86] Combining different theoretical traditions with their

---

83. Peter M. Kristensen and Ras T. Nielsen, 'Constructing a Chinese International Relations Theory: A Sociological Approach to Intellectual Innovation', *International Political Sociology,* Vol. 7, No. 1, 2013, pp. 19-40, pp. 22-30.
84. Wang Jiangli and Barry Buzan, 'The English and Chinese Schools of International Relations: Comparisons and Lessons', *The Chinese Journal of International Politics,* Vol. 7, No. 1, 2014, pp. 1-46, p. 15-19.
85. Rudra Sil and Peter J. Katzenstein, 'Analytic Eclecticism in the Study of World Politics: Reconfiguring Problems and Mechanisms across Research Traditions', *Perspectives on Politics,* Vol. 8, No. 2, June 2010, pp. 411-31, p. 412.
86. Paul Feyerabend, 'Explanation, Reduction, and Empiricism', in Yuri Balashov and Alex Rosenberg (eds.), *Philosophy of Science: Contemporary Readings*; London, UK: Routledge, 2002, pp. 141-63, pp. 152-53.

own unique principles can produce a mixture that is internally incoherent and logically inconsistent. Some argue though this "…is not insurmountable if proper care is taken to consider the premises upon which specific analytic components are operationalized in relation to the empirical world."[87] The task of avoiding incommensurability is easier the narrower the specific 'concrete' circumstance to which analytic eclecticism is applied, but this approach has several shortcomings in the specific case of aiding policymakers' initial thoughts about grand strategic alternatives.

Firstly, a different conceptual framework should be constructed for different problems. This is the converse of the approach taken here where the same framework is used across multiple problems, albeit there are three separate frameworks. Using analytic eclecticism suggests there would be as many frameworks as problems, which would add complexity and impede policymaker cognition. Secondly, there needs to be a comprehensive understanding of the developing problem to ensure the blend of theoretical perspectives crafted using analytic eclecticism is soundly based. For policymakers initially considering a new problem a key difficulty is that the issue is generally confusing, intelligence is patchy and all aspects are not yet realized or understood. Crafting an analytic eclecticism framework on the basis of incomplete or incorrect information could well lead to a flawed framework being devised that in shaping perceptions wrongly may lead to a poor grand strategy. A flawed analytic eclecticism framework may have the same impact as choosing an incorrect historical analogy.

Thirdly, the crafting of new conceptual frameworks is a complex business. Such conceptual development must positively avoid Feyerabend's incommensurability as this could lead to the grand strategy devised using a faulty framework that lacked coherence and when implemented has unintended and undesired consequences. Devising a robust and validated framework then is probably not a function busy policymakers could, or should, undertake suggesting that the default position of policymakers is most likely to be to ignore the concept completely. Fourthly,

---

87. Sil and Katzenstein, p. 415.

policymakers are time constrained and have a tendency to employ the first apparently suitable heuristic available whether it is satisficing, prospect theory, analogies or some other. Creating and verifying new analytic eclecticism frameworks will take some time; by then policymakers could well be beyond the stage in their thinking where abstract conceptual frameworks can bring benefits.

Lastly, foregoing parsimony may make thinking about the future environment much more difficult; proliferating independent variables can add significant complexity. There is a point were analytic eclecticism could become so rich that it takes an ecological view of a situation and effectively becomes a historical study, rather than remaining usefully reductionist like International Relations theory.

If analytic eclecticism may have some shortcomings for the specific use envisaged, theory synthesis is another approach that aims to eliminate the problem of multiple theoretical schools. Theory synthesis envisages a progressive convergence of International Relations theories into a single grand all-encompassing theory.[88] From a policymaker's viewpoint this would be an easier diagnostic process than the three theories used in the grand strategy conceptual framework. While the International Relations discipline appears a considerable distance from developing such a unified synthesis, there is also some scepticism about the concept's fundamental practicality and a corresponding preference for problem-driven pluralism.[89] Some hold that: "No research agenda can lead to synthesis, simply

---

88. There is some confusion between analytic eclecticism and synthesis. Some use the term 'synthesis' when they appear to mean analytic eclecticism as this is now defined. For example, in 2003 Andrew Moravcsik considered synthesis had occurred in several instances but these now appear better described as examples of analytic eclecticism; see Andrew Moravcsik, 'Theory Synthesis in International Relations: Real Not Metaphysical', *International Studies Review,* Vol. 5, No. 1, 2003, pp. 131-36, p. 132.
89. Nuno P. Monteiro and Keven G. Ruby, 'Ir and the False Promise of Philosophical Foundations', *International Theory,* Vol. 1, No. 1, 2009, pp. 15-48.

because different approaches see different worlds...."[90]

Convergence may not lead to a synthesis but there is an alternative path where a hegemonic paradigm becomes the 'common sense' of International Relations.[91] In some respects this may be currently happening in the progressive development of Neoclassical Realism that is gradually incorporating constructivist concepts and liberalist domestic variables into a structural realist framework. This suggests that a single broadened Neoclassical Realist school could in time replace the three separate theoretical schools in the conceptual framework.

While appealing, there seem similar problems to the application of the steadily evolving neoclassical realism to analytic eclecticism in the sense that new variants of neoclassical realism seem tied to certain examples.[92] This may be necessary considering the difficulties of avoiding incommensurability when different schools are merged. While in specific historical case studies such integration might be consistent and coherent, this appears unlikely to be true across all situations. Moreover, as neoclassical realism broadens to both encompass more insights that other schools may offer and to achieve greater explanatory power, the number of variables and their interdependencies increase. This complexity makes it more difficult to project these variables into the future and make forecasts, and runs the danger of obscuring the principal methodological difference between history and international relations.

---

90. Steve Smith, 'Dialogue and the Reinforcement of Orthodoxy in International Relations', *International Studies Review,* Vol. 5, No. 1, 2003, pp. 141-43, pp. 142-43.
91. Mark I. Lichbach, *Is Rational Choice All of Social Science?*; Ann Arbor: University of Michigan Press, 2003, p. 116.
92. For example Layne's development of modified defensive realism "that shades almost imperceptibly into liberal IR theory" appears closely related to the specific case of recommending a specific US grand strategy towards a rising China.
Christopher Layne, 'The Influence of Theory on Grand Strategy: The United States and a Rising China', in Annette Freyberg-Inan, Ewan Harrison, and Patrick James (eds.), *Rethinking Realism in International Relations*; Baltimore: The Johns Hopkins University Press, 2009, pp. 103-35, p. 109.

Neoclassical Realism may be able to generalize about a specific issue in a manner similar to history, but become less convincing in terms of providing universal generalizations applicable to a wider range of circumstances. Explanatory power may be gained at the expense of the predictive power needed in grand strategic policymaking.

The approach that this book takes is a form of methodological pluralism that uses different theoretical perspectives to answer different questions and which tries to exploit the particular analytic strengths of each theory in performing a diagnosis. This is a commonly held – some might say conventional – approach. In this regard, Patrick Thaddeus Jackson declares that: "...the proper response to methodological diversity is an engaged pluralist attitude that seeks neither to maintain different methodological traditions in their splendid isolation from one another nor rest content with eclectic assemblage of notions and concepts drawn from different cells in the typology of philosophical – ontological wagers. An engaged pluralism brings to the foreground...contentious conversations..."[93]

From a policymaking viewpoint there are gains from having different, opposed perspectives available when diagnosing a problem. Using the conceptual framework forces policymakers to consider all three quite different conceptual strategies in searching for the most practical policy goal. Once the most sensible goal has been determined a single perspective is employed to take the deliberations on a potential grand strategy further, but this narrowing down of theoretical viewpoints is done only after applying context and judgment in an examination of all three.

---

93. Patrick Thaddeus Jackson, *The Conduct of Inquiry in International Relations: Philosophy of Science and Its Implications for the Study of World Politics*; Abingdon: Routledge, 2011, p. 207.

4

Making Better Grand Strategies: A Practical Approach

How can we assist people imagine better grand strategies? This chapter builds from the previous, theoretically-oriented and somewhat complicated chapter in setting out in a simple manner the form and the content of the grand strategy diagnostic process. This process is designed to help people structure their initial thinking about a grand strategy problem and provide a useful starting point for developing alternative courses of action. Using this process, people can ascertain what is relevant amongst the typically large amount of information presented, how all this fits together and what further confirmatory information should be sought. It helps thinking to be focused so better judgments can be made.

Chapter Two determined that: *grand strategy is the art of building and applying diverse forms of power in an effective and efficient way to try to purposefully change the order existing between two or more intelligent and adaptive entities.* Chapter Three devised 'building power' and 'applying power' frameworks that when combined creates the complete grand strategy process summarized in Figure 4 opposite. This diagram is the book in a single image.

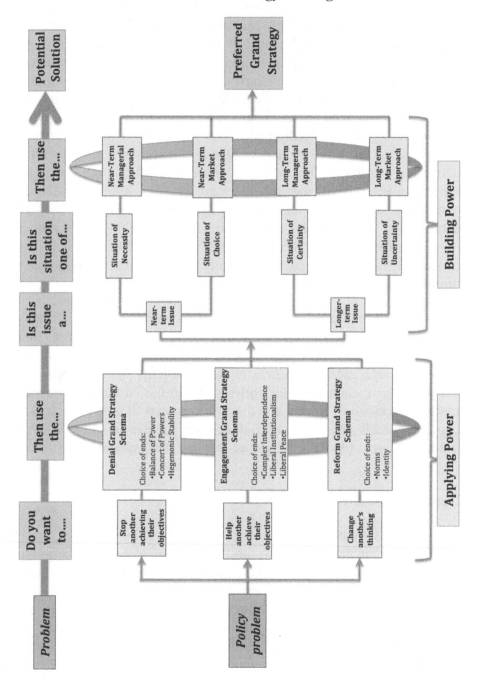

Figure 4. Grand Strategy Process

Some specific characteristics are worth noting. Firstly, while the diagram flows left to right the key issue to initially address is the type of order desired. In this, the process deliberately forces users to be quite precise about the outcomes they wish to achieve. Secondly, ends and ways are directly linked. The type of order sought is related to the way in which the means are used to achieve it. The importance of this is highlighted in the case study of the George W. Bush 2002 grand strategy that sought to use military force to bring democracy to Iraq. Thirdly, the process is explicitly structured on the proposition that the three grand strategy types should be considered as mutually exclusive. The goal sought can only be achieved by the particular type of grand strategy the goal is related to. Blending grand strategy types produces incoherence and confusion as the case study example of the British appeasement grand strategy brings out.

Lastly, the schemas are a crucial element. While their basis and how they were derived were discussed in Chapter Three, they were not detailed. This task is done below. The schemas are the lenses through which grand strategy problems are viewed. The description of each schema follows a similar structure allowing ready comparisons to quickly discern contrasts if needed. It will become quickly apparent that each schema focuses on very different aspects: states (denial), sub-state groups (engagement) or ideas (reform).

Denial Grand Strategy Schema

The fundamental assumption underpinning a denial grand strategy is that the behaviours and actions of states and non-state actors reflect their material power relative to one another. Change in the international system is determined by changes in the distribution of relative power, especially that of the great powers. States can change this distribution through increasing their own power by internal and external means. Internally states can seek to better exploit their resources, develop economically, acquire greater military power and increase societal cohesion. Externally states can enter into alliances to gain access to increased power or undertake wars of conquest.

The structure of the international system is defined not by the sum of all the actors within it but rather by the most powerful. Weak states can be effectively disregarded as operating in the margins of the international system and being simply objects of the major powers' actions.

States are the most important unit of the international system. The nature of a state, democratic or authoritarian, its internal political structures and domestic groups are unimportant. All states act according to the same logic of relative power conflicts regardless of their national culture, political system or leaders.

Each state must be sensitive to the costs involved of pursuing their objectives; actions should strengthen, not weaken, their power relative to others. As rational actors, states only attempt change if their expected gains exceed the expected costs. Accordingly, those that wish to counter change should raise the costs to the other revisionist states actively seeking change.

In a denial grand strategy, the instruments of national power should be used to influence external events in ways that increase one's own national power relative to other states. In assessing another's power, their capabilities - especially military forces - are closely examined. The means of states, not their ends, matter most.

The military instrument of power should be directed against adversary military capabilities but in ways that increase the state's relative power; war is both a legitimate and important strategy. Apposite strategies include blackmail involving making threats of war while avoiding the costs to oneself of actually waging war, 'bait and bleed' through provoking long and costly wars between rivals, and 'bloodletting' in ensuring a war is deliberately prolonged and costly for the adversaries.

The economic instrument of power can be used similarly. Geo-economic actions can enlarge one's own economic might while deliberately impeding the growth of others. The preferred situation is one where one's growth is rapid but that of rivals is negligible or even negative. Intra-alliance trade can deliver positive benefits through the increased economies of scale gained growing the total economic power, and thus potentially military strength, of an alliance. Such considerations also suggest that trade with potential adversaries should be strictly limited as this may have the undesirable effect of increasing their relative power.

The diplomatic instrument can be used to create alliances that increase a state's relative power. This carries risks: firstly, an alliance may entrap them in another's conflicts, secondly abandonment is a constant concern, and thirdly all will try to pass the costs of any action onto others rather than undertaking it themselves.

International institutions are of value mainly as instruments to bind others to specific agreements and so control their behaviour and actions in advantageous ways. In institutions the central issue is both how to maximise the gains for oneself and how to limit the gains of others. Given this conflictual basis, cheating by members is a particular concern.

The denial grand strategy's potential types of international order are a balance of power, a concert of powers and hegemonic stability. In a balance of power order, states or non-state actors develop internally and access external resources to balance the power of others sufficiently to achieve a rough equilibrium. While generally involving alliances, these are impermanent as the continually changing relative power between all parties involved often necessitates new alignments. Conversely, in a concert of powers order the system's great powers act together to ensure a stable power equilibrium; none seeks system dominance, there is a sense of equality and security, systemic roles are not endangered, and each possesses meaningful influence. A hegemonic stability order envisages a uniquely very powerful state providing systemic leadership. The sharply uneven distribution of power allows the hegemon to establish and maintain desired norms across the international system through providing collective goods, enforcing rules and co-opting others to burden-share.

Conditions Favouring Success. The success of the denial type of grand strategy hinges on developing greater relative power appropriate to the circumstances of the order sought. However, the relative power balance is inherently fragile as either side can take steps to change it if desired. Even so, there is less interdependency in denial grand strategies than in others. Denial grand strategies can be used to quickly impose an international order with scant regard or concern for the other parties involved. The downsides are that the range of denial grand strategy international orders is limited and that in being based on relative power may prove short-lived. Others may take action to change the relative power balance again and overthrow the new order.

The shifting nature of the relative power balance lies behind the greatest shortcoming of the denial grand strategy type. While a denial grand strategy may be appropriately chosen and skillfully implemented it is fundamentally unable to resolve the underlying causes of a conflict. A denial grand strategy may be decisive in stopping another achieving their present objectives however, this does not necessarily have the more positive or enduring results a change in the social purpose or social rules of the other state may have. The result of the denial grand strategy may be winning a conflict but losing the peace, unless when it reaches its culminating point another grand strategy succeeds it.

Relative power however has a degree of absoluteness. There may be situations where the state that is the object of a grand strategy has such a preponderance of power that it would be unrealistic for an activist state to adopt a denial grand strategy. A different grand strategy type would then need consideration.

Lastly, there is a specific issue with the denial grand strategy type that may concern. Thinking abstractly, there appears no reason why stopping a state achieving a desired objective could not instead use an engagement or reform grand strategy. The difference in the three alternative grand strategies would then be the 'way' the outcome was achieved: either exploiting a relative material power advantage in the denial type, using another state's domestic interest groups to advance a desired social purpose in the engagement type or favourably changing another state's social rules in the reform type. Importantly, as well as ways, the international orders each alternative type of grand strategy would seek to create in this circumstance would also be distinctly different. While it may be that stopping a state achieving their desired objectives can be met by the other types of grand strategies, this is only true broadly speaking as the ends achieved would differ across each grand strategy type.

The three types of grand strategy do not at the implementation level produce the same ends or use the same ways. Moreover, the reform and engagement types cannot be subsumed solely into the denial type. A denial grand strategy is not appropriate to change a state's social purpose or its social rules, as its focus is particular material aspects quite distinct from those social objectives. Material power works upon certain elements of a target state in a manner that does not lead to change in a state's social purpose or a society's social rules, as the British appeasement and Iraq regime change grand strategy case studies illustrate. A denial grand strategy in itself is not enough.

Engagement Grand Strategy Schema

The fundamental assumption underpinning an engagement grand strategy is that within other states or non-state actors there are groups whose ambitions can be exploited. The behaviours and actions of states and non-state actors reflect their domestic circumstances.

The social purpose of each state is determined by their preferences, and these reflect the capture and recapture of the state by influential coalitions of self-interested, rational individuals and sub-state groups. This social purpose determines what states and non-state actors do. An engagement grand strategy cooperates with useful internal parties to try to ensure their state's or non-state actor's social purpose is as both desire.

Change in the international system is created by a change in the distribution of the constituent states' social purposes, with changes in each states' purposes coming "bottom up" as a product of internal politics and pressures. External factors can also be influential in offering windows of opportunity for domestic individuals and groups to take advantage of or in providing stimuli for change.

The international system is composed of numerous states each with their own individual state preferences that reflect their capture and recapture by their own particular domestic actors. Accordingly, every state is different and distinctive making the international system intrinsically complex. This complexity is exacerbated as states may act at the same time as either unitary or disaggregated actors depending on the issues being considered. In some circumstances they will exhibit strong internal cohesion. In other matters different elements within each may interact with other countries in a semi-autonomous manner.

Multiple transnational linkages can form between a country's sub-state groups and interested foreign parties; these linkages may support, undercut or go around state lines of communication. In these linkages, cooperation is important and involves the different individuals and groups seeking absolute gains irrespective of the distribution of these gains. All will cooperate when each can achieve beneficial outcomes, even if of differing scales.

The ends of states matter most, not their means. In relationships between states some will have stronger preferences over certain outcomes then others. The more motivated states will be more willing and able to mobilize and expend national resources for their desired objectives then states with less strongly held attitudes. This difference in intensity can give a state greater power to decide an issue than an apparent deficiency in relative power capabilities might suggest.

In an engagement grand strategy the instruments of national power should be focused on constructing and supporting useful influential domestic interest groups within other states or non-state actors. The overall intent is to strengthen those groups that hold desirable preferences so that they capture the state or non-state actor and determine its social purpose to be as we desire. Simultaneously, those groups that hold disagreeable preferences should be actively weakened sufficiently enough so that they do not prevail. An engagement grand strategy is based on cooperation in the sense that it seeks to help advance the ambitions of others when these are useful to achieving our objectives.

The diplomatic instrument can be used to gain an understanding of the internal complexities of another state or non-state actor and determine the important individuals and groups, their interests and preferences. Having identified these, the diplomatic instrument can then be focused on shaping and helping key useful individuals and groups through on-going support and encouragement, while actively undermining others.

The economic instruments can be used to provide incentives or apply negative sanctions to those domestic interest groups that profit from transnational economic interactions. Incentives support these domestic groups who then work to sustain these linkages through favourable national policies. Negative measures in imposing costs can instead lead these groups to exert pressure on the state to alter the national behaviours and actions that led to the sanctions.

International institutions can be used instrumentally to advance already established preferences. They are created to realize common interests, advance specific mutual preferences, avoid sub-optimal outcomes and to maximize the potential gains for all parties involved. Such institutions encourage ongoing interaction and information exchange that can build trust and knowledge of others' intentions.

The informational instrument can be used to assist and reinforce the advancement of the preferred individuals and groups. The information means may be able to develop a normative perception in the state or non-state actor targeted that the preferred internal individuals and groups are on the 'right' path whereas others are at best misguided, or at worse have sinister motives detrimental to the parent society. The deliberate branding of particular individuals and groups may help shape perceptions within the target state or non-state actor.

The military instrument can be targeted upon what domestic groups in the other entities value most, which generally would be related to their economic or financial interests. Groups within friendly or adversary countries holding obstructive preferences would be actively undermined; conversely those with useful, helpful preferences would be supported and strengthened.

An engagement grand strategy can build three types of international order: complex interdependence, institutionalism and the liberal peace. A complex interdependence order has three defining characteristics: multiple channels connect states ensuring any actions taken have reciprocal effects, there is no hierarchy of issues, and military force is not threatened. Each party involved perceives benefits but their asymmetrical interdependencies provide useful sources of influence for actors in dealing with another. They can influence another's preferences by establishing linkages between issues, manipulating the setting of agendas to determine how issues are framed, penetrating those domestic groups who shape the preferences of state and non-state actors, and making use of international institutions.

Situated within a stable political system, an institutionalist order involves a shared agreement between all concerned on the order's underpinning principles, the operating rules and the norms. An institutionalist order connects state and societal elites in transnational linkages that benefit those involved and gives them a stake in its continuance. A liberal peace order deepens and extends the other types of order in combining democratic representative governments, international institutions and transnational economic interdependence.

Conditions Favouring Success. The success of an engagement grand strategy hinges on being able to find and work with domestic interest groups in the targeted states or non-state actors that hold preferences compatible with the grand strategic objectives. If so, this type of grand strategy can deliver enduring outcomes. The domestic interest groups involved in being an integral part of the grand strategy may deeply embrace the grand strategy's objectives as their own. These then become self-reinforcing and the grand strategy may no longer require substantial support, effort or resources. Over the longer term an engagement grand strategy may be a more affordable type of grand strategy then a denial type, although start-up costs may be significant. Moreover, it may take some time for the helpful domestic groups being supported to reach an influential size – especially if they are not pre-existing and need to be first created; this situation is discussed in the Iranian grand strategy case study.

The principal shortcoming of an engagement grand strategy is that it is only viable if domestic interest groups willing and able to use the assistance being offered can be developed in countries or organizations important to the grand strategy. Moreover, even if these are present there are some inherent dangers. The interest groups that will be worked with and through need to be carefully chosen; their suitability - not just their availability - needs deep consideration. In trying to exploit useful others, there is a danger that these domestic groups will reverse this and try to exploit the grand strategy for ends opposed to those the engagement grand strategy seeks. Actively, if unintentionally, supporting the wrong groups can be potentially catastrophic as the case study of the British appeasement grand strategy illustrates.

Reform Grand Strategy Schema

The fundamental assumption underpinning a reform grand strategy is that the behaviours and actions of states and non-state actors reflect the social rules that animate them – and these rules can be changed. Such rules arise through social interaction. The actors shape their own social context (structure) and this then shapes the interests, identities, and behaviours of the actors. States behave and act in a manner appropriate to these social rules rather than seeking to maximize desired outcomes.

Change in the international system is driven by changes in norms and identities albeit social rules advocated by great powers are more noteworthy than those of lesser states and non-state actors. Norms are shared understandings of what kinds of actions are appropriate; they define and limit the range of acceptable policy choices and instrumentally rational behaviour. Identities define an actor's characteristics, distinctiveness and uniqueness and are formed by how actors conceive themselves compared to others. Changing a social structure requires altering a tightly integrated network of social expectations and obligations that is mutually reinforcing with an inbuilt resistance to change.

The emergence of a new social rule requires ideational entrepreneurs, be they individuals, organizations or states, to engage in strategic social construction. This has two connected stages: ideational collapse and replacement. A suitable environment is essential for a change in social rules; the old ideas must be understood to have collapsed. Existing ideas are not simply eliminated when they fail. These rules had a social purpose that remains and they must be actively replaced. The new ideas need to advanced by influential advocates who are prominent and authoritative in terms of the social rule being advanced, and able to make use of their organizational platforms to give the desired rules credence and authority. This is influencing ideas from the top-down through the advocacy of the ideational elites.

Ideational entrepreneurs need to progressively persuade sufficient influential advocates to reach a "tipping" point at which a critical mass of the population adopts the new rule thereby redefining appropriate behaviour for the entity concerned. However, for the new social rules to permanently change the population's attitudes the rules need to enter the public sphere and be institutionalized. The new rules should also appear to address the problems that caused the old social rule's collapse. Negative results can lead to renewed ideational turmoil or a return to the old ways.

In a reform grand strategy, the instruments of national power are used to advance and support those social rules they deem attractive. The focus of these instruments should be on the advocates and promoters of new ideas who shape and influence their parent society's social rules. Initially the aim is convincing these ideational elites of the efficaciousness of the new social rules and then as the tipping point is approached, on supporting their efforts to advance the rule cascade and consolidation. A combination of ideational measures and material support is generally needed. New ideas alone unsupported by material means are usually insufficient to have an existing social rule replaced.

The military and economic instruments of power are oriented to support the message of the 'goodness' of the desired particular social rule. The significance of military and economic actions in advancing the desired ideas is more important than the actions themselves. Actions taken must be seen as legitimate in the context of the social rules being advanced; actions considered 'illegitimate' will work against the rule change sought. The ends do not justify the means, instead the means justify, or rather legitimise, the ends.

With social interaction driving change, the diplomatic instrument of national power is important. Interaction is necessary for others to understand and embrace your preferred social rules; without meaningful interaction change is impossible. However, actors at the system, unit, or individual level can readily employ varying means of deception to shape and manipulate others. The face presented in a social interaction may not be the real face. In a reform grand strategy deception may be effective.

The informational instrument is significant both in further assisting productive social interaction but more importantly in ensuring the key ideational messages that explain and justify the desired social rule are understood by all. The use of words is not just to describe or represent events and actions but rather to create a desired understanding of them. Institutions in being mutually constituted can be used to advance desired new identities and norms being internalized by others.

States can take action to build the international orders they prefer based on widening the circle of states that have their desired norms and identities. Those with different social rules can appear particularly illegitimate, dangerous and requiring action to change.

Conditions Favouring Success. The success of this type of grand strategy requires the existing ideas to collapse due to some external shock. Such a collapse may be achieved fortuitously by some unconnected event. While this may substantially reduce overall resource and time demands, the replacement ideas and the plans to have them accepted would need to be already developed and ready for implementation. The alternative is to deliberately engineer the external shock but this can be a costly, difficult and time-consuming business. The advantage in this later approach however, is that the ideational replacement program can then be well-timed and more efficiently implemented.

Choosing between these two alternatives may depend on the resources the state or organization implementing the grand strategy can command and the size of the targeted advocate group that needs persuading. Those organizations with few resources and a large target group may need to be ready to exploit external shocks whereas those with large resources and a small target group may prefer to be proactive.

The principal shortcoming of this type of grand strategy is that deliberately changing the ideas of a selected target audience requires suitable and timely access to them. This may be difficult to achieve or require resources beyond the grand strategy's ability to generate; not all circumstances will lend themselves to the use of reform grand strategies.

Partly offsetting this is that the target audience initially may be small. In the early stages the focus is principally on ideational advocates within the broad target group who are prominent and authoritative in terms of the idea being advanced and who are able to use their organizational platform to give the new ideas credence and clout. This will probably be a relatively limited number of people. While this makes a reform grand strategy more practical then may at first be thought, determining who these key ideational advocates are requires deep insight into the broader target group. Such intelligence may be problematic to obtain in some situations.

In considering the three grand strategy types, a reform grand strategy is the most dependent on the other party to succeed. While a denial grand strategy can simply use force to coerce others, and an engagement grand strategy can make use of another's pre-existing ambitions, it is more difficult to change people's minds. For this, there needs to be a certain degree of acceptance of the need for change and agreement with the new ideas. This matter extends deeper when issues of adequate and timely access and the need for deep knowledge of the broad target group are considered. The success of a reform grand strategy very much depends on adequate interaction between the parties involved and on the receptiveness of the target group.

Building Power

Choosing the type of grand strategy to employ varies with the effect on others that is sought, however the power to achieve this effect also needs to be built. This involves developing and allocating the necessary resources of manpower, money, material, legitimacy and soft power. To develop the necessary resources, domestic and international sources are used. The resourcing base of a grand strategy is determined by the grand strategy not by some particular geographic boundaries.

There are two key aspects. Firstly, the resources needed to support and implement a grand strategy need to be available when required, but not before, or indeed after. Given enough time, considerable resources can be developed and turned into the power needed. If the issue is near-term however, options may be limited. Secondly, in building resources the choices are between a managerial approach – the state or non-state actor becoming deeply involved in building the necessary resources and actively directing society - or a market approach where the state or non-state actor manipulates and exploits local and global market forces by using inducements, incentives, regulations and rules to develop the resources the grand strategy needs.

The four different building power approaches that feature in the Grand Strategy Process (Figure 4) are summarized in Table 1 opposite. Each cell is the schema, the bounded rationality, which is used when thinking about particular situations.[1] These sharp edged,

---

1. Historical works that illustrate these four schema include: Friedberg, Hormats, Mandelbaum, Milward, *War, Economy and Society 1939-1945*.

stylized word pictures are meant to stimulate, provoke, and draw attention to certain aspects important to grand strategy formulation.

	Managerial Approach	Market Approach
Near-Term Issue	Most responsive to needs Provides considerable national autonomy and independence Motivates people by fear, through direct and indirect coercion and emphasizing awful consequences if the strategy fails Finance using principally direct and indirect taxation Maximum use of domestic sources of material Best suited for times of necessity when success is essential	Provides good access to the vast global resources available Limits national autonomy and independence Motivates people through securitization of issue as a serious threat to their individual security and prosperity Finance using taxation, domestic bonds and international bonds subject to market acceptance Maximum use of foreign and domestic commercial sources of material Best suited for situations when the level and timing of involvement and actions can be controlled to keep markets content
Long-Term Issue	Grows considerable national autonomy and self-reliance Limits responsiveness to unforeseen challenges Motivates people by appeals to nationalism or statist ideology Finance using principally taxation and domestic bonds Directed nation-building emphasizing those industries the grand strategy needs Best suited for developing essential capabilities and for lessening both the dependence on others and the constraints on future actions they could impose	Make's best use of the vast global resources available Diminishes autonomy and independence Motivates people through appeals to being in an individual's best self-interest over the longer term Finance using minimum taxation supplemented by bonds, international preferred Most effective method to grow national prosperity. Increasing sensitivity to external shocks over time Best suited for times of uncertainty

Table 1. Building Power Schemas

The four schemas make use of the same theoretical perspectives and accordingly can be combined without problems of incommensurability, unlike the earlier creating change schemas that each had different ontology's i.e. state, sub-state or ideas. While the grand strategy building power framework may suggest a particular managerial or market approach, policymakers in examining a specific context and the constraints it imposes may choose a blend of approaches. A grand strategy can be resourced using one, or a mix of, the four schemas devised. Moreover, the resourcing approach used may evolve over time as the demands of the grand strategy change. Importantly, in considering resourcing there is the possibility of equifinality; there may be several potential resourcing paths that are feasible, albeit of varying effectiveness and efficiency.

Conclusion

The schemas for 'applying power' and 'building power' have been detailed. The grand strategy process (Figure 4) makes explicit at which stages people need to apply these schemas to structure their thinking about their specific grand strategy problem. Importantly, and to reiterate, the grand strategy process is only to help people structure their initial thinking. Context and judgment must still be applied to determine sensible, practical grand strategic options. George saw such a diagnostic process as:

> "...an *aid, not a substitute for policy analysis and for judgments that decision makers make when choosing a policy.* Even the best theoretical conceptualization of a problem and the most highly developed generic knowledge of a strategy cannot substitute for competent analysis by governmental specialists who must consider whether some version of a strategy is likely to be viable in the particular situation at hand. ...for policymakers to judge what action to take, they must take into account a number of considerations that cannot be anticipated or addressed in generic articulations of strategies."[2]

---

2. Emphasis in the original. George and Bennett, p. 276.

The discussion of the grand strategy process has so far been very abstract. The case studies are intended to rebalance this. They involve applying the process to a series of historical grand strategies to allow an understanding to be gained of the design and logic of each type of grand strategy. As George noted, people's eyes glaze over when abstract theory is discussed. The case studies are practical illustrations intended to address his observation and make the grand strategy process real.

A further advantage of the case studies is that the grand strategies are examined as they play out over time. In this way the dynamic nature of grand strategy and their life cycle can be clearly realized. In contrast, an example proposing some future grand strategy would offer only a snapshot perspective in looking forward into an uncertain tomorrow. Importantly, the case studies are not intended to be the complete, disinterested deep studies of particular historical events but rather to support the purpose of this book: providing a grand strategy diagnostic process.

5

Denial Grand Strategies

This chapter applies the grand strategy process to three historical case studies. The case studies are structured to highlight the important policymaking aspects of denial grand strategy formulation, in particular the design requirements, general operating logic and the circumstances and conditions favouring success or failure.

An undemanding case is that of the US grand strategy in the Iraq War of 1991-1992. The time frame is from the grand strategy's origin until it reached the desired end state. The key issues are the desired international order sought, the 'way' this was to be achieved, the use of the four different type of means and the approach taken to build power.

The second case is more problematic, complex and protracted and involves the Liberation Tigers of Tamil Eelam (LTTE) insurgency against the Sri Lankan government during 1990-2002. The LTTE case was the most sophisticated insurgent non-state actor of the post-Cold War period and made unusually extensive use of globalization. Both aspects are at variance with notions of grand strategy being for great powers only and being concerned mainly with territorially constrained internal mobilisation. The time frame chosen begins from the withdrawal of the Indian peacekeeping force when the LTTE became the dominant separatist group battling the Sri Lankan state. From this time the LTTE was able to single-mindedly apply the grand strategy until 2002 when a Norwegian-brokered ceasefire came into effective. While it had not yet created its desired international order, with the ceasefire the grand strategy had reached its culminating point. At this point, the Sri Lankan state was clearly beginning to develop an effective counter grand strategy in response and there were significant adverse changes in the international and domestic environment.

The failure case is that of the USSR's détente grand strategy during 1965-1980 where the desired order sought was matched with an incompatible use of the instruments of national power and an inappropriate approach to building power. The Soviet denial grand strategy case examined begins in the period when the USSR appeared a rising great power that many thought could plausibly overtake a flagging US and become the dominant state in the international system.[1] The case study covers the complete life cycle from the early development of the grand strategy when Leonid Brezhnev gained power as Communist Party Secretary in late 1964, past its culminating point in 1972 when the Basic Principles treaty was signed with the US, through its progressive decline across the mid-1970s, until its final demise in late 1979 with the Soviet invasion of Afghanistan.

US Iraq War Grand Strategy 1991-1992

On the 2nd of August 1991 Iraq invaded its' neighbour Kuwait, seeking to incorporate the oil-rich state as Iraq's 19th province; the economic benefits were seen as great and the costs low from such action.[2] Three days later the American President George H. Bush declared that: "This will not stand. This will not stand, this aggression against Kuwait."[3] A new American grand strategy was hastily formulated to give substance to the President's words.

Several years before this, Iraq did not loom large in US thinking although it did feature in the American denial grand strategy of containing Iran. As part of this, during the 1980-1988 Iran-Iraq war the US on occasion provided limited intelligence information, gave diplomatic support and sold dual-use equipment and food stocks trying to deliberately shift the balance of power towards Iraq.

---

1. William Curti Wohlforth, *The Elusive Balance: Power and Perceptions During the Cold War* Ithaca: Cornell University Press, 1993, p. 185.
2. Andrew T. Parasiliti, 'The Causes and Timing of Iraq's Wars: A Power Cycle Assessment', *International Political Science Review,* Vol. 24, No. 1, 2003, pp. 151-65. Gregory Gause, 'Iraq's Decisions to Go to War, 1980 and 1990', *The Middle East Journal,* Vol. 56, No. 1, 2002, pp. 47-70. Fred H. Lawson, 'Rethinking the Iraqi Invasion of Kuwait', *The Review of International Affairs,* Vol. 1, No. 1, 2001, pp. 1-20.
3. 'Remarks and Exchange with Reporters, August 5, 1990 ', *Public Papers of the Presidents: George Bush*; College Station: George Bush Library, 1990, pp.

In this though, the US focus remained fixed on Iran. When changing its relationship with Iran demanded, the US abruptly began providing intelligence and selling arms to Iran for use against Iraq.[4]

With the end of the war and a new American President, a new grand strategy focused on Iraq was formulated with rather ambitious and, as it eventuated, unrealistic objectives. Steve Yetiv observed America: "tried to alter Iraq's behaviour with a strategy that leaned strongly towards placating it in the hope of co-opting it."[5] The social purpose of the Iraqi state would now be deliberately shaped through an engagement grand strategy. The intent, as National Security Directive 26 (NSD 26) elaborated upon, was to establish normal relations with Iraq, moderate Iraq's behaviour, increase US influence and promote regional stability. This was to be achieved through commercial activities in conjunction with limited military assistance to develop "access to and influence with the Iraqi defence establishment."[6]

Constructive engagement remained in force until the Iraq invasion of Kuwait. While "pursued with few hopes and fewer hopes that it could work", this grand strategy in leading to a major war is ultimately indefensible.[7] A successful engagement grand strategy would have required finding a suitable and willing Iraqi partner that held ambitions useful to America. However, the grand strategy was somewhat confused. The group within Iraq the grand strategy should work with was never made explicit, with Saddam Hussein seen both as the object and as the subject of the grand strategy. Even so, Saddam and his group appeared an unlikely partner to work with. A senior administration official observed that: "Everybody knew Hussein's reputation, and no one thought he was a potential member of the Kiwanis Club. But could he become a better member of the region? It was worth exploring the possibility, and we

---

4. Steve A. Yetiv, *The Absence of Grand Strategy: The United States in the Persian Gulf, 1972-2005*; Baltimore: John Hopkins University Press, 2008, p. 58.
5. Ibid., p. 65.
6. George Bush, *National Security Directive 26*; Washington The White House, 2 October 1989, pp., p. 2-3.
7. Zachary Karabell, 'Backfire: US Policy toward Iraq, 1988 - 2 August 1990 ', *Middle East Journal,* Vol. 49, No. 1, Winter 1995, pp. 28-47, p. 47.

didn't have a lot to lose."[8] The policy was confused and flawed in its original design.

The Iraqi invasion of Kuwait overturned the problematic engagement grand strategy's rationale and made imperative adopting a new approach. Iraq's actions also sharply elevated the nation's importance in American foreign policy. The invasion changed the regional balance of power, worryingly threatened Saudi Arabia and its massive oil reserves and directly challenged American management of the wider international order. Iraq though bordered the USSR and had for many years been a client state. While Eastern Europe was quickly moving out of the communist orbit, the USSR remained intact under First Secretary Gorbachev. The USSR however was now espousing a new basis for international relations including the "de-ideologization of interstate relations", a strengthened United Nations, a democratic world order and entry of the USSR into a range of international institutions.[9]

In determining how to respond to the Iraqi invasion of Kuwait, President George Bush's thinking and that of his inner decision-making team was strongly influenced by two key historical analogies: the appeasement period of the 1930s and the Vietnam War. The appeasement period was considered to show that dictators were untrustworthy; that left longer they would become stronger, more threatening and problematic; and that military force was the only viable option. Bush wrote later that: "I saw a direct analogy between what was occurring in Kuwait and what the Nazis had done..."[10] The Vietnam War analogy showed that using overwhelming force was needed to succeed and in devising policies based on this, Bush hoped that at the conflict's end "we will have kicked, for once and for all, the so-called Vietnam syndrome."[11] Historian Scot MacDonald argued that historical analogies significantly influenced how the crisis was framed and policymaking

8. Interview 27 May 1992 quoted in ibid., p. 33.
9. Mikhail Gorbachev, 'Speech to the 43rd U.N. General Assembly Session'; New York: 7 December 1988, pp.
10. George H.W. Bush and Brent Scowcroft, *A World Transformed*; New York: Knopf, 1998, p. 435.
11. 'Remarks and Exchange with Reporters, August 5, 1990 ', 1990.

determined, although not always favourably.[12] Barbara Spellman and Keith Holyoak wrote that: "It would not be great exaggeration to say that the United States went to war [against Iraq] over an analogy."[13]

President George Bush's "this will not stand" off-the-cuff remark to reporters "...became the defining statement of American aims for the duration of the crisis."[14] The primary objective of the US throughout remained stopping Iraqi from achieving its objective of permanently annexing Kuwait. This goal suggests a denial grand strategy focused on Iraq and indeed this was rapidly instituted. The American response to the Iraqi occupation of Kuwait was formalized in the hastily devised NSD-45 that directed a range of diplomatic, economic, energy and military measures to be taken with the primary aims of the:

> "...the immediate, complete and unconditional withdrawal of all Iraqi forces from Kuwait [and] the restoration of Kuwait's legitimate government to replace the puppet regime installed by Iraq...."[15]

To achieve this a change was sought in the new balance of power order that Iraq had created in the region. The relative power of the US would be increased and that of Iraqi's decreased aiming to coerce Iraq into leaving Kuwait. In the chosen denial type of grand strategy the threat of conflict is fundamental to its operation and this was evident from the start of the American grand strategy. The Chairman of the Joint Chiefs of Staff, General Colin Powell later commented that on hearing George Bush's "this will not stand" remark he felt war had been already been declared. This was a "widespread reaction" with George Bush himself "certainly [feeling]

12. Scot Macdonald, 'Hitler's Shadow: Historical Analogies and the Iraqi Invasion of Kuwait', *Diplomacy & Statecraft*, Vol. 13, No. 4, December 2002, pp. 29-59.
13. Barbara A. Spellman and Keith J. Holyoak, 'If Saddam Is Hitler Then Who Is George Bush? Analogical Mapping Btween Systems of Social Roles', *Journal of Personality and Social Psychology*, Vol. 62, No. 6, 1991, pp. 913-33, p. 913.
14. H. W. Brands, 'George Bush and the Gulf War of 1991', *Presidential Studies Quarterly*, Vol. 34, No. 1, March 2004, pp. 113-31, p. 121.
15. George Bush, *National Security Directive 45*; Washington: The White House, 20 August 1990, pp.

that force *could* be necessary."[16] The US objective of changing its relationship with Iraq though involved using the full range of the instruments of national power - diplomatic, economic, military and informational.

The initial actions involved diplomatic means seeking to gain the active support from as many nations as possible for American actions while simultaneously isolating Iraq. In this the US achieved remarkable success both in bilateral negotiations and at the United Nations; throughout the grand strategy's duration almost all UN member states voted in favour of supportive resolutions.[17] Co-sponsored by Malaysia and Ethiopia, the seminal Resolution 660 passed on 2 August was aligned with the American position in strongly condemning the invasion and calling for Iraq's immediate and unconditional withdrawal from Kuwait.[18] Critically the support – or at least acquiescence - of the USSR and China was gained ensuring that the UN Security Council consistently approved of US intentions and actions. In this America was helped by the rapidly changing international system. Then-Secretary of State James Baker wrote that it was "...apparent that the entire world suddenly wanted to get closer to the United States. The Soviet Empire was gone. ...It seemed as though everybody wanted to be America's best friend."[19]

The initial diplomatic activity was focused on not just condemnation of Iraqi actions but also on instituting a comprehensive range of negative sanctions. Prompted by the US, the UN on 6 August passed Security Council Resolution 661 imposing sweeping mandatory economic sanctions and establishing the 661 Committee to oversee their implementation by member and non-member states. In late August Security Council Resolutions 665 and 666 provided for an armed naval blockade to prevent Iraq exporting

---

16. George H.W. Bush and Brent Scowcroft, *A World Transformed*; New York: Vintage Books, 1999, p. 333.
17. Thomas M.Defrank and James A. Baker, *The Politics of Diplomacy: Revolution, War and Peace, 1989-1992*; New York: G.P.Putnam's Sons, 1995, pp. 275-328.
18. David M Malone, *The International Struggle over Iraq: Politics in the Un Security Council 1980-2005*; Oxford: Oxford University Press, 2006, p. 60.
19. James A. Baker, p. 414.

oil and importing most goods, while setting guidelines for the safe passage of medical and humanitarian aid. Resolution 670 extended this embargo to air cargo. On 29 November in an historic vote that gained the very rare agreement of all the Permanent Members of the Security Council, Resolution 678 was passed authorizing member states "to use all necessary means to uphold and implement resolution 660…" and by implication permitting the use of military force.[20]

The US deployed significant military forces to the region initially to reassure Saudi Arabia that it would be defended from any further Iraqi actions and then to progressively build up a capability to force Iraq out of Kuwait. To assist both objectives the US persuaded some 34 states to send combat forces to the Gulf region. While some were long-time allies such as the UK and France, major Arab countries including Egypt, Saudi Arabia and Syria also actively participated. Ultimately the force comprised almost one million personnel with about 70% from the US. While a multinational coalition though, the operation was firmly commanded by the US not by some collective system. The National Security Adviser, Brent Scrowcroft observed that:

> "The U.S. had to be the leader. No one else could be a focal point for dealing with aggression, but it was not coercion. It was infinite consultation, cajoling, and listening to their views. We led and got our way…."[21]

The informational instrument was employed to persuade others of the legitimacy of American actions and the illegitimacy of Iraq's. Stress was placed on Iraq's violation of the UN Charter that outlawed aggression, that Iraq had disregarded human rights and arms limitations agreements and that the rights of small states against large hostile large neighbours should be upheld. In this process

---

20. Brands, p. 127.
21. Interview quoted in Eric A. Miller and Steve A. Yetiv, 'The New World Order in Theory and Practice: The Bush Administration's Worldview in Transition', *Presidential Studies Quarterly,* Vol. 31, No. 1, March 2001, pp. 56-68, p. 63.

President Bush described Saddam Hussein as evil, morally reprehensible and comparable to Adolf Hitler.[22]

The combination of the perceived illegitimacy of Iraq's actions, that the USSR was now keen to cooperate with the US on global affairs and the apparent failure of the communist paradigm progressively induced a more expansive outlook for future American global influence. On 11 September 1990 President Bush in a speech to a Joint Session of the Congress on the Persian Gulf Crisis and the Federal Budget Deficit added a new American objective, that of helping establish:

> "...a new world order...freer from the threat of terror, stronger in the pursuit of justice and more secure in the quest for peace. An era in which the nations of the world, east and west, north and south, can prosper and live in harmony. ...A world where the rule of law supplants the rule of the jungle. ... A world where the strong respect the rights of the weak."[23]

President Bush's conception was that the Iraq War grand strategy could provide a model of how the US would provide post-Cold War leadership of the international system. This model had three elements: the offensive use of force would be checked, the US would lead collective action by coalitions and the great powers would cooperate in this. The "new world order" construct helped legitimize the Iraq War grand strategy both domestically and internationally although the different audiences may have heard different messages: American exceptionalism versus a new UN-led era. In examining the role played by the new world order concept, Eric Miller and Steve Yetiv observed that it "...allowed Washington to crystallize positive feelings about a new era into more palpable vision and approach while advancing its national interests and asserting its global primacy."[24]

---

22. Lawrence Freedman, *A Choice of Enemies: America Confronts the Middle East*; New York: PublicAffairs, 2008, pp. 230-31.
23. George Bush, *The Public Papers of the President, 1990. Vol. 2*; Washington: Government Printing Office, 1991, p. 1219.
24. Miller and Yetiv, p. 58.

The denial grand strategy applied power in ways that grew American power by exploiting alliances, partnerships and friends while degrading Iraqi power through isolation and broad-ranging sanctions. Simultaneously, America also acted to develop its own power and limit the costs involved through leveraging off others. In building power two criteria are important: whether the matter is near or long term and whether the matter is one of necessity or choice.

In terms of time, the US thought that its ability to evict Iraq would lessen over time making near-term action crucial. Throughout the crisis, calls to wait until sanctions had been given time to act where consistently discounted. In terms of choice, the Iraq War was considered a matter of choice in that America was not itself threatened by the invasion and the US obtained little oil from the region. Senator Daniel Patrick Moynihan called it "a small disturbance in a distant part of the world."[25] This lack of a compelling rationale to become deeply involved and risk war did create difficulties for President Bush in gaining domestic support.[26]

In being near term and a matter of choice, the grand strategy diagnostic process suggests a near-term market approach that makes use of existing domestic and global resources. The access to global resources proved crucial as the US at the time had significant worries over the burgeoning fiscal deficit inherited from the previous Regan Administration in which George Bush had been Vice-President. The grand strategy promised to exacerbate this by being very costly. Baker commented that:

> "We knew that, even without going to war, these costs would be staggering. We were mobilizing hundreds of thousands of soldiers and shipping them and their equipment to the Gulf by air and by sea. Once we had them there, we had to keep them in everything from missiles to mouthwash for months on end. Our preliminary projections of the direct costs to the United States Treasury ran into the tens of billions of dollars. Moreover, we felt an obligation to come up with the money

25. Speech of 10 January 1991 quoted in Freedman, *A Choice of Enemies: America Confronts the Middle East*, p. 226.
26. Brands, p. 127-30.

to help offset the severe economic hardship the trade embargo would impose on several coalition partners, especially Egypt and Turkey."[27]

To overcome this, the US actively sought to extract considerable financial support from its wealthy allies and friends. The war cost the US some $61bn but coalition partners, especially Kuwait, Saudi Arabia, Japan, Germany and South Korea, provided some $48bn in financial transfers. Moreover, these countries also made in-kind contributions of materiel, fuel and other supplies valued at almost $6bn as well as assisting several nations economically damaged by the embargo.[28]

The money extracted markedly reduced the war's impact on the Federal Government's budget but in relying on a market based approach there were other concerns. In the initial days of the grand strategy, it was realized that the oil supply disruption arising from the UN sanctions and a naval blockade of Iraqi oil exports while not directly impacting American stocks, would adversely impact the economy. At a National Security Council meeting on 6 August Treasury Secretary Nicholas Brady declared that: "The financial markets are down badly. The price of oil is rising. The effect of petroleum and home heating oil price increases is already 0.5% in the Consumer Price Index, or 0.6-0.7% of GNP. This would bring our growth down toward zero."[29] It was quickly realized that to avoid a recession in the US, Saudi Arabia needed to be asked to increase crude oil production. A market based approach to building-power for a grand strategy needs to be undertaken in a manner that keeps markets comfortable for it to succeed.

The American denial grand strategy was successful in comprehensively changing the relative balance of power in the region away from Iraq but even so military power had to be used to forcibly eject it from Kuwait. The marked advantage in relative power though meant that the military operation from the US-led coalition perspective was effective and efficient. The Iraqi armed

---

27. James A. Baker, p. 288.
28. Hormats, p. 255.
29. Brady quoted in Brands, p. 116.

forces collapsed when the ground offensive started after having been the target of incessant air strikes for almost a month. The ensuing rout and a perception that too many retreating Iraqi soldiers were being killed led to a swift end to the war.

The war's conclusion quickly proved controversial with some commentators declaring later that the war stopped too soon or that the Allied force should have marched on Baghdad and removed Saddam Hussein from power.[30] The denial grand strategy adopted perhaps made such second thoughts inevitable. The overall intent was to change the balance of power in a way that stopped Iraq occupying Kuwait not to have American forces occupying Iraq.

The US Ambassador to Saudi Arabia at the time, Charles Freeman, warned Colin Powell before the fighting started that: "For a range of reasons we cannot pursue Iraq's unconditional surrender and occupation by us. It is not in our interest to destroy Iraq or weaken it to the point that Iran and/or Syria are not constrained by it."[31] Scowcroft similarly thought the grand strategy's aim was to "to damage his [Saddam's] offensive capability without weakening Iraq to the point that a vacuum was created, and destroying the balance between Iraq and Iran."[32] Additional contributing factors were that a march on Bagdad would have spilt the Arab partners from the coalition some of whom were contributing basing rights and considerable funding, exceeded the UN mandate and risked American forces being embroiled in a long-lasting occupation.[33]

The denial grand strategy was successful because it was carefully designed taking into account the problem's specific conditions. The ends set by President Bush, that Iraq would not achieve its objectives of annexing Kuwait, were appropriate to the denial grand strategy type that seeks to stop another state achieving

---

30. An example is Robert A. Divine, 'The Persian Gulf War Revisited: Tactical Victory, Strategic Failure', *Diplomatic History,* Vol. 24, No. 1, Winter 2000, pp. 129-38.
31. Freeman quoted in With Joseph E. Persico Colin Powell, *My American Journey* New York: Ballantine Books, 1995, p. 527.
32. Bush and Scowcroft, *A World Transformed*, p. 383.
33. Yetiv, p. 88.

their desired objectives. This type of grand strategy stresses the importance of relative power and America made astute use of diplomatic, informational, military and economic means to decisively shift the power balance towards it for the time it needed to succeed. Given a more lengthy confrontation, the relative power balance may have eroded.

The success of the American denial grand strategy against Iraq though also illustrates this type's shortcomings. The limited grand strategic ends chosen skillfully matched available ways and means, but the underlying causes of the conflict remained. Stopping Iraq achieving its objectives was a negative goal that produced the more favourable balance of power order sought, but did not have more positive or enduring results such as a change in the social purpose or the social rules of the Iraqi state may have. This seeming deficiency led some to charge that the President's grand strategy won the war but lost the peace.[34] There is some truth in such criticism of this type of grand strategy.

Even though the grand strategy succeeded, the US could not disengage from the region and return to the *status quo ante* as many wished. Iraq remained a problem in persecuting the Kurds who had staged an unsuccessful uprising that the US encouraged; America now felt obliged to remain and provide humanitarian assistance. Moreover, Iraq's development of Weapons of Mass Destruction needed to be permanently halted and this required constant military pressure on the country from coalition forces based in the Gulf to ensure that UN weapon's inspectors could achieve this. In the end, there was little confidence that Saddam no longer posed a threat to regional peace and security.[35]

The denial grand strategy created the kind of peace that was sought and for which the grand strategy was designed. If this was ultimately unappealing, a new grand strategy needed to be fashioned to continue from where the denial grand strategy had reached its

---

34. Divine, pp. 137-38.
35. Freedman, *A Choice of Enemies: America Confronts the Middle East*, pp. 252-53.

culminating point.   Grand strategies are not a set-and-forget approach.

The LTTE Grand Strategy 1990-2002

The civil war waged in Sri Lanka from 1983 to 2009 was principally between the national government and the Liberation Tigers of Tamil Eeelam (LTTE).   The LTTE sought to create a separate, independent state for the local Tamil community[36] in the northeast of the island adjacent to the southern Indian state of Tamil Nardu.[37]   Sri Lanka for the LTTE leader Velupillai Prabhakaran, comprised only two nations - the Sinhala and the Tamil - and accordingly for him:

" The argument is simple – the Tamils are peaceful people who wish to live in peace in their traditional homeland. However they are subjugated, colonized, and oppressed by the Sinhala nation, from which the Tamils want freedom, and their right to live in peace in their homeland."[38]

In the 1990-2002 period the LTTE could have chosen between denial, engagement or reform grand strategies.   Considering

---

36. The Tamil population of Sri Lankan is divided into those resident in Ceylon when the British colonized the island in 1796 termed Sri Lankan Tamils, and those that migrated from Tamil Nardu in the 19th and 20th Centuries to work in plantation agriculture termed 'Indian' or 'Estate Tamils'. In 1997 the ethnic composition of Sri Lanka was estimated to be 74% Sinhalese, 12.7% Sri Lankan Tamils, 7% Moors (Sri Lankan Muslims), 5.5% 'Indian' Tamils and 1% others. This division was based on religion, caste and language differences as originally discerned by the British. Few Indian Tamils were involved with the LTTE, which was comprised mostly of Sri Lankan Tamils. Deborah Winslow and Michael D. Woost, 'Articulations of Economy and Ethnic Conflict in Sri Lanka', in Deborah Winslow and Michael D. Woost (eds.), *Economy, Culture, and Civil War in Sri Lanka*; Bloomington: Indiana University Press, 2004, pp. 1-30, p. 4-5, p. 25 n9, p. 26 n12.
37. P. Sahadevan, 'Sri Lanka's War for Peace and the LTTE's Commitment to Armed Struggle', in Omprakash Mishra and Sucheta Ghosh (eds.), *Terrorism and Low Intensity Conflict in South Asian Region*; New Delhi: Manak Publications, 2003, pp. 284-315, p. 304.
38. Kasun Ubayasiri, 'An Illusive Leader's Annual Speech ', *Ejournalist: a refereed media journal,* Vol. 6, No. 1, 2006, pp. 1-27, p. 14.

the engagement option, in the three years prior the LTTE had worked with the Sri Lankan government to force an Indian military peacekeeping force deployed to the island under the Indo-Lanka Accord to leave. To achieve this joint goal, the Sri Lankan government covertly provided the LTTE with arms and money and involved them in political negotiations.[39] Even so, the LTTE never attempted an engagement grand strategy, probably because they would not accept any compromise over secession and the various Sri Lankan governments involved only offered autonomy and devolution.[40] The two sides ultimately proved unable to work together for mutual benefit as they could not find common ground and shared objectives. Their earlier alliance of convenience collapsed when both realised they held conflicting values. An engagement grand strategy requires finding partners with whom to cooperate and this proved impossible to find.

Similarly a reform grand strategy was not adopted either, although given the narrow and fragmented elite base of Sri Lankan national politics there may at times have been some opportunities for the LTTE to have acted to transform the extant norms in a favourable direction. In such a grand strategy though the secession agenda would have again proved problematic. Advancing this agenda would have required the idea of a single government ruling the entire island to collapse, and this always seemed unlikely. Accordingly, the LTTE embraced a denial grand strategy aiming to stop the Sri Lankan government retaining control over the whole island.

The denial grand strategy of the LTTE was particularly evident and efficacious in the period 1990-2002 from the Indian Peacekeeping Force withdrawal and until the Norwegian-brokered ceasefire agreement signed on 22 February 2002. This period includes Eelam War II and III, and several ceasefires. The LTTE

---

39. Rohan Edrisinha, 'Trying Times: Constitutional Attempts to Resolve Armed Conflict in Sri Lanka', in Liz Philipson (ed.), *Accord: An International Review of Peace Initiatives - Demanding Sacrifice: War and Negotiation in Sri Lanka*, 4; London: Conciliation Resources, 1998, pp. 28-36, p. 30.
40. Sahadevan, in Mishra and Ghosh (eds.), *Terrorism and Low Intensity Conflict in South Asian Region*; New Delhi: Manak Publications, 2003, pp. 284-315, p. 310.

employed a grand strategy focused on changing the existing relationship with the Sri Lankan state into a balance of power order. In such an order the state would no longer dominate the domestic sub-state system. In this, the LTTE was a revisionist non-state actor endeavouring, through improving its power relative to the Sri Lankan state, to gain the independence of the Sri Lankan Tamil nation.

The LTTE believed that the Sri Lankan state could not impose its will militarily and could be balanced against; academic Sahadevan observed: "It is this factor that determines the Tiger's preference for war...."[41] The preference for this kind of grand strategy however was also partly influenced by the thinking of its leader, Velupillai Prabhakaran, who dominated LTTE central committee decision-making.

While Prabhakaran's thinking was not shaped by a philosophy or ideology, he drew a close historical analogy between the Tamil struggle for an independent Eelam and the Indian nationalist movement that defeated the British colonial state.[42] In this however he considered the armed resistance approaches of Indian's Subash Chandra Bose and Bhagath Singh more appropriate to defeat the Sinhala dominated Sri Lankan government than the non-violent methods of Mahatma Gandhi.[43] The colonial era analogy may have been historically recent but there were significant differences between the two conflicts. Importantly, Prabhakaran overlooked that the British were not defeated by armed force.

The LTTE's denial grand strategy made extensive use of its military, diplomatic and informational instruments of power although as the denial grand strategy schema suggests military power was the central element. The LTTE did not employ positive or negative economic sanctions.

---

41. Ibid., p. 297.
42. 'Obituary: Prabhakaran', *The Economist* 21 May 2009.
43. Chellamuthu Kuppusamy, 'Prabhakaran: The Story of His Struggle for Eelam', 24 October 2013 edn.Kindle Edition, Amazon Digital Services, 2013, Chapter 2. Alastair Lawson, 'The Enigma of Prabhakaran', *BBC News*; London: BBC, 2 May 2000.

The LTTE's military power was principally directed at the Sri Lankan state's opposing military forces although some attacks were made on supporting civilian infrastructures including the Central Bank and the international airport, and against specific political and military leaders.[44]   Compared to other contemporary secessionist groups, the LTTE emphasized more conventional military operations uniquely involving land, sea and air units. The LTTE also formed a specialist suicide arm – the Black Tigers – that undertook numerous attacks; in the 1990-2002 period, the LTTE were the most significant non-state actor globally using this technique. The military instrument positively supported the grand strategy with the LTTE leader declaring in his 1999 Hero's Day Speech that:

> "The spectacular victories that we gained…have turned the balance of military power in our favour. The massive effort made by [Sri Lankan President] Chandrika over the last five years to weaken the LTTE and to achieve military hegemony was shattered by us in the matter of a few days."[45]

The diplomatic instrument was focused on enhancing the LTTE's relative military power, as the framework's denial grand strategy schema thinking would suggest. While several ceasefires were announced and negotiations entered into with the Sri Lankan government, these episodes were used simply to resupply and rebuild the LTTE's armed forces. Jonathan Goodhand wrote that nothing suggested that the LTTE "….acted in good faith in the interests of peace….in spite of the political rhetoric of returning to talks, primacy [was] still accorded to a military course of action in shaping

---

44. Uniquely, the LTTE assassinated three heads of government: Indian Prime Minister Rajiv Gandhi in 1991, Sri Lankan President Ranasinghe Premadasa in 1993, and former Sri Lankan Prime Minister and presidential hopeful Gamini Dissanayake in 1994. Cécile Van De Voorde, 'Sri Lankan Terrorism: Assessing and Responding to the Threat of the Liberation Tigers of Tamil Eelam (LTTE)', *Police Practice and Research,* Vol. 6, No. 2, May 2005, pp. 181-99, p. 187.
45. V. Prabhakaran, 'LTTE Leader Calls Upon Sri Lanka to End Military Oppression for Peace Talks', [accessed 26 November 2010] edn.; London, UK: International Secretariat of LTTE, 1999, pp., p. http://www.infolanka.com/ubb/Forum2/HTML/001166.html [accessed 26 November 2010].

the process."[46]

Internationally, the LTTE established a quasi-diplomatic presence in some 54 countries, principally concentrating on those with large Tamil migrant populations. This presence aimed to harness and integrate international political support for LTTE objectives. Eelam House in London was the LTTE's principal headquarters outside of Sri Lanka, from here overseas political activity was coordinated and all official Tiger statements, memoranda and promulgations originated.[47]

The informational instrument was extensively used by the LTTE with their message disseminated through e-mail, internet, telephone hot lines, community libraries, mailings, Tamil TV and radio, and political, social and cultural gatherings. Websites were established to give the LTTE a: "…truly global presence, permitting the group to 'virtually' and instantaneously transmit propaganda, mobilize active supporters, and sway potential backers." The LTTE promulgated a consistent three part ethno-nationalist message: Tamils are the innocent victims of Sinhalese discrimination and government instigated military repression; only the LTTE can defend and promote the interests of the Sri Lankan Tamil community; and there can be no peace until Sri Lankan Tamils are granted their own independent state governed by the LTTE.[48]

The approach taken to building power was shaped by the ongoing war, the certainty it would continue and that this was a matter of necessity. As the diagnostic process would suggest, the LTTE implemented a near-term managerial approach that emphasized extraction. In this, the LTTE was not limited to simply the territory of Sri Lanka. Since gaining independence from Britain in 1948, there had been five successive waves of chain migration with the third and fifth waves that occurred after the 1983 ethnic

46. Jonathan Goodhand, *Aid, Conflict and Peace Building in Sri Lanka*, Conflict Assessments; London: Conflict, Security and Development Group, King's College, University of London, July 2001, pp. 42-43.
47. Daniel Byman et al., *Trends in Outside Support for Insurgent Movements*; Santa Monica: RAND, 2001, p. 44.
48. Ibid., pp. 43-46.

riots particularly supportive of the LTTE. During 1987-2002 in the fifth and largest wave, some 300,000 Tamils migrated and by 2002 an estimated one-third of the three million Sri Lankan Tamils lived overseas.[49]

Gaining legitimacy presented a particular problem. The LTTE was an authoritarian military organization with no accompanying political party so the option of using democratic means to gain input legitimacy was unavailable.[50] Accordingly, legitimacy was sought through the LTTE presenting itself as the only group able to defend Sri Lankan Tamils from a predatory government. By the early 1990s, the LTTE was the dominant Sri Lankan Tamil insurgent group having actively eliminated most other opposition groups, large and small, through marginalization, assassinations and targeted violence both within Sri Lanka and internationally; this program left the LTTE uniquely positioned to claim resistance legitimacy.[51] The claim of output legitimacy was further advanced though deliberately cultivating an appearance of serving those under its control:

> " The LTTE...accomplished this...through an elaborate effort to direct the service activities of the local and international NGO communities, create its own NGOs, and appoint steering committees to Sri Lankan government agencies that provide services. By creating this public image of a welfare 'state', the LTTE ensures that the population under its control sees it as the primary provider of relief and

---

49. Rohan Gunaratna, 'Sri Lanka: Feeding the Tamil Tigers', in Karen Ballentine and Jake Sherman (eds.), *The Political Economy of Armed Conflict: Beyond Greed and Grievance*; Boulder: Lynne Rienner Publishers, 2003, pp. 197-224, p. 200-02.
50. Liz Philipson and Yuvi Thangarajah, *The Politics of the North-East: Part of the Sri Lanka Strategic Conflict Assessment 2005*; Colombo: The Asia Foundation, 2005, p. 28-29.
51. Gamini Samaranayakea, 'Political Terrorism of the Liberation Tigers of Tamil Eelam (LTTE) in Sri Lanka', *South Asia: Journal of South Asian Studies,* Vol. 30, No. 1, 2007, pp. 171-83, p. 174, 77.

rehabilitation."[52]

The LTTE had to primarily rely on Sri Lankan Tamils living in Sri Lanka and under its control for the majority of its manpower needs. Of the others within its territory, the LTTE persecuted Muslim groups and Indian Tamil participation was marginal.[53] The Sri Lankan Tamil population under LTTE control during 1990-2002 probably oscillated between a half to one million people; by comparison the state's population was around 17 million people.[54] By 2002, the LTTE could only sustain some 8,000-10,000 armed combatants with a core of 3,000–6,000 trained fighters.[55] Many had volunteered in the early phases of the insurgency motivated by Tamil nationalism and indignation against state repression. As enthusiasm waned and losses mounted however, the LTTE introduced conscription and progressively made much greater use of women and children.[56]

About a third of the LTTE were women who undertook many of the suicide attacks and were prominent in conventional military campaigns.[57] RAND military analyst Christine Fair noted that: "In the LTTE's 2000 offensive to retake the Jaffna Peninsula, the LTTE engaged the Sri Lankan Army with about 7,000 light infantry cadre. Of this figure, it is estimated that 3,000 were women."[58] Manpower

---

52. Shawn Teresa Flanigan, 'Nonprofit Service Provision by Insurgent Organizations: The Cases of Hizballah and the Tamil Tigers', *Studies in Conflict and Terrorism,* Vol. 31, No. 6, 2008, pp. 499-519, p. 504.
53. Samaranayakea, p. 174.
54. The key population centre for the LTTE was the city of Jaffna where some 800,000 people lived; across this period the city was often under LTTE control. The estimates of the LTTE population base are derived from: Tamil Information Centre, 'Exodus of Tamils from Jaffna: The Displacement Crisis'; www.tamilcanadian.com/article/469: *TamilCanadian: Tamils True Voice,* December 1995.
55. 'Patterns of Global Terrorism 2001'; Washington: United States Department of State, May 2002, pp., p. 100.
56. Sahadevan, in Mishra and Ghosh (eds.), *Terrorism and Low Intensity Conflict in South Asian Region*; New Delhi: Manak Publications, 2003, pp. 284-315, p. 306.
57. Voorde, p. 186.
58. C. Christine Fair, *Urban Battle Fields of South Asia: Lessons Learned from Sri Lanka, India, and Pakistan*; Santa Monica: RAND, 2004, p. 25.

shortages also saw extensive use of children across the period; by early 1996 half the recruits were between 12 and 16 years old.[59] The child soldiers were reportedly involved in major combat actions from the early 1990s and by 2000 some 2,000 were estimated to be serving in the LTTE. [60]

The LTTE's revenue was derived internally (40%) and externally (60%). The internal funds met operating expenses whereas the external funds were mainly used for arms procurement.[61] Internally, the LTTE taxed Sri Lankan Tamils on an individual income basis and at times solicited or coerced extra donations. There was further taxation of individuals migrating and of those families that had family members abroad. Within LTTE areas, commercial businesses, private passenger buses and lorries transporting food and supplies were also taxed. While outside LTTE areas there was a clandestine tax collection from Tamil business enterprises.[62]

Externally, funds came from four main sources: direct contributions from migrant communities; funds siphoned off contributions given to NGOs, charities, and benevolent donor groups; people smuggling; and investments made in legitimate, Tamil run businesses.[63] In later years, the LTTE also started commercial businesses to obtain a regular funding source.[64] The largest funding source though was from a tax imposed on Sri Lankan Tamils living abroad. This tax was preferred to be given voluntarily but if not threats were made to family members in LTTE- controlled

59. Voorde, p. 186.
60. 'Child Soldiers of the Liberation Tiger of Tamil Eelam (LTTE)'; www. satp.org/satporgtp/countries/shrilanka/terroristoutfits/child_solders.htm [accessed 1 December 2010]: South Asia Terrorism Portal, Institute for Conflict Management, Delhi, India, 2001.
61. Gunaratna, in Ballentine and Sherman (eds.), *The Political Economy of Armed Conflict: Beyond Greed and Grievance*; Boulder: Lynne Rienner Publishers, 2003, pp. 197-224, pp. 209-10.
62. Ibid., pp. 210-11.
63. Byman et al., p. 49.
64. D.B.S. Jeyaraj, 'Ramifications of Crackdown on LTTE in Switzerland'; Toronto, Canada: dbsjeyaraj.com/dbsj/archives/1952, 28 January 2011, p.

areas in Sri Lanka or to the unwilling contributors themselves.[65] The tax collectors, while initially volunteers, later worked on a commission basis that encouraged coercion and intimidation.[66]

In this extraction of external funds, the deliberate LTTE manipulation of Tamil diaspora organizations played the central role. The LTTE gained output legitimacy by providing services and this legitimacy then supported their fund-raising activities. Rohan Gunaratna writes that:

> " Diaspora organizations provided the medium for the LTTE to permeate diasporas and migrants with Tamil nationalist, secessionist, and pro-LTTE rhetoric. The key LTTE strategy aimed at enhancing control over Tamils overseas was to make them dependent on LTTE services for their basic needs and to provide social and cultural fulfilment."[67]

Material was also obtained internally and externally. Internally, arms were captured from the Sri Lankan Army and a rudimentary manufacturing capability was established that could supply mines, grenades and mortar shells for low-intensity guerrilla warfare.[68] Most arms came from overseas, initially from India but after 1987, when overt Government support ceased, from global sources.[69] To support this, the LTTE developed a large-scale shipping organization involving at least 11 deep-sea freighters sailing under Honduran, Liberian or Panamanian flags of convenience. The main logistical transhipment base was in Thailand

---

65. Byman et al., p. 50.
66. Jeyaraj, 28 January 2011.
67. Gunaratna, in Ballentine and Sherman (eds.), *The Political Economy of Armed Conflict: Beyond Greed and Grievance; Boulder*: Lynne Rienner Publishers, 2003, pp. 197-224, pp. 206-07.
68. Sahadevan, in Mishra and Ghosh (eds.), Terrorism and Low Intensity Conflict in South Asian Region; New Delhi: Manak Publications, 2003, pp. 284-315, p. 306. Gunaratna, in Ballentine and Sherman (eds.), *The Political Economy of Armed Conflict: Beyond Greed and Grievance*; Boulder: Lynne Rienner Publishers, 2003, pp. 197-224, p. 208.
69. The major weapon sources were Cambodia, Myanmar and Afghanistan with ammunition supplied from Bulgaria, the Czech Republic and North Korea, and explosives from Ukraine, Croatia and South Africa. Byman et al., pp. 118, 20-21.

with supplies purchased using bank accounts in Germany, Netherlands, Norway, the UK and Canada.[70]

The use of the diaspora for funding military procurement was skilful but may have had some unintentional side effects. The strategic synthesis saw more resources flowing from overseas than domestic sources and this grew in importance as in-country sources became less able or willing to contribute. Stephen Battle writes that overtime:

> "...the LTTE became less concerned in actually representing local Tamil interests and more concerned in selling the perception of being the sole representative of the Tamil struggle to the vast Diaspora. ...it purported itself as the sole representative...not to win a war of succession, but to facilitate the continual flow of monetary support to its coffers. The actual plight of local Tamils became less and less of a concern to the LTTE."[71]

The LTTE saw less need to sustain in-country legitimacy and resorted to the easier option of increasing coercion as a means to extract resources from the in-country Tamil community.[72] The access to external resources allowed the LTTE to be less responsive to local pressures and avoid any reassessments of their grand strategy and its likelihood of long-term success.

The LTTE's denial grand strategy was successful in being matched to the problem's specific context. In the 1990-2002 period the ends sought of denying Sri Lankan government control over the entire island were appropriate to the denial grand strategy type but its ability to be successfully implemented depended on being able to achieve and sustain a suitable relative power balance. The LTTE was able to achieve this by reducing the Sir Lankan government's

---

70. Ibid., p. 119.
71. Stephen L. Battle, *Lessons in Legitimacy: The LTTE End-Game of 2007–2009*, (Naval Postgraduate School, June 2010), pp. 43-44.
72. Jannie Lilja, 'Trapping Constituents or Winning Hearts and Minds? Rebel Strategies to Attain Constituent Support in Sri Lanka', *Terrorism and Political Violence,* Vol. 21, No. 2, 2009, pp. 306-26, pp. 314-18.

power through the use of military, diplomatic and informational means and by building up its own power though a near-term managerial approach. The relative weakness of the Sri Lankan military means was particularly important in the grand strategy's success. At the end of the Eelam III war in 1999 an external observer noted that:

> "The official army is weak strategically, poorly led, poorly paid, demoralized by danger and sustained lack of success, and allegedly riddled with corruption. Strategically, its major handicap is a scarcity of intelligence about the enemy. It has few resources for gathering intelligence, few Tamils to do it, and very few trained analysts of the intelligence that is gathered. So the Sri Lankan army fights a committed, even fanatic, cadre of guerrillas with overwhelming numbers but with insufficient training, knowledge, and motivation."[73]

While achieving its strategic objectives in the 1990-2002 period, the LTTE however, was arguably unwise to continue with a denial grand strategy that stressed relative military power. The Sri Lankan state was inherently much stronger than the LTTE could ever aspire to, making the grand strategy particularly vulnerable to governmental policy changes. A grand strategy involves interacting with intelligent others that can learn from their failures and adopt new or evolved grand strategies in response. The change in the relative balance of power when it came took time and was noted by the LTTE leadership but the denial grand strategy remained in place.

Beyond the period discussed here, the relative power balance changed dramatically as the Sri Lankan government adopted a new grand strategy that used military, diplomatic, informational and economic means to weaken the LTTE while sharply building up its own military power.[74] For the LTTE, this external challenge came at

---

73. Robert I. Rothberg, 'Sri Lanka's Civil War: From Mayhem toward Diplomatic Resolution', in Robert I. Rothberg (ed.), *Creating Peace in Sri Lanka: Civil War and Reconciliation*; Washington: Brookings Institution Press;, 1999, pp. 1-16, p. 2.
74. Ashok Mehta, *Sri Lanka's Ethnic Conflict: How Eelam War Iv Was Won*, Manekshaw Paper No.22; New Delhi: Centre for Land Warfare Studies, 2010.

a time when its internal power had passed its peak and was weakening. The LTTE's near-term managerial approach was highly effective in allowing a small non-state actor drawing on a very limited population base to successfully balance against a much larger state but only for a time. Waging permanent war necessitated the recruitment of women and children and to growing war weariness in the populace.

The Sri Lankan state progressively developed overwhelming military power, took advantage of declining legitimacy to split the LTTE, and in 2009 simply annihilated the intrinsically much weaker non-state actor.[75] The LTTE grand strategy played to the Sri Lankan state's fundamental strengths, as Sahadevan had prophetically observed in 2003 the LTTE: "...is invariably a loser in any conventional battle."[76] This was an outcome that having an understanding of the operation of a denial grand strategy could have foretold.

A denial grand strategy simply aims to stop the actions of another state succeeding and therefore has a negative goal. This type of grand strategy does not seek to change the social purpose of the other state or its social rules. For the LTTE to create a secessionist Tamil state it needed to move at some time from a denial to another type of grand strategy. When the Sir Lankan government decided to change the relative balance of power, the LTTE denial grand strategy reached its culminating point and needed to be replaced. Grand strategies are dynamic not static and must evolve to suit the times.

The USSR's Détente Grand Strategy 1965-1980

By the mid-1960s, the USSR was one of the most successful economies in the world and was militarily rapidly gaining on the

Sinharaja Tammita-Delgoda, *Review Essay: Sri Lanka's Ethnic Conflict* Manekshaw Paper 22a; New Delhi: Centre for Land Warfare Studies, 2010.
75. Sergei Desilva-Ranasinghe, 'Land Warfare Lessons from Sri Lanka', *Asian Defence & Diplomacy,* Vol. 16, No. 6, December 2009/January 2010, pp. 29-37.
76. Sahadevan, in Mishra and Ghosh (eds.), Terrorism and Low Intensity Conflict in South Asian Region; New Delhi: Manak Publications, 2003, pp. 284-315, p. 299.

Western alliance.[77] To observers both within and outside the USSR, the macro-trends appeared to indicate a dynamic and growing USSR and a declining America; the future seemed bright. Soviet political thinking swung to favour the "...stability of the post-war great-power alignments. Even the official ideology...now busied itself with glorifying the status quo as the best of all possible solutions."[78] The new First Party Secretary Leonid Brezhnev led a confident Communist Party that sought to maintain this newly favourable international situation.

The Soviet leadership's thinking was influenced by concerns over the brinkmanship of the previous Party Secretary, Nikita Khrushchev and more distant memories of the Second World War. Brezhnev dismissively talked of Khrushchev's approach to the Cuban missile crisis declaring that: "We almost slipped into nuclear war! And what effort did it cost us to pull ourselves out of this...."[79] This event reinforced his beliefs arising from his World War Two experiences, that wars should be avoided at all costs, and that the US and the USSR had a special responsibility to act together to prevent future major wars.[80]

Using newly available Soviet sources, Vladislav Zubok determined that "...Brezhnev's [détente] strategy came from a disarmingly straightforward premise: two superpowers, the Soviet Union and the United States, had a joint obligation to maintain a stable world order."[81] Brezhnev though, like the rest of the senior Soviet leadership, also drew an historical analogy from the Second World War that maintaining the peace and building military strength in the circumstances of the mid-Cold War were not contradictory. This cognitive dissonance was to later cause the détente grand

77. Robert C. Allen, 'The Rise and Decline of the Soviet Economy', *Canadian Journal of Economics,* Vol. 34, No. 4, November, 2001, p. 861.
78. Wohlforth, p. 193.
79. Brezhnev quoted in Vladislav M. Zubok, *A Failed Empire: The Soviet Union in the Cold War from Stalin to Gorbachev*; Chapel Hill: The University of North Carolina Press, 2009, p. 203.
80. Vladislav Zubok, 'The Soviet Union and Détente of the 1970s', *Cold War History,* Vol. 8, No. 4, November 2008, pp. 427-47, pp. 430-31.
81. Ibid., p. 431.

strategy mortal difficulties.

The Soviet leaderships' predilections and their view that conflict was inherent in the contemporary international system suggested their adopting a denial grand strategy from the beginning. While ostensibly global in coverage, the grand strategy was focused on changing the relationship with the US. The international system was considered by the Soviets to be strongly bipolar with "the US-Soviet relationship...the central one in world politics." [82]

In considering potential international orders to strive for, the hegemonic stability order appeared impractical as the Soviet bloc patently did not, at least yet, have the combination of overwhelming political, military, economic and social power needed to dominate the international system. By contrast a satisfactory balance of power had been already been achieved. Partly from default but also because it conformed to the leadership's world view, Brezhnev's party decided to use a denial grand strategy to create a concert of power order. Historian John Lewis Gaddis observes détente was all about "...turning a dangerous situation into a predictable *system*...to freeze the Cold War in place. Its purpose was not to end the conflict...but rather establish rules by which it should be conducted."[83]

For the USSR these rules were formally codified in the 1972 Basic Principles of Relations between the United States of America and the Union of the Soviet Socialist Republics.[84] US Secretary of State Henry Kissinger called it a roadmap that established "clear rules of conduct."[85] The two states agreed their relations would be based on "...the principles of sovereignty, equality, non-interference

82. Wohlforth, p. 201.
83. John Lewis Gaddis, *The Cold War: A New History*; New York: The Penguin Press, 2005, p. 198.
84. Geoffrey Roberts, *The Soviet Union in World Politics: Coexistence, Revolution and Cold War, 1945-1991*; London: Routledge, 1999, p. 75.
85. Henry Kissinger 29 May 1972 news conference quoted in Jeremi Suri, *Power and Protest: Global Revolution and the Rise of Detente*; Cambridge: Harvard University Press, 2003, p. 257.

in one another's internal affairs, and mutual advantage."[86] Contentious issues would now be resolved not by threats or force but as Brezhnev declared "...by peaceful means, at a conference table."[87] Historian Jeremi Suri writes that it created:

> "...a framework that gave priority to the "security interests" of the superpowers. The signatories rejected spheres of influence...but the provisions for assured boundaries and stability legitimated the current division of authority between East and West....The United States and the Soviet Union would, in essence, [now] collaborate as fireman, putting out flames of conflict around the globe."[88]

As the denial grand strategy type suggests, the military instrument in the Soviet grand strategy was "the primary element of power."[89] The Soviets believed that building military power comparable to the US was central to the strategy's success as without this America would once again resort to intimation and blackmail as it did in the 1950s.[90] The denial grand strategy with its goal of a concert of power order only "...became possible because of a new correlation of forces in the world arena..."[91] In 1968 when Soviet tanks crushed the Prague Spring and the West did not intervene, Brezhnev felt the USSR had now developed the military strength to bargain effectively. The new KGB head Yuri Androprov advised that: "Nobody wants to talk to the weak."[92] Brezhnev thought that only strong Soviet military power could convince the US that "...not brinkmanship but negotiation...not confrontation but peaceful

86. Raymond L. Gathoff, *Detente and Confrontation: American-Soviet Relations from Nixon to Reagan*; Washington: Brookings Institution Press, Revised Edition 1994, p. 327.
87. "The Outstanding Exploit of the Defenders of Tula; Speech of L. I. Brezhnev," Pravda, 19 January 1977 quoted in ibid., p. 40.
88. Suri, p. 257.
89. Wohlforth, p. 201.
90. Melvyn P. Leffler, *For the Soul of Mankind: The United States, the Soviet Union and the Cold War*; New York: Hill and Wang 2007, p. 254.
91. Brezhnev, Lenninskim kursom, 5:317, 1975 quoted in R. Craig Nation, *Black Earth, Red Star: A History of Soviet Security Policy, 1917-1991*; Ithaca: Cornell University, 1992, p. 256.
92. Zubok, pp. 207-11.

cooperation is the natural course of things." [93]

The grand strategy led to an impressive military build-up, but this unintentionally worked against the desired concert of powers order in which no state seeks system dominance, the states involved feel reasonably secure and their status is recognized and not endangered. The rapidly growing Soviet military strength could be misinterpreted as excessive for a concert of powers order and suggestive of a striving for a more ambitious different order. Cold war historian Melvyn Leffler observed that:

> " Between 1965-1970, [Soviet] defence expenditures increased by more than a third and, according to some estimates, came close to doubling. The numbers of strategic weapons...intercontinental ballistic missiles, submarine launched ballistic missiles, and long range bombers...soared from approximately 472 in 1964 to 1,470 in 1969. The annual production of tanks rose from 3,100 in 1966 to more than 4,250 in 1970; armoured vehicle production grew during these same years, from 2,800 to 4,000. Yet Brezhnev and his colleagues did not want to wage war. They yearned for American respect...and demanded equal security."[94]

If the new correlation of forces were held to have bought the West to reason, within this the nuclear forces were considered to have the central role. Deputy Foreign Minister Vladimir Petrovskii asserted that: "...the nuclear equilibrium of the two powers forms the basis of the international equilibrium."[95] The grand strategy accordingly, gave primacy to the strategic missile force, which by 1968 was consuming almost 20% of the Soviet defence budget. The ICBM acquisition program was the "largest single weapons effort in

---

93. L. I. Brezhnev, "Report of the CPSU Central Committee and the Immediate Tasks of the Party in Home and Foreign Policy", 24 February 1976 quoted in Leffler, *For the Soul of Mankind: The United States, the Soviet Union and the Cold War*, p. 254.
94. Ibid., p. 238.
95. V. Petrovskii, "Novaia struktura mira: Formuly i real'nost'," MEiMo, 1977, no.4, 18 quoted in Wohlforth, p. 192.

Soviet history and the most expensive...."[96]

The concert involved considerable diplomatic activity with an important role for institutions including regular summit meetings, international treaties, and new protocols and processes. The Soviet grand strategy became most clearly defined in terms of specific international agreements including the Strategic Arms Limitation Talks, the Basic Principles Agreement, various trade agreements, the agreement on the prevention of nuclear war, the Anti-Ballistic Missile treaty, the Commission on Security and Cooperation in Europe, and the Mutual and Balanced Force Reduction agreements. For the USSR these agreements supported the concert of powers order and were important to keeping the favourable relative balance between Soviet and US military power, in gaining international agreement to the post-World War Two division of Europe and in building economically useful relations with Western nations.

As the denial grand strategy type suggests, the economic and informational instruments of national power were distinctly secondary. Unlike in earlier eras, the USSR now accepted the capitalist world's continuance and there was a reduction in covert and overt agitation in foreign trade unions, academes, and political parties. Economic support remained in place for Soviet client states and this became progressively more draining, but was not a major feature impacting the grand strategy in this period.

The denial grand strategy adopted the long-term managerial approach to create and distribute the required resources. The problem was enduring, while the future was considered certain in that the bi-polar competition was assumed to continue indefinitely. An international strategy was attempted that selectively accessed Western money and material to avoid having to make domestic changes. Comparative politics academic Valerie Bunce observed that:

" The possibility of greater economic contact with the West...provided an optimal solution for political as well as

---

96. Zubok, p. 205.

economic reasons. The prevailing [internal] distribution of power...could be maintained, by using the West to plug up holes rather than engaging in economic reforms which would undercut planner and Party sovereignty."[97]

The long-term managerial approach to building power extracted men, money and materials from Soviet society using corporatist policies that gave distributional preference to the state-owned defence and heavy industries. These corporatist policies of 'developed socialism' envisaged a consensual society managed by an activist state that aimed to:

> "...maximize productivity by incorporating dominant economic and political interests directly into the policy process, while cultivating the support of the mass public through an expanding welfare state....[and] the extension of benefits by the State to all those groups considered vital to the functioning of the economy. In return, the State demanded compliance, moderate demands, and support for the prevailing distribution of power, status, and economic resources."[98]

Output legitimacy was stressed and reinforced by appeals to the universal statist, communist ideology that promised a better future of security and prosperity. This approach recognized that gaining input legitimacy was problematic given the state's authoritarian nature.

The denial grand strategy was successful for several years in that the Soviet Union now felt more secure than during any earlier part of the Cold War.[99] Moreover, the USSR was now more respected globally with considerably more international prestige and consequence. In 1971 Brezhnev declared that:

"At the present time no question of any importance in the

---

97. Valerie Bunce, 'The Political Economy of the Brezhnev Era: The Rise and Fall of Corporatism', *British Journal of Political Science* Vol. 13, No. 2, April 1983, pp. 129-58 p. 148.
98. Ibid., p. 131.
99. Wohlforth, p. 220.

world can be solved without our participation, without taking into account our economic and military might. Never before in its entire history….has our country enjoyed such authority and influence in the world."[100]

There were though intrinsic difficulties in the USSR using this type of grand strategy. As the US extracted itself from the debilitating Vietnam War and made use of an emerging China, the utility for America of a concert with the USSR declined. China was important for both the US and the USSR in this period. Growing worries over the erratic path that Mao was taking and emerging concerns about a possible armed conflict strengthened Soviet interest in détente with the US.[101] The Soviet leadership thought that having a friendly, or at least a neutral, America in some future conflict with China would be advantageous.

The Americans in contrast thought they could enlist Chinese support. In the late 1960s President Nixon and National Security Adviser Kissinger sought Chinese help to extract America from Vietnam and then, as Sino-Soviet tensions deepened and armed conflict emerged on their borders, realized that China could be turned into a useful ally. For China itself these developments offered new opportunities; Yang Kuisong writes:

> "Being threatened with war by Moscow and enticed by diplomatic overtures by Washington created a new environment in which Mao would change some of his fundamental views about China's external relations. …the unprecedented war scare from August 1969 pushed him to alter Chinese foreign policy in unprecedented ways…."[102]

With China now a partner in containing Soviet military power, détente steadily became of less importance to the US. While the USSR prized continued military parity with the US, America

---

100. Brezhnev, Leninskim kursom, 1971, 6: 245-46 quoted in ibid., p. 187.
101. Zubok, pp. 429.
102. Yang Kuisong, 'The Sino-Soviet Border Clash of 1969: From Zhenbao Island to Sino-American Rapprochement', *Cold War History,* Vol. 1, No. 1, August 2000, pp. 21-52, p. 47.

focused on other elements of national power to explain why it alone was uniquely central to world politics.[103] America's position had moved, the USSR was not now seen as an equal and so, as Hedley Bull commented, the US: "...shifted away from the attempt to fashion international order on the basis of an 'adversary partnership' with the Soviet Union...."[104]

By the late 1970s Secretary of State Cyrus Vance observed that Soviet leaders displayed: "...a deepening mood of harshness and frustration at what they saw as our inconsistency and unwillingness to deal with them as equals."[105] Soviet leaders though, even after noticing this crucial change in perspective central to a concert of powers order, stuck doggedly with their grand strategy. There was no "...comparable shift in the policy of the Soviet Union."[106]

Worse for the Soviets, their continuing arms build-up so central to their denial grand strategy acted against them in convincing the US that the USSR was untrustworthy and harboured bad intentions. Not only no longer seen as equal in terms of jointly managing global affairs, the Soviets' now also appeared to many in the US as deceitful and treacherous. It seemed demonstrably evident that the massive military surge ran counter to creating the stable political equilibrium that underpinned a concert of powers order.

American critics and military experts publicly campaigned about the growing "Soviet military threat", progressively undermining relations.[107] Deepening Soviet involvement in the Third World throughout the mid-to-late 1970s exacerbated this deterioration. The Soviet military intervention in Afghanistan, ironically to try to return a worsening political situation to the *status*

---

103. Wohlforth, pp. 211-18.
104. Hedley Bull, *The Anarchical Society: A Study of Order in World Politics*, 2nd Edition edn.; New York: Columbia University Press 1995, p. 220.
105. Cyrus Vance, *Hard Choices: Critical Years in America's Foreign Policy*; New York: Simon and Shuster, 1983, p. 101.
106. Bull, p. 220.
107. Zubok, p. 203.

quo ante, finally seemed to confirm Western fears.[108]

The Soviet leadership did not realize that their grand strategy had passed its culminating point and in being continued was now creating - not addressing - problems. The opportunity to devise a new grand strategy or to evolve the old one was missed. The USSR was now seen as a revisionist power attempting to change the overall international distribution of power in its favour.

At the end of the 1970s, the US and its allies embarked on a new arms build-up and a series of counter-interventions in communist controlled Third World states. If the Soviet's believed their stress on relative military power allowed the concert, it was also instrumental in undermining the grand strategy's objective of maintaining the status quo. Moreover, their approach to building power became progressively less viable over time as the previously high GDP growth rates steadily weakened.[109]

The Soviet leadership, while privileging the military instrument as the denial grand strategy type suggested they would, failed to properly appreciate the importance of matching this with the essential supporting domestic economy. There was a poor grand strategic synthesis inappropriate for the desired concert of powers order.

A long-term managerial approach was adopted as the diagnostic process would recommend, but there was an over-emphasis on military power that damaged the overall health of the Soviet industrial base and the economy. The policies adopted towards building military power were what would be suggested for a short-term managerial state impelled by a strong sense of urgency and necessity. The concert of power order though was one where the Soviet Union as a joint global manager should have felt secure albeit needing to be prudent.

The large defence expenditures undertaken misdirected

---

108. Odd Arne Westad, *The Global Cold War: Third World Interventions and the Making of Our Times*; Cambridge: Cambridge University Press, 2007, pp. 316-26.
109. Allen, pp. 861-62.

investment into the defence and heavy industries damaging the development of other sectors of the economy. [110] In analysing the economy of the USSR in this period, economist Robert Allen wrote that:

> " The [Soviet] growth rate dropped abruptly after 1970 for external and internal reasons. The external reason was the Cold War, which diverted substantial R&D resources from civilian innovation to the military and cut the rate of productivity growth. The internal reason was the end of the surplus labour economy: unemployment in agriculture had been eliminated and the accessible natural resources of the country had been fully exploited. [111]

The grand strategy's use of global financial resources also proved at odds with the long-term managerial approach that recommended financing through domestic means to lessen dependence on others and any constraints they might impose. While the USSR was relatively fiscally prudent, the grand strategy neglected the financial needs of its Warsaw Pact allies. Foreign policy analyst Matthew Ouimet observed that:

> "...Eastern Europe's collective debt rose by 480 percent during the period 1973-1978....Investment funds either went to pay for consumer imports or simply dissipated in the hands of inefficient or corrupt bureaucratic managers. Consequently, the long run impact...was an economic catastrophe in Eastern Europe that invited indebtedness, ensured wide-scale industrial obsolescence, and constrained exports." [112]

---

110. "Growth began to slow down in the 1960s, and success turned to failure after 1970, when the growth rate dropped dramatically. GNP grew in excess of 5 per cent per year from 1928 to 1970, but the annual rate dropped to 3.7 per cent in 1970–75, then to 2.6 per cent in 1975–80...." Vladimir Kontorovicha and Alexander Weinb, 'What Did the Soviet Rulers Maximise?', *Europe-Asia Studies,* Vol. 61, No. 9, 2009, pp. 1579-601, pp. 1594-95.
111.   Allen, pp. 878-79.
112.   Matthew J. Ouimet, *The Rise and Fall of the Brezhnev Doctrine in Soviet Foreign Policy*; Chapel Hill: The University of North Carolina Press, 2003, p. 82.

These economic woes significantly added to the difficulties of maintaining the status quo in the Eastern Bloc. The political instability in Poland in the late 1970s was fuelled by economic decline and eventually proved to be particularly damaging to the USSR's long-term viability.[113]

The institutionalization of the concert was also particularly problematic. There was no attempt to map out a joint strategy to define common objectives and share burdens, nor agreement on "…any theory or ideology of world order…that would give direction and purpose to a Soviet-American concert."[114] Moreover, the denial grand strategy type's position on institutions, that cautions that their use reflects relative power differentials, was too easily disregarded in the intense desire to gain Western recognition of the borders of Eastern Europe. To achieve this, the USSR signed the Helsinki Final Act that in enshrining human rights norms ultimately undermined the internal legitimacy of the Soviet state, calling into question all its actions and policies.[115]

Implementing a short-term managerial approach as regards building military power, but a long-term managerial approach for the remainder of society and the economy, created a damaging level of incoherence. The general managerial approach was effective in allocating massive resources to the favoured military and supporting heavy industry sector. However, in a manner that the diagnostic process cautions, this led to the USSR facing growing inefficiencies, declining productivity, and constraints arising from an inappropriate use made of its limited access to global resources. The grand strategy's incoherence in terms of building power simply expedited the process of collapse.

Overall the Soviet grand strategy while initially successful in constraining the US progressively acted to undermine the desired stable political equilibrium and its own domestic strength across the

---

113. Ibid., pp. 109-13.
114. Bull, p. 219.
115. Daniel C. Thomas, *The Helsinki Effect: International Norms, Human Rights, and the Demise of Communism*; Princeton: Princeton University Press 2001, pp. 257-86.

period 1965-1980. This was the direct opposite to that intended. While the détente grand strategy had internal contradictions working against its success, given that the US was the stronger state by all measures, the weaker USSR was arguably unwise to use a denial grand strategy that privileged relative power. Other options were possible; the Chinese Communist Party's used a successful engagement grand strategy while Mikhail Gorbachev implemented a reform grand strategy albeit unsuccessful from the communist party's viewpoint. The most enduring legacy of the détente denial grand strategy appears to have been its considerable contribution to the internal collapse of the USSR in the late 1980s.[116]

The operating logic of a denial grand strategy suggests the grand strategy as actually implemented by the USSR would probably fail, an outcome historically validated. In retrospect, the framework highlights elements of the USSR's grand strategy that were in conflict with each other. The desired concert of powers order was undermined by the large-scale military build-up which was more appropriate gaining a satisfactory balance of power in a highly threatening situation. On the other hand the grand strategic synthesis was also flawed in using a muddled combined short- and long-term managerial approach.

In the end the grand strategy failed due to internal contradictions. Inappropriate use of the instruments of national power can work against achieving the desired order, while success is made more unlikely if the strategic synthesis is also defective. In the USSR's détente grand strategy, the USSR's reconciliation of ends, ways and means lacked coherence and consistency. This is a mistake that better understanding of the design of a denial grand strategy may have foreseen.

Conclusions

Considered together the three denial grand strategy case studies further emphasize important policymaking aspects both about grand strategies in general and denial grand strategies in particular.

---

116. Vladislav Zubok, 'The Soviet Union and Détent of the 1970s', *Cold War History,* Vol. 8, No. 4, November, 2008, pp. 427-47, pp. 438-44.

All three case studies reveal the dynamic nature of grand strategy. A grand strategy involves interacting with intelligent others that learn from their failures and can adopt new or evolved grand strategies in response. Grand strategies need to be continually monitored to determine if they have reached their culminating point beyond which their utility diminishes. The time to reach this point is determined by the speed with which the targets of the grand strategy respond although notice may also need to be taken of changes in the external environment as well. Grand strategies are not a set-and-forget approach.

In the Iraq War case, Iraq was never going to be able to match America in relative power terms when the US decided to act and focus its diplomatic, informational, military and economic instruments of power on the problem. Similarly, the LTTE could only maintain a relative power advantage while the much larger Sri Lankan state allowed it to by not fully utilising its latent national power. For Iraq and the LTTE to have any reasonable likelihood of success they needed to begin with different grand strategies, or have moved to adopt completely new ones when it became apparent that their adversaries were marshalling their might.

The denial grand strategy's operating logic is built around the importance of relative power. Either side can use internal or external balancing to change their relative power. This means that each participant has considerable autonomy; decisions can be taken independent of the actions of others involved in the grand strategy. In contrast, and as discussed in later chapters, in the engagement and reform grand strategy types there is considerably greater interdependence between all involved. The motive force of denial grand strategies is relative power and this provides a degree of absoluteness.

An important outlier to this general rule-of-thumb was examined in the Détente grand strategy case. In this, the relative *military* power balance between the two sides did not fluctuate greatly. Instead, the US decided to change the rules of the game in determining that the USSR was not its equal across all measures of national power and never would be. A concert of power international order was therefore not an order the US now wished to be a party to making. This order has the greatest degree of interdependency of the three denial grand strategy alternatives in that both sides have to agree to be mutually supporting.

Even with this partial exception, the inherently unstable nature of the relative power balance lies behind the greatest shortcoming of the overall denial grand strategy type. While a denial grand strategy may be appropriately chosen and skillfully implemented, it is fundamentally unable to resolve the underlying causes of a conflict. The Iraq War was decisive in stopping Iraq achieving its objectives. However, this did not have the more positive or enduring results that a change in the social purpose or the social rules of the Iraqi state may have had. The result of this grand strategy was that critics, with the benefit of hindsight, later asserted that the grand strategy won the war but lost the peace and accordingly failed.

Particular types of grand strategy can only create particular types of international orders, particular kinds of 'peace'. A denial grand strategy can only be used to create a balance of power, a concert of power or a hegemonic stability order not some other kind. The way that the means are used does influence the outcomes possible. In the Iraq War and LTTE case studies, the denial grand strategies used created the kind of peace that was sought. If this was ultimately unappealing, new or evolved grand strategies needed to be fashioned to continue from when the denial grand strategies had reached their culminating point.

The Détente grand strategy case is again a variation worthy of note. The order sought was within the choices that a denial grand strategy offers but the desired concert of powers order was undermined by the large-scale Soviet military build-up more appropriate to highly threatening situations. Success requires judicious use of the instruments of power even within the same type. Moreover, when the Soviet leadership became aware that the US was moving away from supporting a concert of powers order, they did not significantly adjust their grand strategy in response. Ultimately they proved unable to learn and instead inflexibly stuck to a fixed course. In grand strategy making, continually matching ends, ways and means is crucial.

6

Engagement Grand Strategies

In the last decade, as the wars waged by Western forces in Afghanistan and Iraq gradually came to be seen as unsuccessful, a new stress has been placed on engagement grand strategies as an all-encompassing solution. In its recent applications in Libya and Syria however, the results have seemed disappointing suggesting that engagement grand strategies are appropriate in some circumstances but perhaps not in others.

Crucially, as discussed earlier, the engagement grand strategy is not a liberal grand strategy. A liberal grand strategy would incorporate the normative positions of liberal philosophers whereas the engagement grand strategy does not. The engagement grand strategy here uses Moravcsik's new liberalism as the basis for how different groups within democratic or authoritarian states can shape an entity's social purpose.

In this, the engagement grand strategy's approach of working with and through domestic groups within a state may appear broadly similar to the use of alliances in a denial grand strategy. However, the two are conceptually dissimilar. The engagement grand strategy focuses on working with useful sub-state groups: the grand strategy is all about these groups. In contrast, in denial grand strategies the focus is on the opponent with the allies simply being additional means bought into play; denial grand strategies are all about the opponent.

The three historical case studies are structured to highlight the important aspects of engagement grand strategy formulation, especially the design requirements, general operating logic and the circumstances favouring success or failure. The first case is the US grand strategy of 1947-1952 to revitalize Western Europe, a particularly well-known example of an engagement grand strategy. The centrepiece of this regional grand strategy was the Marshall

Plan, a long-term program of American economic assistance to Western Europe. The time span chosen for this case study is from the start of the grand strategy with the announcement of the Marshall Plan at Harvard University in 1947 until the Plan finished and the grand strategy culminated in 1952.

In thinking about grand strategy the Marshall Plan is often used as an exemplar with numerous 'new' Marshall Plans proposed over the last thirty years for many regions and nations. For many the Marshall Plan is considered to have been highly successfully and worthy of replication. The Plan is often used as an analogy when a new international problem develops both to frame the key issues and to illustrate potential solutions.[1] Applying the diagnostic process developed to this particular grand strategy can allow policymakers to better understand its design and logic, suggesting circumstances where it may, or may not, be replicated.

The second case is more demanding in examining Iran's grand strategy in partnering with the Hezbollah non-state actor in Lebanon during 1982-2006. The engagement grand strategy framework being based upon new liberalism may be considered relevant only to democratic states. This case study involving authoritarian governance systems indicates an engagement grand strategy type's wider applicability. The time span of this case study begins with the purposeful construction of Hezbollah in 1982 in response to the Israeli intervention in Lebanon until 2006, when Israel again intervened and the grand strategy reached a new maturity but not yet its culminating point.

The failure case examined is that of Britain's interwar appeasement grand strategy 1934-1939. The British used an engagement grand strategy but combined this with elements of a denial grand strategy in an approach Christopher Layne argues

---

1. New Marshall Plans have been proposed over the last 30 years for many regions and nations including Latin America, eastern Europe, the former USSR, the Balkans, the Middle East, Africa, and the Philippines. Barry Machado, *In Search of a Usable Past: The Marshall Plan and Postwar Reconstruction Today*; Lexington: George C. Marshall Foundation, 2007, p. xiii. Curt Tarnoff, *The Marshall Plan: Design, Accomplishments, and Relevance to the Present*, Report 97-62; Washington: Congressional Research Service, The Library of Congress, 1997, p. CRS-1.

"...was logical in its: definition of Britain's interests, ranking of the threats to those interests, and allocation of the limited resources available to meet the strategic challenges that Britain faced."[2] Even so, the grand strategy was disastrous. The application of the engagement grand strategy process to this case reveals inherent and irreconcilable contradictions in its design that could have been avoided.

The time span chosen is from 1934 when the Britain Cabinet formally decided on a grand strategy that cast Germany as the principal threat to the Empire and Britain's position as world power until the start of the Second World War in September 1939. This period covers the grand strategy's beginning, past its culminating point that probably occurred around March 1936 with the German remilitarization of the Rhineland (but not later than German military intervention in mid-1937 in the Spanish Civil War), until its obvious failure with the start of the major war that it was designed to avoid. The grand strategy arguably continued in a fashion during the so-called Phony war period with hopes German moderates would yet stop the war, until the German invasion of France in mid-1940 bought Churchill into power in Britain.

US European Recovery Program Grand Strategy 1947-1952

The end of the Second World War left Europe devastated and concerns soon arose over the possibilities of widespread starvation, chaos and revolution. In 1946 Winston Churchill declared that Europe was " a rubble heap, a charnel house, a breeding ground for pestilence and hate."[3] While the USSR had done little to create this dire situation, the Soviets were perceived to be well-organised and positioned to benefit from it. The U.S. European Recovery Program Grand Strategy aimed to address this through creating a 'liberal peace' international order that strengthened democratic representative governments, developed institutions, and built

---

2. Christopher Layne, 'Security Studies and the Use of History: Neville Chamberlain's Grand Strategy Revisited', *Security Studies,* Vol. 17, No. 3, 2008, pp. 397-437, pp. 399-400.
3. Winston Churchill quoted in Norman Davies, *Europe: A History*; London: Pimlico, 1997, p. 1065.

transnational economic interdependence. The emphasis was on rebuilding "the war-ravaged economic, political, and social institutions of Europe that made communist inroads possible."[4] This emphasis was noticeably different to the stress placed on building alliances and military forces by the later global containment denial grand strategy.

Senior American policymakers drew upon the analogy of the New Deal in thinking about how to assist European reconstruction. From this pre-war policy initiative, policymakers took the underlying assumption that in extreme economic crises government spending was essential. In extending this thinking into the post-war environment, the New Deal analogy directly informed the formulation of strategies to deal with the emerging set of problems in Europe.[5] Mills writes that underpinning the Secretary Of State's thinking about reconstruction options was his "belief in the application of New Deal-style government economic intervention to American foreign policy.[6]" In reviewing the grand strategy 50 years later, Dianne Kunz held that senior policymakers at the time thought that: "The New Deal had made America safe for capitalism: the Marshall Plan would do the same for Europe."[7]

Crucially, American assistance was not to be unilateral; the recipients were deeply involved in planning and implementing their own assistance. US Secretary of State Marshall in announcing the Plan at Harvard University in June 1947 that:

> " It would be neither fitting nor efficacious for this Government to undertake to draw up unilaterally a program designed to place Europe on its feet economically. This is the

4. G. John Ikenberry, *After Victory: Institutions, Strategic Restraint, and the Rebuilding of Order after Major Wars*; Princeton: Princeton University Press, 2001, p. 181.
5. Michael J. Hogan, *The Marshall Plan: America, Britain and the Reconstruction of Western Europe, 1947-1952*; Cambridge: Cambridge University Press, 1987, p. 45.
6. Nicolaus Mills, *Winning the Peace: The Marshall Plan and America's Coming of Age as a Superpower*; Hoboken: John Wiley & Sons, 2008, p. 25.
7. Diane B. Kunz, 'The Marshall Plan Reconsidered: A Complex of Motives', *Foreign Affairs,* Vol. 76, No. 3, May-June 1997, pp. 162-70, p. 164.

business of the Europeans. The initiative, I think, must come from Europe. The role of this country should consist of friendly aid in the drafting of a European program and of later support of such a program so far as it may be practical for us to do so. The program should be a joint one, agreed to by a number, if not all European nations."[8]

The success of the grand strategy hinged on working with the European states and in particular those domestic interest groups that held preferences compatible with the broad American desires. American grand strategic aims were to be advanced through directly and indirectly helping others achieve their preferences. The grand strategy was only viable if domestic interest groups could be found in the countries of interest who were willing and able to use the assistance being offered. The engagement grand strategy was to be as the Head of the Marshall Plan noted " a catalytic agent and never the driving force."[9]

European governments were from the start enthusiastic participants in the Marshall Plan as the funding provided significantly addressed many of their economic problems, and helped buttress them politically. This willing cooperation and collaboration was matched by the rapid acceptance by their voters of the underlying goal of the engagement grand strategy of advancing the prospects of a unified, economically integrated Europe. Opinion polls in 1948 found some 74% of the public favoured such a goal, compared to 16% opposed. Moreover, a unified Europe was also the grand objective of influential government officials and politicians such as Monnet and Schuman in France, Adenauer in Germany and de Gasperi in Italy; all of whom would significantly themselves advance European integration.[10] The engagement grand strategy was able to be successful because of supportive domestic groups and elites in the targeted region holding similar preferences.

8. *The "Marshall Plan" Speech at Harvard University, 5 June 1947* (Organisation for Economic Co-operation and Development 1947), George C. Marshall (Dir.).
9. Paul Hoffman, 'The Marshall Plan: Peace Building-Its Price and Its Profits', *Foreign Service Journal* Vol. 44, No. June, 1967, pp. 19-21, p. 20.
10. Alfred Grosser, *The Western Alliance: European-American Relations since 1945* London: The MacMillan Press, 1980, pp. 73, 101-28.

The economic assistance that defined the engagement grand strategy allowed friendly governments to exclude communists from their cabinets after it became evident that the crucially-important US aid was conditional on having Communist-free Western European governments. The electoral positions of the non-communist parties were thus very usefully strengthened.[11] By comparison, the USSR's parlous economic situation meant it could offer nothing similar and so could not help local communist parties in any meaningful way. In the grand strategy, economic health was considered directly linked to political stability in the sense of limiting communist parties electoral gains in the democratic countries of Western Europe.

The engagement grand strategy also included a deliberate informational element that aimed to keep the European public "sufficiently informed...to assure their cooperation and conversion."[12] The grand strategy in addition guided focused covert activities. The newly established Central Intelligence Agency (CIA) provided discreet funding to the American Federation of Labor allowing them to actively support US-friendly labour organizations and unions in Western Europe and undermine labour movements that had communist sympathies in several Western Europe countries.[13]

In terms of the diplomatic instrument of power, the grand strategy's goal was reflected in the Truman administration's support for the Brussels Pact, the European Defence Community (EDC) and the Schuman Plan. The 1948 Brussels Pact bound the UK, France and the Benelux countries into a security relationship, the EDC of the early 1950s sought an integrated European army, and the Schuman Plan proposed integrating French and German coal and steel production, and eventually lead to the establishment of the European Community institutions.[14] In the military sphere, the NATO agreement signed in April 1949 was also from the American perspective consistent with, and understandable in the terms of, their regional engagement grand strategy. Ikenberry writes that the NATO

---

11. Machado, p. 11.
12. Ibid., p. 26.
13. Grosser, p. 69.
14. Tony Judt, *Postwar: A History of Europe since 1945*; New York: The Penguin Press, 2005, pp. 149, 244-45, 156-57.

pact's "purpose was to lend support to European steps to build stronger economic, political, and security ties within Europe itself. In this sense, the NATO agreement was a continuation of the Marshall Plan strategy..."[15]

The American grand strategy was only viable if suitably cooperative domestic leaders and interest groups holding appropriate preferences could be made use of and worked with. Marshall initially also offered the aid to the Soviets however they were unwilling to be involved and moreover also prevented their Eastern European satellites being involved. Without cooperative domestic interest groups with compatible preferences the grand strategy could not have been implemented in these nations.[16] In this regard, Machado in analysing the Marshall Plan observed that while often overlooked in American accounts, the Plan's "ultimate success depended as much on the attributes of Europe's leadership as on America's role."[17] An engagement grand strategy is dependent for success on being able to work with and through cooperative partners holding compatible, or at least exploitable, preferences.

To build power, the grand strategy used a long-term/ market state approach. In terms of resources, the centrepiece and most costly element was the Marshall Plan where the US provided grants (90%) and loans (10%) to some 15 managerial state West European countries. In GNP terms, the program transferred some 2.1% of American GDP in 1948, 2.4% in 1949 and 1.5% in the remaining two years.[18]

The US Federal Budget at the time was in deficit, and so the monies used came from a mix of taxation and domestic bonds. Across the period Federal taxes constituted about 12% of GDP of which some 7% were individual income taxes and 5% corporate

---

15. Ikenberry, *After Victory: Institutions, Strategic Restraint, and the Rebuilding of Order after Major Wars*, p. 197.
16. Marc Trachtenberg, *A Constructed Peace: The Making of the European Settlement 1945-1963* Princeton Princeton University Press, 1999, pp. 63-64.
17. Machado, p. 114.
18. Alan S. Milward, *The Reconstruction of Western Europe, 1945-51*; London: Routledge, 1987, p. 72.

taxation.[19] An accommodational strategy was used although there was limited choice in this; an international strategy would have been impractical as in this period few nations had excess funds for investment abroad.

The Marshall Plan took a Keynesian approach to restoring and revitalizing the Western European market economies disrupted by World War Two with a long term intent of creating a single, integrated market across the continent that was envisaged to lead to economies of scale, high growth and robust democracies.[20] While Government funded, in keeping with the market states' distrust of government bureaucracies' effectiveness and efficiency, the government's role was carefully constrained. Historian Michael Hogan in a major work on the Marshall Plan wrote that:

> "...the Marshall Plan carefully delimited the [American] government's role in the stabilization process. This role was perceived as a national security imperative and as an aid to private enterprise. It was to be performed as far as possible in collaboration with private elites. Policymakers ruled out a government aid corporation to administer the recovery program and established an independent agency, staffed it with managerial talent from the private sector, and linked it to private groups through a network of advisory committees. Marshall Planners then urged participating countries to replace this administrative system. The result was a series of partnerships that blended public and private power..."[21]

The purpose of the Marshall Plan monies changed over time moving from the initial focus on immediate food-related items such as food, feed, fertilizer and fuel towards an emphasis by 1949 on raw materials and production equipment. While the purchasing decisions were made in Europe, Barry Machado notes that: " relatively few dollars ever left the United States, or even passed through foreign hands – by program's end an estimated 83% of all dollar purchases

19. C. Eugene Steuerle, *Contemporary U.S. Tax Policy: 2nd Edition*; Washington: Urban Institute Press, 2008, p. 34.
20. Machado, pp. 12-14.
21. Hogan, p. 19.

were spent in the United States."[22] This spending aided the stability and long-term development of the US economy, and helped gain support for the Marshall Plan both in Congress and with those American businesses who were significant beneficiaries of the plan.

Input legitimacy was sought although, given the Congressional funding and the strong involvement of private companies, there was a focus on elites rather than the civil society. The government formed the Harriman Committee that included representatives of business, labour and academia to focus principally on moulding elite opinion. An ad hoc group was felt to be more effective than using the government bureaucracy because of distrust in Congress. The quasi-private "Citizens Committee for the Marshall Plan to Aid European Recovery" carried out much of the public effort through using mass media and speaking to select audiences. The legitimacy of the Marshall Plan grand strategy was based on appeals to "idealism, self-interest and ideology" with a growing emphasis on the need to protect the free world from communism and all that this political system entailed.[23]

The American engagement grand strategy was successful because the US was able to find and work with pre-existing domestic interest groups and governments within European nations that held preferences compatible with the broad American desires. These useful partners were assisted in growing, becoming more influential in their respective countries and in achieving their ambitions. Conversely the domestic interest groups and governments that did not hold preferences useful to American grand strategic objectives where directly and indirectly hindered. American instruments of national power were employed to make these unhelpful groups less and less influential within their individual national political, economic and social systems.

The success of the American engagement grand strategy further illustrates a potential gain from this type of grand strategy; it can be enduring. The grand strategy in working with and through useful others led to their capturing of the future of their respective

22. Machado, p. 41.
23. Ibid., pp. 16-22.

countries. The grand strategy's objectives effectively became self-reinforcing across Europe and no longer needing continuing support, effort and resources. Over the longer term an engagement grand strategy may be a lower cost option although, in this example the start-up costs were significant.

This particular grand strategy also illustrates the principal shortcomings of an engagement grand strategy. This type is only viable if domestic interest groups willing and able to use the assistance being offered can be found in countries important to the grand strategy. In the USSR and their Eastern European satellites, access to useful domestic interest groups was denied and as such, in those areas the grand strategy was unsuccessful.

In considering the concept of grand strategy as a policymaking methodology, the European Recovery Program grand strategy is an example of a regional grand strategy within a broader, overarching grand strategy albeit retrospectively (discussed in Chapter 2). The European Recovery Program grand strategy did not begin this way, instead being commenced before the overarching and very different denial grand strategy of containment was devised, agreed and formalised.

Secretary of State Marshall announced the plan named after him at Harvard in June 1947. George Kennan however, did not draw together the basic ideas underlying the new overarching containment grand strategy until 5 November 1947 in Planning Policy Statement (PPS) 13 "Resume of World Situation", a strategic overview prepared for Marshall.[24] Moreover, it was not until early 1948 that this new containment grand strategy began to influence wider policy matters within the Truman Administration, initially as regards the relationship between the U.S. and newly communist mainland China.

The earlier European Recovery Program grand strategy had a different and considerably narrower focus than the later containment grand strategy that took a global perspective. It seems only some of its thinking informed the later overarching grand strategy. It is for example, inconceivable that under the global containment grand strategy Marshall Plan aid would have been offered to the Soviet

---

24. Brands, pp. 29-30.

Union like it was under the European Recovery Program grand strategy. While a suitable level of coherency was achieved between the two grand strategies, it is striking that throughout the long Cold War the highly regarded European Recovery Program grand strategy remained *sui generis* with this approach not used again.

Iranian Hezbollah Grand Strategy 1982-2006

The 1979 Islamic revolution completely reoriented Iran's foreign policy. The state became strongly opposed to Israel and the United States and developed a strong desire to export the revolution both to gain prestige and influence for the new regime, and to help fellow Shia co-religionists elsewhere. These multiple objectives came together in Lebanon, which had a large Shia community with deep religious linkages to Iran dating back to the 16th Century[25], bordered Israel, and in suffering significant political instability suggested revolutionary change might be possible. Iran began supporting the Shiite nationalist movement Amal ('Hope'), the most powerful organization within the Lebanese Shia community and perhaps the largest such non-state group in the country.[26]

In many respects this was a poor fit. Amal did not propose a revolutionary Islamic state but was instead a secular movement trying to unite Lebanon's Shia along communal rather than religious lines.[27] Amal worked inside the extant political system, and was uninterested in taking actions outside Lebanon's borders.[28] Worse, as Middle Eastern specialist Augustus Norton writes:

> "...Amal tacitly welcomed the Israeli invasion of June 1982 because it broke the power of the Palestinian fighters in the

25. Daniel Byman, *Deadly Connections: States That Sponsor Terrorism* Cambridge: Cambridge University Press, 2005, pp. 80-81.
26. Kenneth Katzman, 'Hizbollah: Narrowing Options in Lebanon', in Stephen C. Pelletiere (ed.), *Terrorism: National Security Policy and the Home Front*; Carlisle Barracks: Strategic Studies Institute, U.S. Army War College, 1995, pp. 5-27, p. 24 n22. Robert A. Pape, *Dying to Win: The Strategic Logic of Suicide Terrorism*; New York: Random House 2005, p. 131.
27. Byman, pp. 82-83.
28. Eitan Azani, *Hezbollah: The Story of the Party of God: From Revolution to Institutionalization*; New York: Palgrave Macmillan, 2009, pp. 62-63.

South. Amal leaders…sought a modus vivendi with Israel and the United States. [Their] participation in the National Salvation Committee…created by Lebanese president Elias Sarkis….was castigated by young radicals…who described the Committee as no more than an "American-Israeli bridge" allowing the United States to enter and control Lebanon."[29]

The Lebanese state and Iran's chosen ally in the country were seemingly going in a direction diametrically against Iranian objectives. A new grand strategy was needed.

In considering Iranian options, a reform grand strategy would have been impractical as Iran had limited ideational influence over elites in the secular Amal or in the Lebanese state. The Government furthermore was led by a Maronite Christian and supported by Western governments strongly opposed to the Islamic Republic of Iran. A denial grand strategy to stop Israeli and US actions using mainly military force was also impractical given Iran's very weak regional military presence and complete lack of allies. In this regard, Ali Muhtashimi, Iran's ambassador in Syria between 1982 and 1985, recalls discussing his strong personal preference for a denial grand strategy approach with Grand Ayatollah Ruhollah Khomeini, Iran's Supreme Leader:

> "The Imam cooled me down and said that the forces we send to Syria and Lebanon would need huge logistical support….Reinforcement and support would need to go through Turkey and Iraq. We are in a fierce war with Iraq. As for Turkey, it is a NATO member and an ally of the United States. The only remaining way is to train the Shia men there, and so Hezbollah was born."[30]

Iran decided to work with and through like-minded domestic non-state actors to shape Lebanon in the direction Iran preferred.

---

29. Augustus Richard Norton, *Hezbollah: A Short History*; Princeton: Princeton University Press, 2007, p. 23.

30. Ali Muhtashimi interview with Shargh (Tehran), 3 August 2008 quoted in Michael Rubin, *Deciphering Iranian Decision Making and Strategy Today*, Middle Eastern Outlook; Washington: American Enterprise Institute January 2013, p. 7-8.

This engagement grand strategy accordingly focused on developing these specific groups' social influence and political power so that they could steer Lebanon's social purpose in directions useful to Iran. With this grand strategy, Iran created a complex interdependence order that deliberately connected the state and society through multiple channels to particular Lebanese non-state groups that shared Iranian values and goals. Iran made use of the distinctive political processes within complex interdependence to influence these non-state group's preferences through linking issues, controlling the setting of the agenda to determine how issues were framed, operating within these groups to shape their organizational preferences and making use of institutions. Iran developed and then took advantage of its inherently asymmetric relationship with these non-state groups

Iran deliberately exacerbated and exploited fissures developing within Amal.[31] In late June 1982 the second in command broke away and formed Islamic Amal, an organization more attuned to Iranian objectives. To support him, Iran dispatched some 1500 Iranian Revolutionary Guard Corps (IRGC) military personnel to instruct the Islamic Amal militia in fighting Israel, together with some 35 clerics to strengthen ties and Iranian political and religious influence.[32] With Islamic Amal as the core, an assortment of small pre-existing Shiite organizations rapidly coalesced into Hezbollah (Party of God), which while officially created in a June 1982 meeting of Islamists and other religious clerics was not announced publically until 1985.[33] Hezbollah's general secretary, Sheikh Hassan Nasrallah, explains that:

"This new group or new framework had the conditions for its formation before the Israeli invasion. But the invasion

---

31. Frederic Wehrey et al., *Dangerous but Not Omnipotent: Exploring the Reach and Limitations of Iranian Power in the Middle East*; Santa Monica: RAND Corporation, 2009, pp. 88-90.
32. Pape, p. 131. Amal Saad-Ghorayeb, *Hizbu'llah: Politics and Religion*; London: Pluto Press, 2002, pp. 14-15.
33. Krista E. Wiegand, 'Reformation of a Terrorist Group: Hezbollah as a Lebanese Political Party', *Studies in Conflict & Terrorism,* Vol. 32, No. 8, 2009, pp. 669-80, p. 670.

accelerated its existence, and Hezbollah was born as a resistance force in the reaction to the occupation.... Contrary to the accusations...that it was Iranian – it was a Lebanese decision, founded by a group of Lebanese with Lebanese leadership, Lebanese grassroots, and the freedom fighters are Lebanese.... Naturally we asked for assistance. From any party...From then on relations began with...Iran.[34]

Norton is less charitable observing that: "...at the beginning, Hezbollah was hardly a popular movement, but a conspiracy of a handful of men funded by the nascent Islamic Republic of Iran."[35] Certainly Iran provided the new organization with considerable support and assistance. In addition to military training, and ideological indoctrination provided by the IRGC personnel and clerics, there was substantial Iranian funding for community services such as schools, clinics, hospitals, and cash subsidies to the poor. While the Iranian revolutionary paradigm was deeply inspirational, Iran's material assistance was crucial to Hezbollah's development. Lebanese academic Amal Saad-Ghorayeb in her major study of Hezbollah observed:

> "...without Iran's political, financial, and logistical support, [Hizbu'llah's] military capability and organisational development would have been greatly retarded. Even by Hizbu'llah's reckoning, it would have taken an additional 50 years for the movement to score the same achievements in the absence of Iranian backing."[36]

Iran "deserves considerable credit for Hezbollah's political successes and large social network" however Hezbollah also significantly helped Iran achieve its objectives.[37] Hezbollah brought Iranian Islamic revolutionary ideology and theology deep into

---

34. Hassan Nasrallah from "An Interview with Sheikh Hassan Nasrallah" Middle East Insight, Vol.12, Nos. 4-5, May-August 1996 quoted in: Pape, p. 132.
35. Augustus Richard Norton, 'Hizballah and the Israeli Withdrawal from Southern Lebanon', *Journal of Palestine Studies* Vol. 30, No. 1, 2000, pp. 22-35, p. 24.
36. Saad-Ghorayeb, p. 14.
37. Byman, p. 98.

Levantine politics, and made Iran politically more influential. Hezbollah was central to Iran's war with Israel as the group provided a unique toehold for Iran in the region. If Iran had not been involved against Israel, it would have been hard to portray itself as being at the revolutionary vanguard of the Muslim world.[38] Iranian prestige and influence in the Muslim and Arab worlds at the time rested significantly on the benefits gained from its astute development of a complex interdependence order relationship with Hezbollah.

In the engagement grand strategy, economic and institutional instruments of national power are more important than military means. The case of Iran and Hezbollah across the 1982-2006 period reflects this.

Economically, Iran consistently provided Hezbollah with significant support. Of the Hezbollah annual budget of some US$500m, direct funding from Iran constituted about US$100-$200m.[39] This money allowed Hezbollah to sustain a large social welfare network that included schools, clinics, agricultural cooperatives, TV and radio stations, hospitals and mosques. In the mid-1980s Iran was financing an estimated 80% of Hezbollah's social programs.[40] This involvement was more than by the Iranian state alone with the extensive involvement of Iranian parastatal charitable foundations in building hospitals and schools, and aiding widows, orphans, and the disabled.[41] Iranian direct and indirect funding and support allowed Hezbollah to have a deep and continuing influence on Lebanese society.

---

38   ibid., pp. 94-96.
39. Apart from Iranian funding, Hezbollah also received money from charitable fund raising, legitimate commercial activity, enforced tax levies, criminal activity, financial defalcation, and transfers from the Lebanese government. Martin Rudner, 'Hizbullah: An Organizational and Operational Profile', *International Journal of Intelligence and CounterIntelligence,* Vol. 23, No. 2, 2010, pp. 226-46, p. 232.
US Department Of Defense, 'Report on Military Power of Iran '; Washington, DC US Department of Defense, April 2010, p. 8.
40. Byman, p. 88.
41. Abbas William Samii, 'A Stable Structure on Shifting Sands: Assessing the Hizbullah-Iran-Syria Relationship', *Middle East Journal,* Vol. 62, No. 1, Winter 2008, pp. 32-53, p. 41.

Iranian economic aid was also pivotal in helping Hezbollah support the Lebanese Shia community in recovering from several conflicts with Israel. In the 2006 conflict, Christine Hamieh and Roger Mac Ginty observed that:

> "As soon as the fighting came to a halt...Hezbollah leader Hassan Nasrallah appeared on television pledging that his organisation would help to rebuild homes and compensate those whose homes had been destroyed. Well in excess of US$100 million in cash was distributed within 72 hours of the cessation of hostilities. Hezbollah seemed the most effective on-the-ground actor as it directed bulldozers to raze damaged buildings and its volunteers staffed registration centres to assess the needs of returnees...for many Lebanese, Hezbollah's reconstruction activism contrasted with the seeming inefficiency of the state.[42]

The Iranian government declared it would assist in the reconstruction without any funding ceiling. The Lebanese media later estimated some US$1 billion was provided directly through Hezbollah - rather than through the Lebanese state - giving Iran and Hezbollah an enormous reconstruction presence. Hezbollah's use of Iranian reconstruction funding allowed it to make:

> "...connections to citizens, political parties, and other groups, and because reconstruction assistance was regularly disbursed through municipalities, it oiled the traditional patronage and clientelistic political system. Thus, it reinforced the existing political system....[43]

The Iranian funding was used by Hezbollah to build output legitimacy amongst the Lebanese Shia. The organization was perceived as competent in service delivery and responsive to the community's welfare needs. Iran did not seek legitimacy directly but rather indirectly through funding Hezbollah. This overcame

---

42. Christine Sylva Hamieh and Roger Mac Ginty, 'A Very Political Reconstruction: Governance and Reconstruction in Lebanon after the 2006 War', *Disasters*, No. 34(S1), 2010, pp. S103–S23, p. S106.
43. Ibid., p. S119.

problems Iran may have had in regard to being perceived as a Persian power involving itself deeply in an Arab country.

The leverage Iran received from its economic instrument was reinforced by astute use of the diplomatic instrument, particularly in institutionalizing Iranian influence. Across this period, Hezbollah's governing body, the Shura Council, was composed of nine members, two of whom were Iranian representatives.[44] Moreover, whenever Hezbollah's leaders were deadlocked, Iran's Supreme Leader was asked to make the final decision.[45] Reflecting this integration, in 1995, Supreme Leader Ayatollah Khamenei appointed the leader of Hezbollah as his deputy in Lebanon.[46] Hezbollah officials and Iranian government leaders also regularly talked and met to discuss their mutual interests.[47]

The formal ties though understated Iran's institutional influence. Hezbollah was deliberately structured in accordance with the Iranian model and established on the principle of the authority of the religious sage.[48] The majority of the Lebanese members of the leadership were Shia clerics who possessed strong religious linkages with senior Iranian clerics, gained while studying together in Najaf.[49] The Shia concept of the Guardianship of the Islamic Jurists reinforced these linkages. At the time, Martin Rudner observed that:

> "Hizbullah shares its political and religious ideology with Iran and the doctrines of the late ayatollahs Baqir as Sadr and Ruhollah Khomeini, who held that a religious jurist should hold supreme authority over the Shia community. Hizbullah looks to Iran's Supreme leader, Ayatollah Ali Khamenei and to Grand Ayatollah Muhammad Hussein Fadlallah, the leading Lebanese Shia religious authority, for political and

44. Rudner, p. 227.
45. Byman, p. 89.
46. Graham E. Fuller, 'The Hizballah-Iran Connection: Model for Sunni Resistance', in Alexander T. J. Lennon (ed.), *The Epicenter of Crisis: The New Middle East*; Cambridge: The MIT Press, 2008, pp. 207-20, p. 211.
47. Wiegand, p. 671.
48. Azani, p. 179.
49. Magnus Ranstorp, *Hizb'allah in Lebanon: The Politics of the Western Hostage Crisis*; Basingstoke: MacMillan Press, 1997, p. 181.

policy guidance in advancing the Islamic revolution in Lebanon."[50]

These links cut both ways though. Religious factions within Hezbollah at times were involved in clerical power struggles in Iran.[51]

Militarily, the main Iranian involvement was in providing supplies and training. Iran gave large quantities of arms including sophisticated missiles and rocketry, and the maintenance items needed to support these. Hezbollah would have been hard-pressed to pay for these with its own resources. Iran also provided training for Hezbollah members in both Lebanon and Iran, making them considerably more skilled and allowing the movement to undertake highly effective combat operations. There were reportedly close ties between Hezbollah's terrorist wing and the Iranian officials involved in coordinating and directing Hezbollah terrorist operations, especially those undertaken outside Lebanon. Some favoured Hezbollah terrorists even had Iranian diplomatic passports.[52]

In passing it is important to note that Hezbollah also received considerable assistance from Syria. This was mostly indirect and, with Hezbollah and Iran not sharing similar ideological or religious values, the aid given was for more tactical and short-term objectives than that with Iran.[53] The relationship between Syria and Hezbollah was described as a: "...loveless marriage that endures because their common interests demand it."[54] The association between Syria and Hezbollah was of a denial grand strategy alliance type relationship rather than an engagement grand strategy complex independence type.

---

50. Rudner, p. 226.
51. Ranstorp, p. 181.
52. Byman, p. 87, 90 and 98.
53. Samii, p. 37-40. Rola El Husseini, 'Hezbollah and the Axis of Refusal: Hamas, Iran and Syria', *Third World Quarterly,* Vol. 31, No. 5, 2010, pp. 803-15, pp. 810-11.
54. Al-Nahar (Beirut), 5 April 2001 quoted in: Gary C. Gambill and Ziad K. Abdelnour, 'Hezbollah between Tehran and Damascus', *Middle East Intelligence Bulletin,* Vol. 4, No. 2, February 2002, meforum.org/meib/articles/0202_11.htm.

To implement its engagement grand strategy, Iran embraced a long-term managerial approach with an accommodational strategy that made use of existing extraction policies. The state at this time played a major role in the Iranian economy through central planning, the extensive use of five-year plans and being deeply involved through large public and quasi-public enterprises in the manufacturing and finance sectors.[55] During this period, Hezbollah's annual fiscal demands of some US$100-200m were readily manageable within the Iranian government revenue base (US$29.6 billion in 2005/6) although, some three quarters of this revenue base was derived from oil sales and varied considerably with oil prices. The revenue from oil was US$11 billion in 2001/2 but had almost doubled to US$21.3 billion in 2005/6.[56] While funding for Hezbollah across 1982 - 2006 was relatively stable and meagre, occasionally large unanticipated sums were required, such as in 2006 for Lebanese reconstruction. At these times, Iranian generosity appeared more munificent when oil prices were high.

The grand strategy's manpower and material needs during this period were readily met internally by the armed forces and Iranian industry. State ownership of the necessary armament factories allowed most of Hezbollah's military arms requirements to be met by Iranian industry although, some equipment like anti-ship missiles were acquired from foreign sources.

The limited domestic legitimacy the grand strategy required was gained through a combination of input legitimacy granted based on the Iranian state's constrained electoral processes, and output legitimacy based on the state being the most appropriate institution to support foreign Shia groups and having demonstrated competence.

Iran achieved a durable grand strategic synthesis with its

---

55. World Bank, 'Country Brief - Iran'; go.worldbank.org/ME0HZPWIB0: World Bank, September 2010.
56. In 2005/6 Iran had a GDP of some US$188.5 billion and was the second largest economy in the Middle East and North Africa after Saudi Arabia. Juan Carlos Di Tata et al., *IMF Country Report No. 07/101: Islamic Republic of Iran: Statistical Appendix*; Washington, D.C.: International Monetary Fund, 9 February 2007, p. 3.

order building well matched with its building power approach. Iran's use of an engagement grand strategy produced outcomes that other grand strategy types would have struggled to achieve, especially with such a low impact on the Iranian domestic base. This was only possible because of the existence of Lebanese domestic groups that shared Iranian objectives and which were able to be assisted to become so influential and powerful that they were able to achieve tangible outcomes.

While Iran initially supported Amal, its values and goals steadily diverged from Iran's and it became progressively less useful in meeting Iranian objectives. Iran's decision to create Hezbollah and then actively support the group - especially with economic aid - was crucial to Hezbollah being able to realistically challenge Amal for leadership of the Lebanese Shia community. Even so, much of Hezbollah's success must be accredited to the movement itself. Hezbollah consistently generated inspiring and competent leaders able both to rally and unite their community, and wield a deft political touch that has enhanced their stature in Lebanon.[57] Hezbollah and Iran had a complex interdependent relationship where both relied on each other to achieve their shared objectives. As Norton writes:

> "The rapid growth and popularity of the Hiz'ballah...was achieved not only by a successful combination of ideological indoctrination and material inducement by Hizb'allah through the infusion of Iranian aid and military assistance. It was also achieved by the ability of the Hizb'allah leaders to mobilize a destitute Shi'a community, disaffected with the continuing Israeli occupation, and unite it within the framework of an organisation with clearly defined and articulated political objectives. This was achieved through the provision of concrete and workable solutions to the fundamental political, social, and economic needs of the Shi'a community in the absence of any central Lebanese authority and in the presence

---

57. Byman, p. 99.

of the civil war."[58]

In the later years of the grand strategy period, there was a perception that with Hezbollah joining the political process, contesting elections and having representatives in Parliament that the organization had been Lebanonized and was moving away from being as useful to Iran.[59] However the logic of the engagement grand strategy type suggests that Iran would be keenly self-interested in making Hezbollah steadily more influential in Lebanon as the organization intrinsically shared Iranian values and goals, even as these evolved over time. Iran's fundamental interest was to shape Lebanon's social purposes and having Hezbollah embedded deep in the country's political structures undoubtedly advanced this.

The decision to enter the Lebanese political process was indeed contested within Hezbollah's leadership Shura Council. The deadlock was only resolved in favour of participation by the Iranian Supreme Leader, Ayatollah Khamenei during a large conclave held in 1989 in Tehran; his decision was supported by President Rafsanjan.[60] The Shia religious and the Iranian state networks both agreed on the direction Hezbollah should take indicating that from a grand strategy perspective this step was considered advantageous to Iran.

The Iranian engagement grand strategy was successful because Iran was able to work with domestic interest groups that held preferences compatible with broad Iranian desires. In the early 1980s though Iran's Lebanese partners were few in number and politically marginalized. In response, Iran actively created the Hezbollah group and then assisted it to grow dramatically in size, to become much more influential in Lebanese society and to be able to shape the country's social purpose. Conversely, those Lebanese groups that did not hold preferences useful to Iranian grand strategic

---

58. Ranstorp, p. 39.
59. Wiegand, p. 673-78. Husseini, p. 809-10. Wehrey et al., p. 100-02. Byman et al., pp. 102-05.
60. Nizar Hamzeh, 'Lebanon's Hizbullah: From Islamic Revolution to Parliamentary Accommodation', *Third World Quarterly,* Vol. 14, No. 2, 1993, pp. 321-37, pp. 323-25.

objectives were directly and indirectly targeted. Iran worked to make these unhelpful groups progressively less influential within Lebanon's political, economic and social systems.

Iran's successful grand strategy further illustrates that this type of grand strategy can be enduring. Iranian grand strategic objectives to a large extent became self-reinforcing as Hezbollah progressively deeply embraced them and incorporated them within Hezbollah's own social purposes. An important aspect of this example was that lacking an effective Lebanese partner to advance its aims Iran carefully crafted one, but this partner was intended from the start to be more than a puppet. The building of a complex interdependence order meant that Hezbollah as it developed and grew remained loyal to the social purposes that Iran wished advanced. Iran did not need to instruct or run its partner, rather Hezbollah even when acting alone and independently could be relied on to act in a manner that Iran would generally agree with.

Iran's grand strategy proved to be remarkably cost-effective. The majority of the resource costs over this period were borne by Hezbollah rather than Iran although there were some start-up costs that Iran alone paid. Even so, the key shortcoming of this type of grand strategy remains: viable domestic interest groups in the society of concern must be able to found or built. If not, then this type of grand strategy is impractical.

British Appeasement Grand Strategy 1934-1939

In the 1930s the British government adopted a grand strategy of appeasement to counter the dangers evident from a rearming and revisionist Nazi Germany.[61] The grand strategy carefully combined elements from both the denial and engagement grand strategy types. In this typology, appeasement could be considered as a variety of engagement grand strategy. To avoid confusion however, and in accord with common usage, this British grand strategy will be labeled the Appeasement grand strategy. The denial grand strategy type component will be considered as one of the two strands of the

---

61. In the 1930s appeasement referred to the ends sought rather than the means used as it does today. David Gillard, *Appeasement in Crisis: From Munich to Prague, October 1938-March 1939* Basingstoke: Palgrave Macmillan, 2007, p. 18.

all-encompassing Appeasement grand strategy.

The Appeasement grand strategy employed sought to pacify Germany through conciliation and negotiation and hopefully avoid war but as insurance, in parallel also implemented a measured rearmament program. At worse, the denial strand of the Appeasement grand strategy would mean the UK was able to defend itself against German military actions.[62] While intuitively sensible, this hedging strategy in merging grand strategic perspectives proved a significant failure.

By the interwar period the British Empire had grown to its largest ever extent and sprawled around the globe. Britain was a satisfied great power whose national interest lay in maintaining the status quo. In 1926 a Foreign Office memorandum observed: "We have got all that we want, perhaps more. Our sole object is to keep what we have and live in peace."[63] However, in the early 1930s the Great Depression led to a breakdown of globalization, a rise of economic nationalism, a turning away from free trade towards protectionism, and the formation of semi-autarkic currency and trading blocs. The severe economic woes strengthened a broad societal move towards authoritarian governments, with those of Japan, Italy and Germany potentially posing particularly worrying security problems for the British Empire. A grand strategy was needed to meet the gathering storm.

The objective of stopping other states from taking actions that interfered with the British Empire initially suggested adopting a denial type grand strategy. In this time of economic hardship though, British resources were considered insufficient to meet the threats posed by the three dictatorships if they made war against Britain simultaneously. The resource shortfall suggested that the perceived threats from the three nations needed to be prioritized with manpower, material and money focused on addressing the most

---

62. Norrin M. Ripsman and Jack S. Levy, 'Wishful Thinking or Buying Time?: The Logic of British Appeasement in the 1930s', *International Security,* Vol. 33, No. 2, Fall 2008, pp. 66-67, 148-81, 159.
63. Keith Middlemas, *The Strategy of Appeasement: The British Government and Germany, 1937-39*; Chicago: Quadrangle Books, 1972, p. 17.

serious problems. Accompanying this was a debate over adopting a grand strategy involving changing several interstate relations or a grand strategy addressing the most important bi-lateral relationship.

While the protection of the security and interests of the British Empire was global in scope perhaps implying a multilateral grand strategy, some held that Britain could better solve the matter on a bilateral basis. Historian Michael Roi writes: " In other words, Britain should approach Germany, Japan and Italy directly to settle outstanding disputes. [Others believed though that]…the interdependence of events in every region of the globe militated against bilateral solutions."[64]

In contrasting the two options, a bilateral approach was considered to give Britain greater autonomy and flexibility compared to dealing with several states in an integrated multilateral manner that would inevitably impose constraints on the national freedom of action. In the 1930s, a major cause of the First World War was considered to be entangling alliances that prevented timely action to settle differences; multilateralism appeared dangerous, even provocative.[65] For policymakers, this historical analogy was compelling.

British policymaking moreover deliberately discounted any contribution allies might make to the balance of power with reliance placed solely on national military capabilities.[66] The strategic culture further favoured bilateralism for as historian David Gillard notes: "…the traditional preference of British governments [was] for a diplomacy of deals rather than one of alliances."[67]

In 1934 the British Cabinet decided on a grand strategy that focused the nation's scarce resources principally towards meeting the

---

64. Michael L. Roi, *Alternative to Appeasement: Sir Robert Vansittart and Alliance Diplomacy, 1934-1937*; Westport: Praeger Publishers, 1997, p. 162.
65. Gustav Schmidt, *The Politics and Economics of Appeasement: British Foreign Policy in the 1930s*; New York: St Martin's Press, 1986, p. 371.
66. Ripsman and Levy, pp. 180-81.
67. Gillard, p. 18.

German threat.[68] The grand strategy devised and implemented drew upon appeasement to try to avert war and rearmament to deter war should diplomacy fail. The engagement and denial types were merged into a single comprehensive grand strategy colloquially labelled Appeasement. There was a strong perception that another great European war would finish the Empire, and Britain's systemic position as a great power. War was to be avoided if at all possible. Neville Chamberlain, initially as Chancellor of the Exchequer and from June 1937 as Prime Minister emerged as the primary driver of Britain's new grand strategy.[69]

The grand strategy's engagement strand aimed to change the social purpose of the German state.[70] Britain did not seek the political reform of the Nazi state and was well aware that alone it could not militarily coerce Germany. Instead, as historian David Gillard observed:

> "The essential problem...was how to convince Hitler or any post-Nazi leadership that it was in Germany's long-term interests to exercise restraint in its use of power and to rely on negotiated change in the international order, despite Germany's undoubted power to disrupt that order."[71]

British governments of the period considered that Germany had some legitimate grievances arising out of the 1919 Peace Treaty of Versailles that necessitated revision. The Foreign Office wrote in 1935 that: "from the earliest years following the war, it was our

---

68. 'Appeasement Reconsidered: Some Neglected Factors', *The Round Table,* Vol. 53, No. 212, 1963, pp. 358-71, p. 362.
69. Layne, 'Security Studies and the Use of History: Neville Chamberlain's Grand Strategy Revisited', pp. 403-09.
70. In an oft-quoted definition grand strategy historian Paul Kennedy declared that appeasement is: "...the policy of settling international...quarrels by admitting and satisfying grievances through rational negotiation and compromise, thereby avoiding the resort to armed conflict which would be expensive, boldly, and possibly very dangerous. It is in essence a positive policy, based upon certain optimistic assumptions about man's inherent reasonableness...." Paul Kennedy, *Strategy and Diplomacy 1870-1945: Eight Studies*; Aylesbury: Fontana Paperbacks, 1984, p. 16.
71. Gillard, p. 18.

policy to eliminate those parts of the Peace Settlement which, as practical people, we knew were untenable and indefensible."[72] The belief was that working with Germany to resolve the shortcomings of the Peace Treaty would convince Germany that her goals could be achieved peacefully rather than through using force. Such Anglo-German cooperation would led to better and more lasting results than simply relying on a denial grand strategy that sought a balance of power order through military force.

Historian R.A.C. Parker noted that the British "...relied on a sympathetic treatment of German grievances to win Hitler, or failing him, influential Germans, to peaceful ways."[73] In this, the Nazi leadership was not seen as monolithic. There were considered to be four distinct power centres: firstly the officer class of the armed forces led by the Commander in Chief Bloomberg; secondly the economic policy bureaucrats, bankers and the business heads especially those from the heavy industries in the Rhineland and Ruhr; thirdly the Nazi party; and lastly the SS led by Himmler. The British believed that there were struggles between the moderate and the extremist power centres that could be exploited.[74]

The British grand strategy's engagement strand sought to strengthen the moderate's position in the German state through working with them to address their concerns about the Peace Treaty and by offering tempting political and economic policy incentives. Chamberlain felt that Britain should "do all in its power to encourage the moderates."[75] Crucially in this grand strategy, "...Hitler was thought to be a comparatively moderate exponent of German discontents so that the more unquestioned his power, the easier appeasement would be."[76] Until September 1939, Chamberlain had a particularly strong belief in Hitler as a moderate, and so helping him

72. Middlemas, p. 11.
73. R.A.C. Parker, *Chamberlain and Appeasement: British Policy and the Coming of the Second World War*; Basingstoke: Palgrave Macmillan, 1993, p. 346.
74. C. A. Macdonald, 'Economic Appeasement and the German "Moderates" 1937-1939: An Introductory Essay', *Past & Present* No. 56, August 1972, pp. 105-35, p. 110.
75. Ibid., p. 121.
76. Parker, pp. 23-24.

achieve his demanded revisions to the Peace Treaty without using force was considered likely to lead to better relations and positive policy responses, including disarmament.

The British Appeasement grand strategy sought to build a complex interdependence order where the British state could favourably manipulate the German state's preferences, where there were multiple influence channels and where the use of military force was inconceivable. This was an engagement grand strategy type of international order however, the British grand strategy had a dual nature that included a denial component; "For Britain, appeasement was…a complement to a strategy of rearmament and balancing, not an alternative to it."[77] Chamberlain believed this dual policy gave the best chance of Britain avoiding war.

Rearmament though implied seeking a denial grand strategy balance of power order where military power was privileged, war was a legitimate instrument of policy and states created alliances to counter systemic threats. The engagement grand strategy complex interdependence order and the denial grand strategy balance of power order are inherently mutually incompatible. It was not surprising at the 20 November 1938 cabinet meeting Chamberlain remarked that: "In our foreign policy we were doing our best to drive two horses abreast, conciliation and rearmament. It was a very nice art to keep these two steeds in step."[78] The difficulties inherent in seeking incompatible orders are particularly evident when the use of the instruments of national power in implementing the grand strategy is considered.

Britain primarily internally balanced against Germany by re-equipping and expanding its armed forces. While Britain had limited resources, the dual policy militated against using external balancing as making firm alliances with other European nations would be seen under Appeasement as militarily threatening Germany through encirclement. Germany would then perceive that Britain harboured aggressive intentions justifying its own large-scale military build-up.

---

77. Ripsman and Levy.
78. Parker, p. 291.

Accordingly, the important entente with France was deliberately downplayed.[79] In early 1938 the Service chiefs rejected military-to-military talks with France, as these would cause "the very situation we wish to avoid, namely the irreconcilable suspicion and hostility of Germany."[80] The other large European power, Russia, was also disregarded as: "…western association with the USSR would annoy and provoke, rather than restrain, the Nazis and non-Nazi Germans."[81]

The logic of the engagement strand of the grand strategy meant allies were not enlisted to contribute to the denial strand's balance of power element; such a stance was in strong opposition to the fundamental operating logic of the denial grand strategy. This disregard of allies was reflected in the military strategy that downplayed any formal continental commitment of large-scale land forces in the event of war, instead the British Army was to concentrate on imperial policing and home defence. The armed forces as a whole were to adopt a deterrent posture with the Royal Air Force the primary element re-equipped to threaten German civilian industrial targets.[82] The Royal Navy would contribute by threatening to blockade German raw material supplies, and by ensuring Germany could not cut off Britain's crucial lines of supply. Keeping the sea trade routes with the Empire open was considered essential for Britain to win what was envisaged to be a long war if it came.

The economic instrument of the grand strategy was focused on strengthening the position of the German moderates. In the 1930s, Britain and Germany were the two largest capitalist economies in Europe, and strong economic connections existed between the major financial and commercial institutions in London and Berlin. These "informal channels between British and German business and industrial groups lay at the heart of efforts towards economic

79. Middlemas, p. 2-3. Martin Gilbert and Richard Gott, *The Appeasers*, 2nd edn.; London: Weidenfield and Nicholson, 2nd Edn 1967, pp. 8-9.
80. Michael Howard, *Continental Commitment: The Dilemma of British Defence Policy in the Era of the Two World Wars*; London: Temple Smith, 1972, p. 118.
81. Parker, p. 347.
82. Howard, pp. 96-118.

appeasement."[83]   British government economic management and
Foreign   Office   officials   encouraged   the   intensification   of
commercial interactions to assist tipping the domestic balance of
political power in favour of the moderate German groups.[84] To help
this, the British government granted an increasing volume of export
credits to firms involved in commerce with Germany right up to late
August 1939 immediately before the war started.[85]   This commercial
activity was in accord with the grand strategy; Scott Newton
observes:

> "...[the] private interests of finance and large-scale industry
> worked with the grain of public policy. Indeed the level of
> political access enjoyed by organizations such as the Anglo-
> German Fellowship and the extent of ministerial support for
> the industrial diplomacy of the Federation of British
> Industries make it hard to distinguish between the
> international interests of the state and the foreign policy of
> powerful economic pressure groups.[86]

Inter-governmental activities actively complemented this.
The Standstill negotiations of the early 1930s had generated an
unusually   close   working   relationship   between   the   banking

---

83. Frank Mcdonough, *Neville Chamberlain, Appeasement and the British Road
to War*; Manchester: Manchester University Press, 1998, p. 135.
84. Steven E. Lobell, 'The Second Face of Security: Britain's 'Smart'
Appeasement Policy Towards Japan and Germany', *International Relations of the
Asia-Pacific*, Vol. 7, No. 1, 2007, pp. 73-98, pp. 84-85.
85. Scott Newton, 'The 'Anglo-German Connection' and the Political Economy of
Appeasement', *Diplomacy & Statecraft*, Vol. 2, No. 3, 1991, pp. 178-207, pp. 196-
97.
86. Ibid., p. 191. The Anglo-German Fellowship was formed in 1935 to foster
good relations between Britain and Germany. The Fellowship became a powerful
lobby group that provided the City with a source of pressure for harmony between
the two countries additional to the one created by the German Central Bank's ·
historic, but more informal ties with the Treasury. Corporate members included
large firms, such as Firth-Vickers Stainless Steels, Unilever and Dunlop, whilst the
directors of leading industrial concerns, for example Imperial Chemical Industries,
Anglo-Iranian Oil, Tate and Lyle and the Distillers Company, joined as private
individuals, as did Lord Stamp and Sir Robert Kindersley, both Governors of the
Bank of England, and Lord Magowan, Chairman of the Midland Bank. Ibid., pp.
186-87.

representatives of each nation. The Governor of the Bank of England held that behind the new Nazi regime were sensible financial figures able to steer Hitler towards less militaristic policies.[87] One of the key German moderates targeted was Hjalmar Schacht, President of the Reichsbank (German Central Bank, 1933–1939) and Minister of Economics (1934–1937). Schacht asserted that economic concessions bolstered him and the other moderates within the inner-German power struggle.[88] In mid-1937, the British also began cultivating Herman Goring, then Commissioner for the Four Year-Plan and an important Nazi Party figure.[89]

The British stressed the strong linkages between economic possibilities and their sought-after political agreements. This continued right up until mid-1939 with the British offering a full-scale economic partnership, including a very large loan, provided Germany stepped back from the use of force to achieve its political aims.[90] McDonald writes:

> "...Chamberlain attempted to demonstrate to this group [of Germans] that Germany would benefit economically from a political settlement, which led to the termination of autarky and rearmament. He hoped that this section of German opinion would then use its influence with Hitler in favour of a negotiated settlement, in contrast to Party "extremists" like Goebbels and Himmler, who argued that Germany could only attain its aims by war."[91]

Economic appeasement though worked against the logic of the denial grand strategy strand that underlay Britain's rearmament. Germany used its economic and financial relationship with Britain to help build and finance its rapid military build-up. The 1931

---

87. Ibid., pp. 185-86.
88. British officials approached other German moderates such as Helmut Wohltat, a senior official of the German Economics Ministry, Field Marshal von Blomberg, Dr Frick, Minister of the Interior, Baron Konstantin von Neurath, the former Foreign Minister, Walther Funk, Schacht's successor, and Ernst von Weizsacker under-secretary in the Foreign Office. Lobell, p. 85-86.
89. Macdonald, p. 110.
90. Newton, pp. 196-97.
91. Macdonald, p. 105.

Standstill Agreement, renewed annually, aided German bank solvency and provided important credit. [92] Trade with Britain furnished crucial international currency needed to pay for essential food and raw material imports. As was recognized at the time, this all facilitated German rearmament[93]; Reginald McKenna chairman of Midland Bank and Member of Parliament in 1936 campaigned against economic concessions to Germany on these grounds.[94] The Foreign Office countered though that this economic and financial interaction "strengthened the peace party" helping "reasonable people in Germany to exert their influence."[95]

The diplomatic instrument was used as part of the programme of political appeasement under the engagement strand. Britain assisted, or at least acquiesced, in the German, often unilateral, violation of the Peace Treaty provisions. These included the Germans reintroducing conscription, full-scale rearmament including the building of a new navy and air force, the March 1936 remilitarization of the Rhineland, and the progressive annexation of Austria, the Sudetenland and the non-German lands of Czechoslovakia. Only in the case of the Sudetenland annexation did Britain gain some promises of future cooperation as part of the Munich Agreement.[96] These political compromises undoubtedly strengthened Hitler's position as leader but did not lead to moderate policies as envisaged. Worse, diplomacy further worked against the denial grand strategy strand and Britain's rearmament. The

---

92. Newton, p. 183.
93. Newton writes that" "The commercial attaché in Berlin, Magowan, advocated denouncing the Anglo-German Payments Agreement, on the grounds that Germany was only using it to procure raw materials for rearmament. He believed that the Nazi regime was now openly hostile to Britain, and that its main prop was the Payments Agreement. Denounce the agreement and German rearmament would collapse for lack of foreign exchange." Macdonald, p. 121.
94. Adam Tooze, *The Wages of Destruction: The Making and the Breaking of the Nazi Economy*; New York: Viking, 2007, p. 233.
95. Frank Ashton-Gwatkin, Head of the Economic section of the Foreign Office quoted in Macdonald, pp. 116-17.
96. After the Munich talks, Chamberlain thought he had convinced Hitler of the need for peaceful negotiated change rather than change by force, as well as the UK having a central role in European affairs. Hitler post-Munich bitterly regretted his agreement. Gillard, p. 19.

violations of the Peace Treaty all acted to strengthen German military might relative to Britain's and the balance of power steadily tilted Germany's way. Steven Lobell commenting on the example of dismemberment of Czechoslovakia writes:

> "The Munich Agreement, intended to defuse the immediate danger of war, strengthened Germany's immediate warmaking capacity by granting Berlin foreign exchange, strategic raw materials, industrial power (especially the Skoda armament works), and equipment to arm forty German divisions."[97]

Moreover Britain, which at the time only had some five Regular Army divisions, lost a potential ally with some thirty-five well-equipped divisions.[98]

The engagement strand of the Appeasement grand strategy did though boost the effectiveness of the informational instrument in supporting the British position. Few could doubt that Britain had tried very hard to avoid conflict, albeit sometimes at the expense of others such as Austria and Czechoslovakia. Britain hoped that in appearing willing to settle genuine grievances without war, Germany's leaders might find it harder to mobilize their people for war. Indeed, there is evidence that the German people would have welcomed a settlement built on the 1936 status quo.[99] Gustav Schmidt writes that the Appeasement grand strategy reasoned that:

> "Whereas…economic offers would help to upvalue the position of the 'moderates' in Germany and would further Germany's willingness to compromise, the political approach [sought]…to bring the German people into play and that this, accompanied by the measures suggested, would restrain Germany's ruling classes from adventurism."[100]

---

97. Steven E. Lobell, 'The Grand Strategy of Hegemonic Decline: Dilemmas of Strategy and Finance', *Security Studies,* Vol. 10, No. 1, 2000, pp. 86-111, p. 104.
98. Howard, pp. 125-30.
99. Tooze, p. 205.
100. Schmidt, p. 201.

This approach however, again worked against the logic of rearmament and the denial strand of the grand strategy. The British public were not rallied to support the sacrifices needed to expedite rearmament. Even after the 1938 Munich Agreement, Chamberlain opposed mobilizing the public as this would work against better, more productive relations with Germany.[101] Moreover, the elections of the period were not fought on preparing the country for war but rather for avoiding it through appeasement; gaining the necessary input legitimacy for the dual policy was inherently problematic.

Britain never achieved a sound grand strategic synthesis. There were consistently tensions between the engagement and denial strands and the building of power to support them. As the grand strategy process would suggest, the Appeasement grand strategy initially adopted a long-term market state approach that reflected the uncertain nature of future developments. Conveniently, such an approach was also in harmony with the liberal, free trade beliefs of the government. Over time however, as the earlier uncertainties steadily resolved themselves and the future became clearer if darker, Britain moved progressively towards a managerial approach, much as the grand strategy process would propose.

In this evolution, the building of power for the Appeasement grand strategy was dominated by concerns over finance. The British experience reflected an attempt to limit the impact of the grand strategy on the society through using an accommodational strategy initially, then seeking foreign monies and only as a last resort moving to a restructural strategy.

The economic orthodoxy of the time stressed balanced budgets and Britain's experience of a relatively quick recovery from the Great Depression seemed to support this. Existing income and indirect taxes were steadily raised to support a measured rearmament program constrained to stay firmly within balanced budget limits.[102]

---

101. Parker, pp. 182-86.
102. Judged in relative terms however, the British commitment to defence increased consistently from 1935. British defence spending increased by more than 35 percent in 1936 and a further 38 percent in 1937; defence spending as a

Deficit financing was to be avoided if at all possible.[103] In 1937 when this accommodational strategy was clearly inadequate, the Government passed the Defence Loans Act that sought to borrow a limited sum of money from private domestic and international sources.[104] However, the earlier Johnson Act of 1934 meant that unlike during World War One the American government was prohibited from loaning Britain money.[105] With other nations also rearming and seeking foreign monies, the lingering effects of the Great Depression, and the need to enforce rearmament priorities Britain then finally adopted a restructural strategy that moved the country decisively towards a managerial state.[106]

The overall economy was strongly oriented towards international trade albeit as an outcome of the Great Depression mainly with the Empire. Britain needed to import food and acquire the raw materials required for its exporting manufacturing industries. Britain's exports then financed the essential imports needed for the denial strand of the grand strategy but worryingly rearmament in itself meant greater imports and potentially less exports. Layne observes that:

"As rearmament began, British policy makers were impaled on the horns of an economic dilemma. The armaments and export industries competed directly against each other for scarce factors of production such as raw materials, skilled labor, and factory floor space. Simply put, if the tempo of rearmament was increased, the volume of British exports

---

percentage of total government expenditures rose to 21 percent in 1936, and 26 percent in 1937. Ripsman and Levy, pp. 176-77.

103. Chamberlain was particularly proud of the balanced budgets achieved while he was Chancellor of the Exchequer; he was disdainful of deficits which he thought were accompanied by "deepening depression and by a constantly falling price level." Middlemas, p. 126.

104. F. Coghlan, 'Armaments, Economic Policy and Appeasement. Background to British Foreign Policy, 1931-7', *History* Vol. 57, No. 190, June 1972, pp. 205-16, p. 213.

105. G.C. Peden, *Arms, Economics and British Strategy: From Dreadnoughts to Hydrogen Bombs*; Cambridge: Cambridge University Press, 2007, p. 133.

106. David Edgerton, *Warfare State: Britain 1920-1970*; Cambridge: Cambridge University Press, 2006, p. 15-190. Peden, pp. 125-44.

would decrease. As its export earnings declined, it would become more difficult for Britain to pay for rearmament."[107]

A stable currency and sound fiscal management was considered central to the planned long war strategy. British war planning was based on a belief that if hostilities broke out, Germany given its economic and raw material constraints could only fight a short war.[108] If Britain could hold out long enough it would prevail. In a long war international loans would be easier to secure if the British peacetime balance of payments were strong while, if loans were unavailable, then the gold reserves built up from peacetime surpluses would be the only financial alternative to selling British capital assets overseas. A strong balance of payments had the leading role in reinforcing what the Treasury and the Minister for Coordination of Defence, Thomas Inskip, called the 'fourth arm of defence'.[109] Economic historian G.C. Peden observed, Britain: "had to try to strike a balance between financing armaments now and maintaining sufficient economic strength to finance a war later."[110]

The result was that the rate of the military build-up was limited to that which did not cause interference with normal civilian production. Rearmament was added to existing production and did not substitute or replace any of it. Rearmament was further delayed by a significant lack of both skilled labour and the requisite industrial capacity. In keeping with its market economy Britain relied mainly on its private industry for rearming.[111]

---

107. Layne, 'Security Studies and the Use of History: Neville Chamberlain's Grand Strategy Revisited', pp. 406-07.
108. British policy makers assumed that if Germany did not win a war quickly, the superior economic and financial strength of the British Empire and France would result in an Allied victory. British policymakers believed that for economic reasons, principally a shortage of key raw materials, Germany could not wage a prolonged conflict. Chamberlain observed "The Allies are bound to win in the end...the only question is how long it will take them to achieve their purpose." ibid., p. 408.
109. Parker, p. 275.
110. G.C. Peden, *British Rearmament and the Treasury, 1932–1939*; Edinburgh: Scottish Academic Press, 1979, p. 66.
111. Parker, pp. 274-73. Coghlan, pp. 213-14.

The combination of an engagement grand strategy and a denial grand strategy patently failed, resulting in for the British Empire a cataclysmic war. The pre-war fears of the British government were fully validated. The ultimate reason for the failure of the grand strategy was that British:

> "...hopes [for peace] rested on a reasonable but incorrect interpretation of the way the Third Reich worked. Hitler, this view assumed, must be interested in keeping power and the policies that set off the Second World War did not seem a sound method; if he were foolish enough to follow them, however, sensible Germans would stop him."[112]

An engagement grand strategy to be successful needs to work through others to achieve mutual beneficial goals. The British Cabinet made a profound error in assuming that Hitler and the Nazi state held to the same assumptions as they did and shared their strong interest in peace and prosperity.[113] At the same time, the adoption of an engagement grand strategy strand meant that the building of a balance of power order and of greater relative power as the denial strand sought was actively prevented. The British Appeasement grand strategy 1934-1939 was fatally flawed in trying to blend two mutually incompatible grand strategy types. The Appeasement grand strategy was deliberately, if unknowingly, designed from the start to be incoherent. The likelihood of failure in terms of avoiding war, maintaining the British Empire and keeping Britain a first-rate power was built-in.

There is a strong case to be made that war with Nazi Germany was inevitable regardless of the grand strategy Britain adopted. Choosing a different grand strategy in 1934 though may have made the war less total and prevented that which British policymakers most wished to avoid: the loss of the Empire and the relegation to being a second-rate power. A denial grand strategy may have lead to an earlier war in 1938 over the Austria *Anschluss* or the dismemberment of Czechoslovakia but such a grand strategy

---

112. Parker, p. 346.
113. Middlemas, p. 413.

in stressing building up military forces and building alliances may have seen Britain much better prepared and the conflict may have been more contained. Moreover Britain in ceasing trade and finance with Germany may significantly have impeded German rearmament. The relative power balances may have been much more favourable. Conversely a fully-fledged engagement grand strategy may have seen a stress placed on collective defence and working with like-minded states across Europe, perhaps even with Russia, again allowing Britain to leverage off others. There is no doubt though that the confused and incoherent grand strategy chosen failed to achieve its aim.

Policymakers at the time may have benefited from being aware that mixing two types of grand strategy would create inherent contradictions with a real danger of complete failure. The UK unintentionally choose an intrinsically risky grand strategy. Separating grand strategy types seems more likely to lead to success than merging them in some integrated manner.

In terms of developing general knowledge about engagement grand strategies, the British Appeasement grand strategy reveals the dangers of deciding to work with the wrong domestic interest groups, ones that do not hold your desired preferences. The British unintentionally strengthened the Nazi Party's grip on power and supported Hitler's ambitions to create a reordered Europe through military might. The catastrophic results of the British grand strategy suggests that very close attention needs to be paid to the domestic interest groups an engagement grand strategy is supporting, to ensure their ambitions accord with yours.

In this regard, the earlier discussion (Chapter 3) on the cognition of policymakers is particularly germane. People can worryingly see what they both expect to see and wish to see. Chamberlain continued to give Hitler the benefit of any doubts even when presented with lucid counter-arguments. In early 1938 when reading Stephen Robert's 'The House that Hitler Built' Chamberlain observed that it was "an extremely clever and well informed but very pessimistic book. If I accepted the author's conclusions I should despair but I don't and won't."[114]

In crafting an engagement grand strategy policymakers need to draw a sharp distinction between the availability of an influential interest group in a country of interest and their fundamental suitability. Easy access may not be the same as usefulness. A related consideration is that domestic interest groups by their nature will generally always seek out external help and assistance. Such groups will be looking to exploit others as much as others may seek to exploit them. The key issue is whether they hold preferences that the grand strategy can usefully and confidently take advantage of.

Conclusions

Considered together the three engagement grand strategy case studies reveal important policymaking aspects concerning grand strategies in general and engagement grand strategies in particular.

In general terms, the failure of the British Appeasement grand strategy highlights that policymakers may be more successful if they build a coherent grand strategy rather than attempt to combine types in an attempt to make some optimum blend. There is a real danger that in being ontologically different (i.e. states, sub-states, or ideas) that the various elements of some integrated grand strategy may unintentionally work against each other, make the situation worse and lead to grand strategic failure.

More specifically, engagement grand strategies rely on being able to find and work with domestic interest groups that hold preferences compatible with the broad grand strategic objectives. The grand strategy then aims to assist these useful partners in developing, becoming more influential in their respective countries and in achieving their ambitions to favourably alter the social purpose of their state. Conversely unhelpful domestic groups should be actively hindered and damaged to ensure they do not prevail in

114. Neville Chamberlain to Hilda Chamberlain, 30 Jan. 1938. NC 18/1/1037 quoted in Erik Goldstein, 'Neville Chamberlain, the British Official Mind and the Munich Crisis,' *Diplomacy & Statecraft,* Vol. 10, No. 2-3, 1999, pp. 276-92, p. 287.

shaping the social purpose of their country. In this, the Iranian example revealed that groups useful for an engagement grand strategy to exploit do not need to be pre-existing but can also be created, and from a very small base.

The success of the American and Iranian grand strategies further illustrates a feature of engagement grand strategies: they can be enduring. This grand strategy type which works with and through useful others can lead to their deeply embracing the grand strategy's objectives. These may then become self-reinforcing and therefore no longer needing continual support, effort and resources. Over the longer term an engagement grand strategy may be a more affordable type of grand strategy than a denial type although, initial start-up costs may be significant.

Both grand strategy case studies also illustrate the principal shortcomings of an engagement grand strategy. This type is only viable if domestic interest groups willing and able to use the assistance being offered can be found in countries important to the grand strategy. In the Marshall Plan only those nations outside the Soviet orbit could participate while, in the Iranian case, the absence of a suitable pre-existing group meant one needed to be created before the grand strategy could fully commence.

The British Appeasement grand strategy showed some of the real dangers inherent in an engagement grand strategy type. The interest groups to be worked with and through need to be carefully chosen; their suitability, not just their availability, needs deep consideration. In trying to exploit useful others, there is a danger that these domestic groups will turn the tables and try to exploit the grand strategy for ends opposed to those the engagement grand strategy seeks. Actively supporting the wrong groups can be potentially catastrophic as the British example showed.

7

Reform Grand Strategies

Reform has an appealing finality but in being so ambitious is the most problematic of all grand strategies. This chapter's case studies highlight important aspects of reform grand strategies including their design requirements, general operating logic and the circumstances that favour success or failure.

The first case is the United Kingdom's grand strategy of 1948-1960 that defeated the communist insurgency in Malaya through shaping conceptions of national and adversary identity. The Malayan Emergency is often seen as being a counterinsurgency exemplar but at its core involved two parties both seeking to gain the ideational edge over the other. As a colonial power the UK may be intuitively considered as unlikely to have prevailed. The time span chosen is from when the need for a grand strategy was first realised with the start of the insurgency in 1948 until its effective end in 1960. The grand strategies used by the British both changed and progressively evolved making this also a useful example of the life cycles of grand strategies.

The second, more demanding case is the International Campaign to Ban Landmines grand strategy during 1992-1999. This involved a unique coalition of non-state actors that sought an international humanitarian law reform objective. The campaign faced considerable opposition from many states and the use of materialist International Relations theories to assist crafting a suitable grand strategy would offer little insight and suggest certain failure. The time span chosen is from the realisation that a new grand strategy was needed until it culminated with achieving its desired end state.

The failure case is that of the US Iraq regime change grand strategy 2002-2003. This period spans the initial thinking about the grand strategy to its culmination in mid-2003 with the collapse of the

Ba'athist regime of Saddam Hussein and the realization that the grand strategic end state desired had not been achieved. This is a useful failure case as the aim, changing Iraqi political norms, was attempted using a denial grand strategy rather than as the grand strategy process would recommend, a reform grand strategy. The operating logic of denial and reform grand strategies would suggest that the US Iraq regime change grand strategy would fail in a particular manner: the Iraqi regime would be stopped from realizing its objectives of survival but the American desired change in Iraqi social rules would not be achieved.

British Malayan Emergency Grand Strategy 1948-1960

The reform grand strategy in Malaya was nested within a much broader UK engagement grand strategy concerning Cold War decolonization. The British concept was that cooperative pro-Western governments could be installed in many countries as they dismantled their Empire if the process of decolonization was carefully managed and avoided any divisiveness that left openings for pro-communist groups. The UK sought to prevent the Communists from capturing anti-colonialist movements and by so doing gaining the allegiance of the new states.[1] This global grand strategy required a capacity to regulate and control the course of events as countries decolonized. The global grand strategy used an engagement approach of working with and through local preferences for, as Nicholas Tarling wrote:

"The British would not frustrate initiatives, but would aim to shape them, trying to work with those who would collaborate, to adopt regional approaches, to influence rather than dominate."[2]

The development of a communist insurgency in the 1940s led to the British colonial government in Malaya declaring a state of emergency in mid-1948. After the Second World War, the Malayan

---

1. Benjamin Grob-Fitzgibbon, *Imperial Endgame: Britain's Dirty Wars and the End of Empire*; Basingstoke: Palgrave Macmillan, 2011, p. 2.
2. Nicholas Tarling, "Ah-Ah': Britain and the Bandung Conference of 1955', *Journal of Southeast Asian Studies,* Vol. 23, No. 1, March 1992, pp. 74-111, p. 74.

Communist Party (MCP) had progressively developed an effective and efficient support base albeit mainly only amongst the ethnic Chinese population. While some 40% of the overall population were Chinese, they constituted some 90-95% of the armed MCP insurgents.[3]

In October 1948 a new British High Commissioner, Sir Henry Gurney, was appointed and he initially attempted an engagement grand strategy. Gurney sought to build up a Chinese political party that would act as a means to bring the Chinese community and their grievances into the mechanism of government. The Malayan Chinese Association (MCA) was formally established in February 1949. Gurney's approach was based on an assumption that the wealthy urban elite of the new MCA had useful connections with the poorer rural Chinese and could favourably influence them; this turned out to be untrue.[4] In reality, the MCP were more widely known and trusted. While the MCA gradually developed in importance as a useful domestic group, at this stage they had inadequacies including the lack of a well-defined political role and a constituency, "...initially the MCA was a group of leaders in search of followers."[5] The later Briggs Plan partly addressed these shortcomings and incorporated the MCA into its reform grand strategy.

The MCP initially implemented a denial type grand strategy that stressed armed struggle to mobilize the people and win independence from the British.[6] With their engagement grand strategy concept stillborn, the British in response also adopted a denial grand strategy. This stressed counter-force activities involving offensive operations to seek out and destroy armed

3. Karl Hack, 'British Intelligence and Counter Insurgency in the Era of Decolonisation: The Example of Malaya', *Intelligence and National Security,* Vol. 14, No. 2, Summer 1999, pp. 124-55, p. 125.
4. Kumar Ramakrishna, *Emergency Propaganda: The Winning of Malayan Hearts and Minds 1948-1958*; Richmond: Curzon Press, 2002, p. 58.
5. Richard Stubbs, *Hearts and Minds in Guerrilla Warfare: The Malayan Emergency 1948-1960*; Oxford: Oxford University Press, 1989, p. 203 and 48.
6. Ramakrishna, pp. 26-53.

Communist guerrillas operating in particular areas.[7] By 1950 though it was apparent that this grand strategy was failing; Colonel Richard Clutterbuck wrote that:

> "...the Communists were fast building up their strength...[they] could get all the support they needed...[and] there was a growing danger that the ...civilian population would lose confidence in the government and conclude that the guerrillas must in the end win."[8]

To wrest the initiative from the MCP, the newly appointed General Briggs in May 1950 issued the *Federation Plan for the Elimination of the Communist Organisation and Armed Forces in Malaya*, often referred to as the Briggs Plan. The plan held that the MCP relied mainly upon the rural Chinese communities for recruitment, food, funding and material and that without this support the insurgency would fail. The intention was to physically separate the rural Chinese from the MCP but more importantly in so doing convince the rural Chinese to identify with the state as their protector and provider. Briggs wrote that "we must give [them] security and...we must win them over".[9] The earlier denial grand strategy had treated the rural Chinese as a community to be denied the MCP. As the grand strategy process would suggest, this approach was insensitive to the social rules of the rural Chinese and did not see these as important to success.[10] Under the Briggs Plan though, British actions would now address previously overlooked ideational matters and deliberately try to change the identity of the rural Chinese.

The rural Chinese at this stage had few dealings with the

7. Stubbs, p. 66-93. John A. Nagal, *Learning to Eat Soup with a Knife: Counterinsurgency Lessons from Malaya and Vietnam*; Chicago: The University of Chicago Press, 2005, pp. 66-67.
8. Richard L. Clutterbuck, *The Long. Long War: Counterinsurgency in Malaya and Vietnam*; New York: Frederick A Praeger, 1966, p. 89.
9. Lieutenant-General sir Harold Briggs, Report on the Emergency in Malaya from April 1950-November 1951, Kuala Lumpur, 1951, pp 3-5, quoted in Anthony Short, *The Communist Insurrection in Malaya, 1948-1960*; London: Frederick Muller Limited, 1975, p. 235. Ramakrishna, p. 89.
10. Ramakrishna, p. 57.

state, which they saw as distant and irrelevant. They had more in common with the MCP and were inclined to take grievances to them to be resolved, even if only because they were known to them, near by and also Chinese.[11] The Briggs Plan now sought to change this. General Briggs wrote that:

> "One of the most vital aims throughout the Emergency must be to commit the Chinese to our side, partly by making them feel that Malaya and not Red China is their home. Without their cooperation it will indeed be difficult to bring the Emergency to a successful conclusion."[12]

The constitutive norms of the rural Chinese that defined the boundaries and practices of the group, their social purposes and worldviews would now be reoriented away from the MCP and their ideology to that of the British colonial state. Importantly, a sharp ideational distinction would be made between the rural Chinese and the MCP who would become the 'other'. This was not a simple undertaking as the extant Chinese social rules favourably viewed the MCP who had earned considerable goodwill resisting the Japanese in the Second World War, were persuasive in the post-war period in arguing for social and economic improvements, included close relatives and were part of many people's friendship networks.[13]

The rural Chinese were dispersed along the internal frontier in numerous small communities but under the Briggs Plan a massive program of resettlement was undertaken that relocated 570,000 people into some 480 new villages and created 216 new urban centres.[14] There was also a 'regroupment' of some 600,000 estate

---

11. Stubbs, p. 248.
12. Lieutenant-General Sir Harold Briggs, CAB 21 / 1861, Federation Plan for the Elimination of the Communist Organisation and Armed Forces in Malaya, May 24, 1950 quoted in Short, p. 240.
13. Stubbs, pp. 89-90.
14. Of the 570,000, some 86% were Chinese, 9% Malaya, 4% Indian and 1% others. T. N. Harper, *The End of Empire and the Making of Malaya*; Cambridge: Cambridge University Press, 2001, p. 175-76. Cheah Boon Kheng, 'The Communist Insurgency in Malaysia, 1948-90: Contesting the Nation-State and Social Change', *New Zealand Journal of Asian Studies,* Vol. 11, No. 1, June 2009, pp. 132-52, pp. 144-45.

labourers into more secure communities.[15] Over one seventh of the entire population of Malaya were moved during the emergency, reversing the demographic effects of the Second World War and transforming the rural Chinese into townsmen. The urban element of the Chinese population increased from about 40% to almost 75%.[16]

The resettlement broke up old established communities, some of which went back centuries, undermining social cohesion and causing existing identities to fracture and collapse.[17] Briggs replacement, General Templer, decreed that the resettlement areas were to be renamed as New Villages emphasising the sharp break with the old, abandoned communities.[18] With resettlement, new heterogeneous communities abruptly came into being, comprised of Chinese of many different backgrounds, occupations and language dialects.[19] The resettlement program in completely disrupting the old community leadership structures allowed new influences from new ideational advocates to readily enter the public sphere.

These constructed settlements provided a captive following for the kind of Chinese leadership the British desired, a role the British encouraged and supported the MCA to play. The urban business elites of the MCA were provided an opportunity to work to re-establish their authority across the Chinese communities that they had lost in the aftermath of the Second World War. [20] The British incorporated the MCA into the new village programmes and instituted new local governance structures that featured a mix of democratically elected representatives and government officials.[21] These structures had mixed successes but brought the state deep into the lives of the rural Chinese and provided them a ready way to have their grievances addressed. This had the critical effect of freezing

15. Hack, p. 126.
16. Kheng, p. 145.
17. Harper, p. 168, 77.
18. Ramakrishna, p. 126.
19. Harper, p. 177.
20. Ibid., p. 151.
21. Ibid., p. 188. Ramakrishna, p. 129, 208.

the MCP out of the picture.[22]

Importantly, this was materially supported and buttressed by the wide range of government services that the Briggs Plan sought to be provided to the new communities. The Briggs Plan envisaged that the local administration would be improved to be more effective and efficient than anything the MCP could offer.[23] Schools, medical services, sporting facilities and community centres were to be built and staffed, an adequate water supply established, effective security provided and roads constructed.[24] These material actions would hopefully help convince the affected people that the government both protected and provided for them. Meeting concrete needs was seen as central to winning rural Chinese hearts and minds.[25] Benjamin Grob-Fitzgibbon wrote: "The key aspect of this strategy was to inculcate within the population a sense of British benevolence contrasted with Communist autocracy."[26] The program succeeded in as much most people when given the choice later, choose to stay living in the New Villages.[27]

The dominant theme of the Briggs approach to which material and non-material means were employed was "the creation of community" although this was a very particular, deliberately constructed community . Historian T.N.Harper continues that:

> "... Community development was an invitation to citizenship, but also a statement of the rules to which civic life had to conform. ...the aim was to absorb individual

22. Ramakrishna, p. 170.
23. Benjamin Grob-Fitzgibbon, 'Securing the Colonies for the Commonwealth: Counterinsurgency, Decolonization, and the Development of British Imperial Strategy in the Postwar Empire', *British Scholar,* Vol. II, No. 1, September 2009, pp. 12-39, p. 28. Clutterbuck, p. 57.
24. Stubbs, p. 173.
25. Ramakrishna, p. 2, 127.
26. Grob-Fitzgibbon, 'Securing the Colonies for the Commonwealth: Counterinsurgency, Decolonization, and the Development of British Imperial Strategy in the Postwar Empire', p. 29.
27. R. W. Komer, 'The Malayan Emergency in Retrospect: Organization of a Successful Counterinsurgency Effort'; Santa Monica, CA: RAND, 1972, pp. 54-58.

citizens, and thereby whole communities, into a common identity with the state through identifying a constructive civic role for the individual in his community. The ideal was 'a sense of oneness' with the government. "[28]

While raising the salience of the state's ideas in the social rules of the rural Chinese, the Briggs Plan also sought to make the MCP and its ideology seem unattractive, insignificant and inappropriate. Considerable effort was made to discredit the MCP on an ideational level through the use of "good propaganda, both constructive and destructive."[29] General Briggs considered that while striving to win over the rural Chinese a simultaneous effort needed to be made to destroy Communist confidence in their beliefs.[30] Over time the rural Chinese identified with the state not with the MCP, and the MCP's influence progressively declined.

In considering the use of the instruments of national power the key matter was to ensure, as this was a reform grand strategy, all actions taken supported the words. The full range of instruments were used, with military actions seen at the time to represent "…only 25 per cent of the struggle against the Communists."[31] While coercion was used to counter the armed communist insurgencies this was meant to be undertaken in a manner that supported the overall grand strategy, albeit at times the coercion involved was unhelpfully heavy-handed.

All actions and activities undertaken taken were intended to support the message that the government was legitimate and helped the people, and it was the MCP instead that was uncaring, vindictive and violent. The UK Secretary of State for War, J. Strachey, noted that it was important "to appear in the role of protectors of the population against the Communists and their destructive and terrorist

---

28. Harper, p. 313 and 10.
29.   Lieutenant-General Sir Harold Briggs, CAB 21 / 1861, Federation Plan for the Elimination of the Communist Organisation and Armed Forces in Malaya, May 24, 1950 quoted in Short, p. 237.
30.   Ramakrishna, p. 102.
31.   Sir Rob Lockhart, Deputy Director of Operations quoted in: 'Winning the Shooting War in Malaya', *Observer,* 4 January 1953.

activities."[32] It took time for government actions to be so focused, at some detriment to the state's message however, the arrival of General Templer in 1952 considerably reinvigorated the Briggs grand strategy in this regard.

The military instrument, which included the police and the Home Guard, undertook defensive and offensive operations. In both, the gradual identification of the rural Chinese with the state led to them providing increasingly more actionable intelligence. Defensively the resettlement of the rural Chinese concentrated them allowing for higher levels of protective security to be enforced. This also allowed food denial and control operations to be practised that helped cut supplies reaching the MCP in the surrounding jungle.[33] These security activities were led by a greatly expanded and professionalized police force supported by the Home Guards. This later group were volunteer, part-time personnel from the settlements being protected.[34] By 1952 the Chinese Home Guard had some 50,000 personnel with units in almost all New Villages. While of variable effectiveness, the Home Guard in involving and arming the rural Chinese proved useful in further convincing them to identify with the state, its control and its administration.[35]

The principal role of military forces was offensive operations although there was significant support given to the police in their defensive activities and military engineers built roads into the more isolated areas to better connect all Malayans to the British state structure.[36] Under the Briggs Plan, military operations largely

---

32. Nagal, p. 71.
33. Stubbs, pp. 166-67.
34. Briggs wrote "Security of the population and the elimination of the Communist cells must be the primary tasks of the Police." Lieutenant-General Sir Harold Briggs, *Report on the Emergency in Malaya from April 1950-November 1951*, Kuala Lumpur, 1951, pp 3-5, quoted in Short, p. 236.
35. Stubbs, pp. 156-59.
36. Briggs wrote "The primary task of the Army must be to destroy the bandits and jungle penetration." Lieutenant-General sir Harold Briggs, *Report on the Emergency in Malaya from April 1950-November 1951*, Kuala Lumpur, 1951, pp 3-5, quoted in Short, p. 236. Grob-Fitzgibbon, 'Securing the Colonies for the Commonwealth: Counterinsurgency, Decolonization, and the Development of British Imperial Strategy in the Postwar Empire', p. 28.

involved jungle penetrations by small army units to disrupt MCP camps, recruitment, training and logistics. The military response to the insurgency though emphasized the primacy of the civilian government and that the government was provider and protector. All measures were meant to be undertaken within a recognized legal framework that stressed impartiality, was carefully modulated, subject to public debate and firmly enforced.[37] Major Joel Hamby noted in an assessment of civil-military relations:

> "Operating under these rules, published for all the population to see, the security forces were able to establish the perception that their actions were honourable, legitimate, and right for Malaya. Safeguards such as judicial appeal and the view of a benevolent hand in charge of the Emergency simplified the task of convincing the people that the government was acting in their best interests."[38]

The economic instrument was employed to make payments directly to rural Chinese to help ease their resettlement difficulties. The MCP was also directly targeted through a rewards-for-surrender program that handsomely bribed insurgents to capitulate. The Government had greater economic resources than the MCP and made effective use of them leading Edgar O'Ballance to remark "the war was won by bribing the rank-and-file Reds to give up".[39]

Diplomacy was used to try to prevent other states supporting the MCP. The main concern was the border with Thailand but the Thai government was supportive and while the Thai border police had shortcomings this potential resupply route was progressively closed off. In the late 1950s the MCP sought sanctuary in southern Thailand were they were little troubled by the Thai authorities providing they avoided causing local difficulties.[40] The Emergency was declared won in 1960 although the small group of MCP

---

37. Komer, 1972, p. 34.
38. Joel E. Hamby, 'Civil-Military Operations: Joint Doctrine and the Malayan Emergency ', *JFQ: Joint Force Quarterly*, No. 32, Autumn 2002, pp. 54-61, p. 58.
39. Edgar O'ballance, *Malaya: The Communist Insurgent War: 1948-1960*; London: Faber and Faber, 1966, p. 151.
40. Short, pp. 373-75, 487.

remaining in Thailand occasionally undertook cross-border skirmishes for the next couple of decades.[41]

In early 1950 British diplomacy worked against the Briggs Plan in recognizing the Chinese Communist Party as the legitimate government of mainland China. Elite urban Chinese became concerned about whether the British would continue fighting until a local government was established. While rural Chinese with memories of World War Two thought that perhaps the British would collapse allowing Communist Chinese forces in.[42]

The diplomatic instrument in its' broader sense was used in the negotiations with the MCP in late 1955. The MCP sought an amnesty, recognition as a legitimate political party and the right to contest elections. The Malayan Government at this stage was not British but indigenous and the Chief Minister Tunku Abdul Rahman rejected the MCP's proposals. After 1957 there was no further such diplomatic interaction with the MCP.[43]

The informational instrument played a crucial role. A highly sophisticated propaganda operation was undertaken to convince all of the virtues of the state and the vices of the MCP. In a major study of the Malayan Emergency Kumar Ramakrishna considered that its' success owed much to the close coordination of the state's actions with the message being broadcast.[44] The actions reinforced the 'words' that the British colonial government was both protector and provider. The operation was greatly helped by the new technologies of film and radio particularly as many rural Chinese were illiterate. The government installed some 700 low-cost battery powered radios in the New Village community centres and coffee shops. By end of 1951 Radio Malaya reached into the rural areas for the first time, becoming an important medium of information, education and entertainment for the more isolated populations who had been outside of its coverage. The rural Chinese placed considerable store on personal contact as a demonstration of the value of the

41. Stubbs, pp. 241-42.
42. Ramakrishna, p. 85, 119.
43. Stubbs, pp. 226-27.
44. Ramakrishna, p. 205.

informational message. The placement of government officials into resettlement camps greatly assisted with this as the merit of the state could be assessed locally.[45]

The term used to describe the insurgents was given careful thought to ensure this dovetailed in with the overall shaping of the societal social rules. The labeling of the MCP by the government as 'bandits' was important in framing the public's perception of the MCP's identity; historian Phillip Deery notes:

> "In all instances the aim was to deny the legitimacy of the opponent. The term 'bandit' is an epithet which invokes negative reactions and which, if it sticks, can isolate and detach the guerrillas from the population they are trying to influence or penetrate. ... the vocabulary employed became ...a critical part of counterinsurgency operations....The political motivations of the communist insurgents could be stripped, their widespread support from the Malayan Chinese diminished, and their nationalistic credentials maligned. The aura of patriotism would be replaced by the stigma of illegitimacy."[46]

The term 'bandit' though was replaced in 1952 with 'Communist terrorist' when the UK Government wanted to reframe the perception of the Malayan Emergency in the outside world. 'Bandit' seemed to downplay the seriousness of the situation, although by this time the situation had clearly turned in favour of the British. The use of the 'Communist' adjective however firmly located the Emergency in the Cold War struggle, assisting efforts to obtain American support for what appeared a purely colonial issue. The word also helped justify to the British public the not inconsiderable material, financial and personnel resources being expended. Conversely, the noun 'terrorist' was intended to demonize the MCP and further emphasize their illegitimacy.[47]   The securitization of the threat was an issue whose importance was well

---

45. Ibid., p. 109 and 19.
46. Phillip Deery, 'The Terminology of Terrorism: Malaya, 1948-52', *Journal of Southeast Asian Studies,* Vol. 34, No. 2, June 2003, pp. 231-47, p. 236.
47. Ibid., pp. 244-46.

understood during the Malaya Emergency.

This description of the reform grand strategy has focused on the rural Chinese however, beyond this other activities were also underway. Significant efforts were made to bring the urban Chinese and ethnic Indian elites into Malayan political life. The British encouraged the growth of the Malayan civil service and the formation of political parties to contest elections for local government. Local élites were co-opted through being given important administrative and political responsibilities. The overall MCP objective of full independence was undercut when the British Government announced this would be granted after a series of phased steps over ten years.[48] Advancing the target date for independence allowed the population's incipient but growing nationalism to be directed against the MCP rather than driving them towards supporting the communists. The UK was able to create the idea of a particular kind of imagined Malayan state amongst the population.

The Malayan Emergency was a near-term matter and perceived as an issue of necessity. Accordingly, the near-term managerial approach to building power was adopted. This approach has the least dependence on others for its accomplishment and suits times when success is deemed essential, as was the case of the Malayan Emergency.

The Emergency's start found a Labour Government in the UK and a colonial government in Malaya that were both managerial states. The colonial government saw its role as accelerating national development through activist measures and direct intervention in society and the economy.[49] A partnership between public and private capital was envisaged with the Government aiming to "attract or guide private enterprise to directions which are the most desirable for

---

48. Komer, 1972, p. 64.
49. Nicholas J. White, 'The Frustrations of Development: British Business and the Late Colonial State in Malaya, 1945 -57 ', *Journal of Southeast Asian Studies* Vol. 28, No. 1, March, 1997, pp. 103-19, pp. 105-10.

progress in accordance with decided policy."[50]

The colonial government bore the majority of the war's financial costs with a significant portion of its spending diverted annually into the Emergency.[51] At its peak in 1952, some 40% of GOM outlays went to the conflict.[52] Fortuitously, the colonial government immediately before the Emergency had significantly revamped taxation policies including introducing new income, corporate and export taxes to meet demands for reconstruction, social services and economic development. The state had gained considerable extractive powers and was able to use these to increase taxes as Emergency funding demands necessitated; this was an accommodational strategy that extended extraction when needed. The quantum of extraction was further dramatically increased with the Korean War export boom. Nicholas White writes that:

> "...in 1951 there was an eight-fold increase over 1949 in revenues from exported rubber, while that from tin doubled over the same period. ....the improved fortunes of rubber and tin during the Korean War, combined with fiscal reforms, provided the funding needed for the Federation's resettlement policy, the seven-fold increase in police numbers, the raising of 240,000 Home Guards and an extra four battalions of the Malay Regiment, and additional funds for social and economic development."[53]

The Malay Army was gradually built up through volunteer recruitment and eventually provided about half of the infantry deployed. Assisting the Army was a considerable force of part-time Home Guards recruited locally and constituting almost five percent of the population. The majority of the police force of 60,000 was also recruited locally. The security forces equipment was mainly of

50. 1947 Colonial Government document quoted in ibid., p. 106.
51. The UK government also provided some direct grants when Malay's finances became stretched.
52. Komer, 1972, p. 22.
53. Nicholas J. White, 'Capitalism and Counter-Insurgency? Business and Government in the Malayan Emergency, 1948-57 ', *Modern Asian Studies* Vol. 32, No. 1, Feburary, 1998, pp. 149-77, p. 175.

British origin as Malaya had little industrial capacity.

The British Government provided the majority of the military forces with deployed Army units reaching some 30,000 troops in 1952. These forces included considerable numbers of conscript national service soldiers; by 1952 "...many of the British Army battalions serving in Malaya...were virtually National Service battalions."[54] The costs were met from annual Government budgets through an accommodational strategy focused on extraction. In this period Britain had significant defence commitments with defence spending consuming some 25% of general government expenditures. Government spending was about 35% of the GDP with revenues roughly split halfway between direct and indirect taxation.[55] However, large defence spending contributed to Britain running deficit budgets of some 2-3% GDP in this period.[56] This was funded by domestic and international borrowings, including significant American Marshall Plan grants during the 1948-1951 period which represented some 1.3% of GDP annually.

In the 1947-1952 period of continual British economic crisis, Malaya was economically very important in the defence of Sterling and the reconstruction of the British domestic economy. With British companies dominating Malay's rubber industry, businessman Sir John Hay in 1949 remarked that:

> " Malaya's rubber production ... produces dollars to an amount that exceeds in total value all...exports from Britain to the US ... if, for any reason, the operations of the great rubber industry are interrupted or seriously impaired, Britain's dollar situation would be rendered more acute than ever. This country would then have less food, less clothes, and there would be fewer dollars with which to buy raw materials - and that would mean unemployment. All of us are

---

54. Robert Jackson, *The Malayan Emergency: The Commonwealth's Wars 1948-1960*; London: Routledge, 1991, p. 45.
55. Tom Clark and Andrew Dilnot, *Long-Term Trends in British Taxation and Spending* London: Institute for Fiscal Studies, 2002a, p. 3-6.
56. Tom Clark and Andrew Dilnot, *Measuring the Uk Fiscal Stance since the Second World War* London: Institute for Fiscal Studies, 2002b, pp. 4-6.

thus deeply concerned in what is happening in Malaya." [57]

In common with the Malayan government, the funding of the demands of the Emergency was undertaken at a time when the British state was strongly expansionist, particularly as regards social welfare and public health.

The reform grand strategy was ultimately successful because the ideas advocated by the British gained acceptance whereas the MCP was unable to convince the population of their value and legitimacy. The British reform grand strategy ensured that the identities of both the state and the MCP that prevailed were those the UK sought. The British desired social rules were embraced by Malayan society and in particular the rural Chinese. The UK was able to successfully create and inculcate its idea of a particular kind of Malayan state amongst the population.

The population structure, the ethnic groupings and the nature of the MCP adversary allowed the British to focus their efforts on a readily identifiable subset of the overall population: the rural Chinese. This group was of a scale appropriate to British resources, allowing them the ability to deliberately fragment the group's identity and then rebuild it in the desired form. If the target group had been significantly larger the fragmentation of the identity would have been even more difficult and costly to achieve. Changing the identity of the rural Chinese was further aided by the earlier formation of the MCA that meant the British could make use of the wealthy urban elite as ideational advocates in the New Village Chinese communities when the time came.

In more general terms however, the British owed their success to their on-going assessment of the effectiveness of their three successive grand strategies. The initial response to the Communist challenge was to attempt an engagement grand strategy but it was soon realized that a suitable domestic partner was not readily available and there was insufficient time to develop the MCA

---

57. Sir John Hay in a BBC Radio Broadcast, 3 January, 1949 quoted in White, 'Capitalism and Counter-Insurgency? Business and Government in the Malayan Emergency, 1948-57 ', p. 152.

to meet this role. The British quickly shifted to a denial grand strategy in a symmetrical response to the now armed insurgency but after several months it became apparent that this new approach was failing to win over the civilian population and the MCP was gaining the political and military initiative. To reverse this, the British then developed and began implementing a sophisticated reform grand strategy.

The British reform grand strategy continued to evolve throughout the Emergency as continuing self-assessment revealed new ways to improve its effectiveness and efficiency. In terms of timing the British took two years of trial and error before adopting the reform grand strategy, a further two years before this grand strategy had reached a suitably refined stage, and another two to three years to achieve demonstrable success. A grand strategy is not a set-and-forget approach but rather needs continuing monitoring, critical assessment and on-going improvements to succeed.

The success of the Malayan Emergency reform grand strategy also illustrates this type's shortcomings. The key to success is the collapse of existing norms and identities and this requires some external shock that demonstrates these ideas need replacing. The British implemented a large-scale resettlement campaign and set up hundreds of New Villages to achieve this. It was a costly, difficult and controversial program – and remains so.

Landmines Ban Campaign Grand Strategy 1992-1999

At the end of the Cold War, Non-Governmental Organizations (NGOs) involved in humanitarian work in Afghanistan, Cambodia and Somalia encountered significant difficulties caused by the very large numbers of anti-personnel landmines sown across these countries. Landmines were causing large numbers of deaths and injuries to non-combatants and severely hampering reconstruction efforts.[58] As these NGOs shared

---

58. Jody Williams and Stephen Goose, 'The International Campaign to Ban Landmines', in Maxwell A. Cameron, Brian W. Tomlin, and Robert J. Lawson (eds.), *To Walk without Fear: The Global Movement to Ban Landmines*; Don Mills: Oxford University Press, 1998, pp. 20-47, p. 20-21.

information with other NGOs working across the world, it became apparent that this was a global issue.[59] Accordingly, in October 1992, six NGOs created an umbrella organization, the International Campaign to Ban Landmines (ICBL), that sought an international ban on the use, production, stockpiling and transfer of anti-personnel mines, and greater resources for humanitarian mine clearance and victim assistance.[60] The NGOs agreed that the organization's core focus should be the ban rather than the humanitarian issues created, as the problems of mined areas and victims would not be resolved until deployment and production permanently stopped.[61]

The ICBL achieved remarkable success. The convention banning landmines entered into force on March 1, 1999, the swiftest major international agreement so far to enter into force.[62] To achieve this, the ICBL adopted a grand strategy to build a broadly based international coalition of NGOs that would: firstly, educate publics, mobilize domestic support and apply pressure on national governments and other relevant parties; and secondly urge governments worldwide to work for a complete ban.[63] At the time,

---

59. Richard Price, 'Reversing the Gun Sights: Transnational Civil Society Targets Land Mines', *International Organization,* Vol. 52, No. 3, Summer 1998, pp. 613-44, p. 622.

60. The six NGOs were: Handicap International (France); Human Rights Watch (US); Medico International (Germany); Mines Advisory Group (UK), Physicians for Human Rights (US) and Vietnam Veterans of America Foundation (US). These six NGOs became the steering committee of the ICBL and appointed Jody Williams as the coordinator. Williams and Goose, in Cameron, Tomlin, and Lawson (eds.), *To Walk without Fear: The Global Movement to Ban Landmines*; Don Mills: Oxford University Press, 1998, pp. 20-47, p. 22.

61. Kenneth R. Rutherford, 'Nongovernmental Organisations and the Landmine Ban', in Richard Anthony Matthew, Bryan Mcdonald, and Kenneth R. Rutherford (eds.), *Landmines and Human Security: International Politics and War's Hidden Legacy*; Albany: State University of New York Press, 2006, pp. 51-66, p. 57.

62. Kenneth R. Rutherford, 'The Evolving Arms Control Agenda: Implications of the Role of NGOs in Banning Antipersonnel Landmines', *World Politics,* Vol. 53, No. 1, October 2000, pp. 74-114, p. 74.

63. Richard A. Matthew, 'Human Security and the Mine Ban Movement 1: Introduction', in Richard Anthony Matthew, Bryan Mcdonald, and Kenneth R. Rutherford (eds.), *Landmines and Human Security: International Politics and War's Hidden Legacy*; Albany: State University of New York Press, 2006, pp. 3-20, p. 6.

states were unconcerned about landmines as an important arms control issue although, there were some minimal international legal restrictions on their use arising from the Landmines Protocol of the 1980 Convention on Certain Conventional Weapons.[64]

In considering grand strategy types, the ICBL could not coerce states to outlaw landmines, and no state was strongly supportive or indeed concerned. This suggested that the denial and engagement grand strategy types were inappropriate. Instead given the goal of changing the international social rules that related to a very specific type of military equipment, a reform grand strategy was suggested. This was a reform grand strategy of changing norms, the shared understandings of what kinds of actions are appropriate, not of changing identities which define an actors' characteristics, distinctiveness and uniqueness. In this, the grand strategy was somewhat ambitious in trying to change a social rule across the complete international system. In seeking to purposefully change the existing order, the ICBL emphasized the use of the informational and diplomatic instruments; the ICBL's characteristics precluded using military instruments and the campaign decided not to use economic ones. The informational instruments produced ideational change with the diplomatic instrument institutionalizing this change.

The ICBL's informational strategy was to shift the debate about landmines from being a political or military matter to being a humanitarian issue.[65] During the Cold War, intrastate conflict in the Third World was perceived in terms of ideological and geopolitical competition with the USSR however, in the post-Cold War era such conflict became depoliticized and was seen instead in humanitarian terms. The focus shifted from state security to human security, and this allowed non-state actors to legitimately discuss the impact of landmines, not only governments and the professional military.[66] In

64. The International Committee of the Red Cross was instrumental in having these restrictions enacted. Rutherford, p. 81.
65. Ibid., p. 87.
66. Miguel De Larrinaga and Claire Turenne Sjolander, '(Re)Presenting Landmines from the Protector to Enemy: The Discursive Framing of a New Multilateralism ', in Maxwell A. Cameron, Brian W. Tomlin, and Robert J.

opening up this space in the social system for norm changes, the ICBL used extant norms as the basis for arguing that landmine use was inhumane and not legally justifiable as the humanitarian impact was more severe than its military utility.[67] The old norms were held to be no longer appropriate and, having collapsed, in need of replacement

International laws of armed conflict stress that the damage inflicted by the use of force must be proportional to the expected benefits, and that force must be used discriminately with any accidental harm to non-combatants minimized. The ICBL argued that landmines in being designed to kill and injure remotely at an indefinite time in the future were weapons that inherently did not allow military commanders to abide by the dictates of proportionality and discrimination.[68] The ICBL informational strategy accordingly emphasized the impact of landmines on civilians, women and children. The campaign claimed that 80% of the victims of landmines annually were civilians[69] and that of this almost half were women and children.[70] The ICBL continually featured landmine victims prominently in their educational, fundraising, and promotional literature and sponsored their participation in international conferences.[71] The military utility of landmines was not disputed, simply that it was significantly less than the long-term human security costs.

Landmine supporters were left to argue that the military utility was sufficiently high to outweigh the highly publicized unintentional deaths and maiming landmines caused. In this moral argument, the ICBL's ideational framing went uncontested.

Lawson (eds.), *To Walk without Fear: The Global Movement to Ban Landmines*; Don MIlls: Oxford University Press, 1998, pp. 364-91, p. 371. Rutherford, p. 94.
67. Rutherford, in Matthew, Mcdonald, and Rutherford (eds.), *Landmines and Human Security: International Politics and War's Hidden Legacy*; Albany: State University of New York Press, 2006, pp. 51-66, p. 57.
68. Rutherford, p. 92.
69. Ibid., p. 87.
70. Larrinaga and Sjolander, in Cameron, Tomlin, and Lawson (eds.), *To Walk without Fear: The Global Movement to Ban Landmines*; Don Mills: Oxford University Press, 1998, pp. 364-91, p. 376.
71. Rutherford, p. 91.

International relations academic and landmine victim, Ken Rutherford wrote that:

" There was no real attempt by states opposed to the ban to dispute the humanitarian arguments. Instead, these anti-ban states made strong military and political arguments as to why landmines should not be banned but at the same time expressed humanitarian concern for the landmine victims. These strategies produced incoherent policies that were not compatible with how and why the landmine issue was established [by the ICBL] on the international agenda.[72]"

The informational campaign further exploited existing weapon ban norms. Landmines were linked to other indiscriminate weapons such as poison gas explicitly noting that, as these had already been banned, a similar norm against landmines would be both feasible and right.[73] The ICBL held that landmines were not a 'normal' weapon but belonged in a special class about which there were already strong taboos.

The informational campaign's thrust did not question the state's role in the humanitarian problems landmines caused but rather was designed to lead to landmines being seen as an enemy against which both the state and civil society must stand together.[74] The role of the state as protector was reinforced, not questioned, and this helped states distance themselves from landmines.[75] Richard Rice writes that:

"Through framing the issue as a humanitarian disaster and educating the public and policymakers about the

72. Ibid., p. 105.
73. Price, p. 629.
74. J. Marshal Beier and Ann Denholm Crosby, 'Harnessing Change for Continuity: The Play of Political and Economic Forces Behind the Ottawa Process', in Maxwell A. Cameron, Brian W. Tomlin, and Robert J. Lawson (eds.), *To Walk without Fear: The Global Movement to Ban Landmines*; Don MIlls: Oxford University Press, 1998, pp. 269-92, p. 276.
75. Larrinaga and Sjolander, in Cameron, Tomlin, and Lawson (eds.), *To Walk without Fear: The Global Movement to Ban Landmines*; Don Mills: Oxford University Press, 1998, pp. 364-91, p. 380.

indiscriminate nature of the weapon, these moral entrepreneurs [of the ICBL] set the stage for a widespread and rapid response. This sense of crisis made a ban seem desirable; however, it was the grafting of taboos from previously delegitimized practices of warfare, especially chemical weapons, that allowed a ban to be considered the art of the possible for many states."[76]

Changes to social rules to be both advanced and made permanent need to be embedded in institutions. The ICBL made use of the diplomatic instruments of persuasion and negotiation in both interacting with states and in partnering with specific like-minded states.

The ICBL grand strategy required pressure to be placed on individual states to persuade them of the need for a landmine ban. In this, while the ideational message was consistent across all ICBL members, the actual lobbying methods to be employed were left up to the NGOs in each country. Similarly, there was no overarching media strategy, simply a common message.[77] Each country's NGOs were responsible for determining the best approach to use. American NGOs were able to work with sympathetic congressmen and thus did not need to build extensive public support. European NGOs by contrast gave higher priority to directly engaging the public than working with government officials or members.[78] This reliance on the knowledge and expertise of local NGOs was particularly important in convincing non-state groups to give up landmines. Paul Wapner observes that:

> "...the Pakistan Campaign to Ban Landmines and the Afghan Campaign to Ban Landmines, both of which were staffed by local people but financed with international funds, worked to convince the Taliban that antipersonnel mines were un-Islamic. In 1998, the Taliban issued a statement to this effect

---

76. Price, p. 639-40.
77. Williams and Goose, in Cameron, Tomlin, and Lawson (eds.), *To Walk without Fear: The Global Movement to Ban Landmines; Don Mills*: Oxford University Press, 1998, pp. 20-47, p. 23.
78. Ibid., p. 28.

and both campaigns reported no subsequent use of landmines by the Taliban (though the opposition Northern alliance continued to deploy mines within Afghanistan through 2001)."[79]

Internationally, the ideational message was pressed through a series of ICBL convened large-scale international conferences and seminars held in the US, Europe, Asia and Africa. [80] These publicized the landmine cause and also help bring international organizations like the United Nations, and especially UNICEF, into giving active support.

The ICBL diplomatic strategy made good use of celebrities to pressure governments and advance the landmine ban agenda. In South Africa, Nelson Mandela's and US General Norman Schwarzkopf's support of a landmine ban proved influential; the later in helping counter domestic military utility arguments.[81] In the UK Princess Diana brought the issue to the media's attention; Rutherford writes that:

" Princess Diana's support of NGOs and their arguments to ban landmines helped transfer the issue from a political to a humanitarian problem. Moreover, she was able to leverage the media into covering the landmine issue from locations such as Angola and Bosnia and thereby helped to marshal public support for the ban and against the British [government] anti-ban position. Each of her trips to landmine infested states was organized and planned by humanitarian

79. Paul Wapner, 'The Campaign to Ban Antipersonnel Landmines and Global Civil Society', in Richard Anthony Matthew, Bryan Mcdonald, and Kenneth R. Rutherford (eds.), *Landmines and Human Security: International Politics and War's Hidden Legacy*; Albany: State University of New York Press, 2006, pp. 251-68, p. 255.
80. Maxwell A. Cameron, 'Democratization of Foreign Policy: The Ottawa Process as a Model', in Maxwell A. Cameron, Brian W. Tomlin, and Robert J. Lawson (eds.), *To Walk without Fear: The Global Movement to Ban Landmines*; Don MIlls: Oxford University Press, 1998, pp. 424-47, p. 431.
81. Rutherford, p. 102.

NGOs."[82]

The ICBL grand strategy had initially been based on working through the existing United Nations Convention on Certain Conventional Weapons (CCW) institution to achieve change however this proved impractical. The CCW relied on a consensus-based approach that meant that reform proposals were stymied by the larger states that opposed a ban such as the US, India, China and Russia and the September 1995 meeting stalemated. In response the ICBL developed a strategy that involved working with like-minded middle-power states outside the CCW framework.[83]

While only a small number of states were persuaded about the landmine ban, there were sufficient to develop an alternative institution, termed the Ottawa process, able to progress the ban proposal outside of the normal diplomatic forums for international humanitarian law. In January 1996 Canada agreed to host a meeting in October that year involving eleven likeminded states and the ICBL. This meeting proved seminal and quickly lead to several more involving ever-increasing numbers of states and the ICBL.

The ICBL was given invited observer status and became an active participant being deeply involved in the development and negotiation of the proposed convention as it evolved.[84] The organization developed its own draft treaty proposal and attempted to have as much of this as possible incorporated into the final ban treaty.[85] In bringing the ICBL coalition into the Ottawa process

---

82. Ibid.
83. Kenneth Rutherford, 'Post-Cold War Superpower? Mid-Size State and Ngo Collaboration in Banning Landmines', in Kenneth Rutherford, Stefan Brem, and Richard Matthew (eds.), *Reframing the Agenda: The Impact of NGO and Middle Power Cooperation in International Security Policy*; Westport Praeger, 2003, pp. 23-38Collaboration, p. 25.
84. Maxwell A. Cameron et al., 'To Walk without Fear', in Maxwell A. Cameron, Brian W. Tomlin, and Robert J. Lawson (eds.), *To Walk without Fear: The Global Movement to Ban Landmines*; Don MIlls: Oxford University Press, 1998, pp. 1-19, p. 5. ibid., p. 11.
85. Williams and Goose, in Cameron, Tomlin, and Lawson (eds.), *To Walk without Fear: The Global Movement to Ban Landmines*; Don Mills: Oxford University Press, 1998, pp. 20-47, p. 35.

however, policymakers were exposed to criticism from civil society and made to feel compelled to provide public reasons for their activities.[86] At the successful conclusion of the Ottawa process in December 1997 when the convention was signed, a survey of state delegates revealed that the pressure exercised by the ICBL, particularly at the negotiating table, had been a very significant influence.[87] Even so the Ottawa process was a state-based approach that made extensive use of traditional diplomatic methods tools albeit enhanced by the selective use of NGOs.[88] This institutionalization of the landmine ban objective was crucial for success.

The ICBL was adroit at using domestic pressure on states and as the Ottawa process continued with more states joining, there developed a feeling of inevitability. States could not isolate themselves from what was perceived to be a powerful and growing world movement against mines. States began to feel: "…that in the end they would be forced to conform and sign."[89] As the number of crucial states supporting a ban reached critical mass, concerns of reputation and identity fostered emulation, which as the reform grand strategy schema would suggest, became an increasingly powerful mechanism through which the new norm was adopted.[90]

The ICBL grand strategy devised a successful grand strategic synthesis were the way changes to the existing order were sought and the way power was built were well integrated. For a coalition of NGOs resources were always problematic with success requiring their prudent employment. The issue was a matter of choice and near-term; the ICBL could be involved as much or as little as

---

86. Cameron, in Cameron, Tomlin, and Lawson (eds.), *To Walk without Fear: The Global Movement to Ban Landmines; Don Mills*: Oxford University Press, 1998, pp. 424-47, p. 443.

87. Cameron et al., in Cameron, Tomlin, and Lawson (eds.), *To Walk without Fear: The Global Movement to Ban Landmines*; Don Mills: Oxford University Press, 1998, pp. 1-19, p. 10.

88. Larrinaga and Sjolander, in Cameron, Tomlin, and Lawson (eds.), *To Walk without Fear: The Global Movement to Ban Landmines*; Don Mills: Oxford University Press, 1998, pp. 364-91, pp. 381-82.

89. Price, pp. 639-40.

90. Ibid.

desired. These factors suggested a near-term market state approach would be employed and it was. In terms of strategies to develop resources, the ICBL started with an accommodational strategy that made use of the coalition's internal resources of people, money and material but as campaign's momentum grew and the call on resources increased an international strategy that sought significant funding external to the ICBL was adopted.

The ICBL made the maximum use of internal resources through being a collection of self-organized national campaigns under the auspices of a coordinator.[91] The grand strategy provided the guidance and coherence but the campaign used a decentralized and informal organizational structure. There was no central headquarters, secretariat, or authority and the ICBL did not dictate the direction of campaigns in other nations.[92]

At the top of the ICBL structure was a 13-member coordination committee made up of rotating members and representatives from every continent that oversaw campaign strategy and set general policy.[93] Below this were some 1,000 NGOs worldwide which shared the overall objective of working towards a comprehensive landmine ban but who were allowed to choose and implement the tactics they considered best suited for their local circumstances. ICBL coordinator Jody Williams noted that members: "…met regularly to plot out overall strategies and plan joint actions, but beyond that each NGO and each National Campaign was free to develop its own work best suited to its mandate, culture, and circumstances."[94]

While there were many NGOs involved, the ICBL spoke for

91. Nicola Short, 'The Role of NGOs in the Ottawa Process to Ban Landmines', *International Negotiation,* Vol. 4, No. 3, 1999, pp. 481-502, p. 483.
92. Lesley Wexler, 'The International Deployment of Shame, Second–Best Responses, and Norm Entrepreneurship: The Campaign to Ban Landmines and the Landmine Ban Treaty ', *Arizona Journal of International and Comparative Law,* Vol. 20, No. 3, 2003, pp. 561-606, p. 589.
93. Wapner, in Matthew, *Mcdonald, and Rutherford (eds.), Landmines and Human Security: International Politics and War's Hidden Legacy*; Albany: State University of New York Press, 2006, pp. 251-68, p. 261.
94. Wexler, p. 589.

them as a single entity and represented them at international conferences for states; "A multitude of voices arose with a single viewpoint on a narrow issue." [95] During the Ottawa process, the ICBL was highly centralized particularly in its interaction with the Canadian government and functioned as a single, homogenous bargaining voice with a unitary position. This distinguished the ICBL from other NGO efforts to affect international policy making, which have been characterized more as a constellation of concerns.[96] Moreover, the ICBL functioned as a single actor for the media coverage surrounding the negotiations, with the ICBL coordinator responsible for all official ICBL press releases while the national campaigns dealt with their respective national media.[97]

The ICBL's human resources came from the many diverse NGOs that included people with many different interests including human rights, arms control, humanitarian assistance, the environment, veterans' affairs, women's and children's rights, demining, and victim rehabilitation.[98] Most people joined the campaign driven by a belief that banning landmines was the right thing for governments to do. They generally contributed social power and authority rather than any specific expertise on landmines.[99] The ICBL assisted them in developing useful campaign skills through providing specific training and capacity building workshops. The ICBL was built deliberately around a self-organizing mass participation model that intrinsically had considerable input legitimacy.

Without significant financing the ICBL would not have been able to play such a central a role, as becoming deeply involved in the Ottawa process proved particularly expensive. The campaign was

95. Rutherford, in Matthew, Mcdonald, and Rutherford (eds.), *Landmines and Human Security: International Politics and War's Hidden Legacy*; Albany: State University of New York Press, 2006, pp. 51-66, p. 60.
96. Short, p. 484.
97. Ibid.
98. Wexler, p. 589.
99. Rutherford, in Matthew, Mcdonald, and Rutherford (eds.), *Landmines and Human Security: International Politics and War's Hidden Legacy*; Albany: State University of New York Press, 2006, pp. 51-66, p. 57.

financed through many sources although the grand strategy also meant that costs were widely dispersed.

Initially the ICBL depended solely on money from well-established member NGOs such as Human Rights Watch, Save the Children and the Lutheran World Federation; foundations such as the Open Society Institute, Merck, and the Dianna Princess of Wales Fund; and the public at large. All the NGOs involved paid no dues to the ICBL to be part of the campaign but were expected to be self-financing in their participation. These various NGOs seconded and funded individuals who worked on the campaign.[100] While there were many small NGOs with sharply limited funding some, like the founding members, were organizations with significant budgets. The Vietnam Veterans of America Foundation (VVAF) alone contributed over \$4.5 million to the effort across 1992-1997.[101] The ICBL Coordinator worked through the VVAF during the campaign, functioning as a non-profit NGO that received funding from government and private sources.[102]

In the late 1990s, the ICBL began receiving funding from several governments including Canada, Switzerland and Denmark.[103] Of these, the Canadian government actively championed the involvement of NGOs in the Ottawa Process and made significant funds available specifically for participation.[104] Across the complete campaign period the ICBL is believed to have received roughly one third of its funding from the Open Society Institute, one third from governments (particularly Canada, Norway, and Sweden) and one third from other NGOs and international organizations such as

---

100. Stephen Goose and Jody Williams, 'The Campaign to Ban Antipersonnel Landmines', in Richard Anthony Matthew, Bryan Mcdonald, and Kenneth R. Rutherford (eds.), *Landmines and Human Security: International Politics and War's Hidden Legacy*; Albany: State University of New York Press, 2006, pp. 239-50, p. 242.
101. Short, p. 493.
102. Ibid., p. 484.
103. Wapner, in Matthew, Mcdonald, and Rutherford (eds.), *Landmines and Human Security: International Politics and War's Hidden Legacy*; Albany: State University of New York Press, 2006, pp. 251-68, p. 260.
104. Short, p. 492.

UNICEF. [105]

The grand strategy was heavily reliant on communications both to keep the coalition coherent and working together effectively, and in the implementation of the informational competent. From the start it was apparent that a grand strategy built upon a large number of diverse NGOs widely dispersed across the globe could only be effective if each NGO felt an immediate and important part of the campaign.[106] Constant exchange of information was key to give members a sense of overall campaign activities and to create and sustain the momentum.[107] For this, the ICBL made extensive use of fax technology and then from 1996 the Internet; Rutherford observes that the:

> " Internet allowed the ICBL to reach out to NGOs across geographic space in an effort to broaden and expand its membership base to the [global] South, most importantly the internet allowed the ICBL to expand to southern states at minimal cost. The low cost and easy use of the internet enhanced the ICBL's political strategy to get as many states on board to counter the opposition of the major powers – China, Russia, India and the United States."[108]

Quickly and efficiently sharing successes and failures empowered the whole organization and lessened the isolation of distant NGOs. With a strong communication backbone, the ICBL often knew of developments before governments, which made it a focal point of information for states and NGOs alike.[109]

---

105. Ibid., p. 484.
106. Williams and Goose, in Cameron, Tomlin, and Lawson (eds.), *To Walk without Fear: The Global Movement to Ban Landmines*; Don Mills: Oxford University Press, 1998, pp. 20-47, p. 24.
107. Ibid., p. 23.
108. Rutherford, in Matthew, Mcdonald, and Rutherford (eds.), *Landmines and Human Security: International Politics and War's Hidden Legacy*; Albany: State University of New York Press, 2006, pp. 51-66, p. 58.
109. Goose and Williams, in Matthew, Mcdonald, and Rutherford (eds.), *Landmines and Human Security: International Politics and War's Hidden Legacy*; Albany: State University of New York Press, 2006, pp. 239-50, p. 244.

While e-mail was used heavily internally, most external meetings were face-to-face. The ICBL built a strong network amongst states and international organizations and applying pressure to these groups necessitated travel. The holding of large-scale international conferences and seminars also required considerable organization. This eased when for the second conference UNICEF provided all logistical support, meeting accommodation and support staff.[110]

The reform grand strategy was successful because it was carefully designed taking into account the problem's specific conditions. The end of the Cold War led to third world conflicts being conceived as humanitarian crises rather than geopolitical battlefields. This major shift in public and governmental attitudes was cleverly exploited by the ICBL to cause the norms supporting land mine usage to almost completely collapse with no real attempt made to dispute their arguments. The external shock of the Cold War ending though was an essential precursor; without this it is very unlikely the ICBL's grand strategy would have been successful.

The ICBL's grand strategy was further aided by being able to take advantage of existing institutions, governmental structures and public society organizations to quickly advance their new ideas. Moreover, the specialized nature of the issue allowed the ICBL to both determine and then focus their efforts on persuading a relatively small number of potential ideational advocates that held germane authoritative positions within these institutions and structures. Reaching a critical mass of relevant actors that had accepted the new norm was therefore achieved reasonably quickly.

While startlingly successful, the ICBL's grand strategy also highlights some shortcomings of the reform type of grand strategy. If the existing norms had not been ripe for complete collapse, it is doubtful the ICBL would have had the ability or the resources to succeed; there was a degree of fortuitousness involved. Moreover if the key issue in a reform grand strategy is this ideational collapse,

---

110. Williams and Goose, in Cameron, Tomlin, and Lawson (eds.), To Walk without Fear: The Global Movement to Ban Landmines; Don MIlls: Oxford University Press, 1998, pp. 20-47, p. 28.

there must also be a suitable new idea at hand ready to deploy to fill the gap. The ICBL relatively quickly developed comprehensive and apparently well-considered ideas that seemed to meet this need and proved broadly acceptable. The ICBL was also fortunate in operating in a virtually uncontested field. Not already having devised new ideas to be ready immediately the old order collapsed could have proved fatal if other groups had been prepared at that time to advance their well-developed ideas. In other circumstances there may be a true clash of opposing ideas that are seeking to fill the gap left by the collapse of the old ideas. This would be a considerably harsher environment to operate and succeed within than that the ICBL faced.

US Iraq Regime Change Grand Strategy 2002-2003

The 1991 multinational war against Iraq liberated Kuwait but left the Ba'athist regime of Saddam Hussein in place and subject, with Iran, to an American-led dual containment grand strategy. In October 1998 the US Congress passed the Iraq Liberation Act, which changed US policy towards Iraq to include regime change to be undertaken mainly by providing aid to dissident groups espousing democracy.[111] This was effectively a small-scale engagement grand strategy.

Motivated by the Al Qaeda attacks on 11 September 2001, the Bush administration on 29 September 2001 began developing plans to remove the Iraqi regime using American military forces.[112] The successful replacement of this authoritarian regime by a democratic government would it was held usher in a new era of peace and prosperity in Iraq and, through this example, across the Middle East.

The order sought was for Iraq to adopt liberal democratic norms that other countries, in particular the US, used. In sharing these norms Iraq would be secure, prosperous and not pose a danger to other states. The order sought was outlined in a classified

---

111. Yetiv, op.cit., pp. 111-12.
112. Douglas J. Feith, *War and Decision: Inside the Pentagon at the Dawn of the War on Terrorism*; New York: Harper, 2008, p. 218.

document signed by President Bush in August 2002 titled "Iraq: Goals, Objectives and Strategy." Michael Gordon and retired General Bernard Trainor write that:

> "...the document proclaimed that the United States would midwife a new Iraq whose society would be "based on moderation, pluralism, and democracy." With his reversal of Iraq's invasion of Kuwait, the president's father had vowed to preserve international norms against the forces of chaos; this new president would upset the established order to spread the gospel of freedom."[113]

The effort taken by the Bush Administration to clearly define the grand strategy's objectives and desired end state was commendable. As well as guiding grand strategy development it also gave a benchmark against which the grand strategy could be judged. The later aspect is of some importance to democratic states (discussed further in Chapter 8).

The order sought is associated in the diagnostic process with a reform grand strategy that aims to reform another country through changing its social rules. This grand strategy type privileges societal ideas, not states or sub-state groups as the denial and engagement types do respectively. The American objective was to reform Iraq by putting in place a new type of government that the Iraqi people considered legitimate. However, the US chose a denial grand strategy. The logic of a denial grand strategy suggests it is suitable only when trying to actively stop a state achieving its desired objectives, not to reform it.

A denial grand strategy judges states mainly on their relative military power, considers war a legitimate policy means, that a state's actions should be judged solely by their results, and that military power is the key determinant of change. The American Iraq regime change grand strategy accordingly privileged the military instrument of national power, and employed the diplomatic,

113. Michael R. Gordon and Bernard E. Trainor, *The Endgame: The inside Story of the Struggle for Iraq, from George W. Bush to Barack Obama*; New York: Vintage Books, 2013, p. 8.

economic and informational instruments principally as supporting elements.

The policy planning to impose regime change on Iraq gained momentum in the first quarter of 2002 after the Taliban regime in Afghanistan was overthrown. The operational planning for the post-Saddam Iraq of "moderation, pluralism, and democracy" though was only begun in earnest in January 2003, some three months before the occupation began, when a decision was finally made that the Department of Defense, and in particular Central Command (CENTCOM) would be responsible.[114]

The CENTCOM Commander General Franks saw the overthrow of the Saddam regime as a separate issue both fundamentally distinct from events beyond its demise and more important than them.[115] The post-Saddam period when Iraq would become an embryonic democracy was called Phase IV as it was seen as an integral part of the overall invasion and subsequent occupation in terms of meeting the President's specified objectives. This phase focussed on regime replacement but received only limited attention within CENTCOM compared to Phase III, the intense combat phase that sought regime removal.[116] Colonel Benson, the chief Combined Force Land Component Command planner said later that: "We were extraordinarily focused on Phase III. There should have been more than just one Army colonel, me, really worrying about the details of Phase IV."[117]

As a denial type grand strategy's logic would suggest the military strategy was a counter-force plan focused on defeating the Iraqi army. The military campaign was designed to damage as little of Iraq's infrastructure as possible, focusing instead on the regime's

114. Donald P. Wright and Timothy R. Reese, *On Point II: Transition to the New Campaign: The United States Army in Operation Iraqi Freedom, May 2003-January 2005*; Fort Leavenworth: Combat Studies Institute Press, US Army Combined Arms Center, 2008, p. 70.
115. Metz, *Iraq and the Evolution of American Strategy*, p. 129-30.
116. Michael R. Gordon and Bernard E. Trainor, *Cobra II: The inside Story of the Invasion and Occupation of Iraq*; New York: Pantheon Books, 2006, p. 139.
117. Wright and Reese, p. 76.

centres of power. The oil sector, the power grid, and other key aspects of Iraq's infrastructure were planned to be mostly unaffected by the war, requiring only minimal reconstruction required afterward.[118] A military planner at the time explained that: "Our interest is to get there very quickly, decapitate the regime, and open the place up, demonstrating that we're there to liberate the country."[119]

The post-Saddam plan assumed that the Iraqi people would greet the American forces as liberators and support the US presence, that the institutions of the government including the army and the police would remain intact and functioning, and that Iraqi exiles recruited by America would assume political power and quickly form the desired new democratic government.[120] The National Security Adviser Condoleezza Rice explained that:"...the concept was that we would defeat the army, but the institutions would hold, everything from ministries to police...You would be able to bring in new leadership but we were going to keep the body in place"[121]

A temporary organization, the Office of Reconstruction and Humanitarian Assistance headed by retired Lieutenant General Jay Garner, a humanitarian aid and relief expert, was set up to assist the new Iraqi government during the envisaged short transitional period.[122] With only limited planning elsewhere, ORHA quickly devised its own post-war plan focused on addressing the four most likely crises anticipated to occur after regime overthrow: oil field fires, large numbers of refugees, food shortages, and the outbreak of epidemics.[123] None was related to regime replacement.

As the denial grand strategy logic would suggest, the

118. Nora Bensahel et al., *After Saddam: Prewar Planning and the Occupation of Iraq*; Santa Monica: RAND Corporation, 2008, p. 234.
119. Thomas E. Ricks, 'War Plans Target Hussein Power Base: Scenarios Feature a Smaller Force, Narrower Strikes ', *Washington Post,* 22 September 2002 pp. A01, A01.
120. Bensahel et al., pp. 234-35.
121. An Interview with Condoleezza Rice quoted in:Gordon and Trainor, *Cobra II: The Inside Story of the Invasion and Occupation of Iraq*, p. 142.
122. Metz, *Iraq and the Evolution of American Strategy*, pp. 131-32.
123. Wright and Reese, p. 70.

economic instrument was used to support the military instrument. While economic sanctions on Iraq remained in place from the earlier grand strategy, the new regime change denial grand strategy also used positive and negative economic sanctions in an endeavour to favourably influence American allies, partners and friends. The US offered to increase or cut economic and military aid, sign trade agreements[124] and help forge investment links[125] depending on the support given by foreign nations for the war. States were also offered reconstruction contracts and a more likely repayment of Iraqi debts post-war if they participated.[126]

The largest aid packages directly linked to specific states supporting the regime change grand strategy military action went to Jordan, Egypt, Israel, and Turkey. Jordan received $700 million in economic aid and $406 million in military support, Egypt received $300 million in economic aid and Israel gained a billion dollars in military aid.[127] Geographically important Turkey was reportedly offered up to $24 billion, but the government felt obligated to take the matter to the Turkish parliament, which voted against supporting the war.[128] The Turkish government though did allow overflights, use of airbases and other quiet support; accordingly the annual

---

124. Supporters such as Singapore and Australia had Free Trade Agreements expedited while dissenters such as Chile had theirs conspicuously delayed. Randall Newnham, "'Coalition of the Bribed and Bullied?'' U.S. Economic Linkage and the Iraq War Coalition', *International Studies Perspectives,* Vol. 9, No. 2, 2008, pp. 183-200, p. 189. Ian Jackson, 'The Geopolitics of President George W. Bush's Foreign Economic Policy', *International Politics,* Vol. 44, No. 5, 2007, pp. 572-95, p. 577.
125. Romanian and Bulgarian support was rewarded with a major effort by the Bush administration to portray them as attractive investment sites. Newnham, p. 192.
126. Bulgaria, for example, was owed $1.7 billion. After President Bush visited in February, 2003, Bulgarian Prime Minister Simeon Saxe-Coburg-Gotha remarked: "The President said very clearly and categorically that ... the countries which have provided support or assistance in the joint effort and have helped the US, and to which Iraq owes a debt, will have a priority when those sums are repaid....''Ivan Vatahov, 'US Recognises 'Functioning' Economy', *The Sofia Echo: http://sofiaecho.com/2003/03/06/630528_us-recognises-functioning-economy,* 6 March 2003.
127. Newnham, p. 188.
128. Ibid., p. 187.

American military aid increased to some $50m, and Turkey received some $200m to mitigate economic stress from the Iraq war.[129] States in Micronesia, Eastern Europe and the Gulf region also received monetary assistance to support the American grand strategy.[130]

Diplomacy was similarly used principally to support the planned military action. The main focus was to secure basing and staging rights to allow US forces to deploy into the region. While considerable diplomatic pressure was applied to regional nations, most remained reticent but did provide limited support.[131] Ultimately the institutions of diplomacy, as the denial grand strategy logic suggests, served the interests of the most powerful state. This approach though was at variance to the grand strategy objective of regime change where such institutions under the diagnostic process would have been used to advance and support the desired social change in Iraq. Regional state and societal support for the Iraqi war's regime change objectives may have considerably assisted in giving a sense of legitimacy to the invasion.

Instead, the denial type grand strategy approach that guided American diplomacy was mirrored regionally, especially by the Gulf States. From the start, regional nations were ambivalent about regime change in Iraq. Many were authoritarian regimes themselves and fretted that, if the Iraq war succeeded, their own populations might grow restive.[132] Under diplomatic pressure regional states acted to sustain their relationships with America, granted military

129. Ibid.
130. Ibid., p. 186, 89. Anders Wivel and Kajsa Ji Noe Oest, 'Security, Profit or Shadow of the Past? Explaining the Security Strategies of Microstates', *Cambridge Review of International Affairs,* Vol. 23, No. 3, September 2010, p. 446. Atsushi Tago, 'Is There an Aid-for-Participation Deal?: US Economic and Military Aid Policy to Coalition Forces (Non)Participants', *International Relations of the Asia-Pacific,* Vol. 8, No. 3, 2008, pp. 379-98, p. 380.
131. For example: The US wished to put 14,000 troops into Jordan, only 5,000 were eventually allowed due to internal Jordanian domestic unease. Similarly, Egypt while formally opposing the war gave access to the Suez canal and accepted US cruise missile strikes fired from the Red Sea. Gordon and Trainor, *Cobra II: The inside Story of the Invasion and Occupation of Iraq,* pp. 110-12.
132. Jon B. Alterman, 'Not in My Backyard: Iraq's Neighbors' Interests', *The Washington Quarterly,* Vol. 26, No. 3, Summer 2003, pp. 149-60.

basing and overflight rights, and provided some support to combat operations. This did not imply their support for the reform goal for as Jon B. Alterman commented:

> "...these governments supported U.S. efforts in order to preserve the status quo—a weak and self-absorbed Iraq— rather than impose a new one. These governments have little interest in catastrophic failure in Iraq, but their interest in the broader goals that the U.S. government... articulated has been similarly limited. ...the leaders of the countries neighbouring Iraq...supported U.S. war efforts as a quest for stability, not radical positive change."[133]

Reflecting their denial grand strategy type underpinnings, American diplomatic efforts were more muscular than calculated to enlist regional support for reform of Iraqi political norms. Rhetoric by US government officials spoke of the post-Saddam Iraq being an exemplar to the region that as Deputy Secretary of Defense Paul Wolfowitz said would: "...cast a very large shadow, starting with Syria and Iran, but across the whole Arab world...."[134] This was echoed by prominent individuals with ex-CIA Director James Woolsey declaring:

> " As we move toward a new Middle East ...we will make a lot of people very nervous. And we will scare, for example, the Mubarak regime in Egypt, or the Saudi royal family, thinking about this idea that these Americans are spreading of democracy in this part of the world. They will say, you make us very nervous, and our response should be, good. We want you nervous."[135]

In Europe, denial grand strategy type impulses similarly

---

133. Jon B. Alterman, *Iraq and the Gulf States: The Balance of Fear*, Washington: United States Institute of Peace August 2007, p. 6.
134. Bill Keller, 'The Sunshine Warrior', *The New York Times Magazine,* 22 September 2002 pp. 50-54, 88, 52.
135. Seth Leibsohn et al., 'Transcript: America, Iraq and the War on Terrorism, UCLA (April 2, 2003)';
http://www.claremont.org/projects/pageID.2499/default.asp: The Claremont Institute.

motivated American diplomacy and its use to support the military instrument. The US sought specific NATO assistance to be given to particular regional nations. While NATO had operated throughout its history on a consensus basis, Nicolas Burns, the US Ambassador to NATO, now demanded that NATO comply with these US desires.[136]

The use of the informational instrument was perceived in the grand strategy as a secondary matter. There were concerns over the legality under international law of the war given its preventative nature.[137] To offset this, an effort was made to obtain UN approval for the invasion and thereby establish the war as legitimate if not strictly legal although, in agreement with the denial grand strategy logic, the UN granting of approval was not seen by the Bush administration as essential.[138] The informational campaign stressed widely accepted, but unverified, beliefs regarding the existence, scale and future potential use of Iraq's weapons of mass destruction capabilities.[139]

In early November 2002 the US received unanimous UN Security Council support for Resolution 1441 that called on Iraq to comply with its disarmament obligations or face serious consequences. However, a second resolution introduced by the US in February 2003 calling for the Council to authorize military action against Iraq was eventually withdrawn in March amidst acrimonious debate. This setback had a significant impact on the international community's perception of the legitimacy of the invasion but as the

---

136. Gordon and Trainor, *Cobra II: The inside Story of the Invasion and Occupation of Iraq*, p. 113.
137. David Krieger, 'The War in Iraq as Illegal and Illegitimate', in Ramesh Chandra Thakur and Waheguru Pal Singh Sidhu (eds.), *Iraq Crisis and World Order: Structural, Institutional and Normative Challenges*; Tokyo: United Nations University Press, 2006, pp. 381-96, pp. 383-86.
138. Charlotte Ku, 'Legitimacy as an Assessment of Existing Legal Standards: The Case of the 2003 Iraq War', in Ramesh Chandra Thakur and Waheguru Pal Singh Sidhu (eds.), *Iraq Crisis and World Order: Structural, Institutional and Normative Challenges*; Tokyo: United Nations University Press, 2006, pp. 397-412, pp. 397-99.
139. Freedman, *A Choice of Enemies: America Confronts the Middle East*, pp. 416-22.

denial grand strategy schema logic suggests had only a limited effect on the grand strategy's implementation.

Considering the approaches used concerning building power, the grand strategy was both one of choice and near term, and accordingly the US adopted a near-term market approach. This approach was nested within, and conformed to, the approach of the wider Global War on Terror (GWOT) grand strategy.

Shortly before the 9/11 attacks, the administration had sharply reduced taxes and increased subsidies as part of a plan to address sluggish economic growth. After the attacks this general approach continued with Republican House majority leader Tom DeLay declaring that "...nothing is more important in the face of war then cutting taxes."[140] The tax cuts did stimulate economic growth as their advocates predicted but this was insufficient to offset the loss of Federal Government revenue caused by the tax cuts.[141] The grand strategy was accordingly funded through deficit financing using domestic and international bonds.[142] Of this, some 40% of the grand strategy's financing is estimated to come through the sale of US Government bonds to foreign governments and international companies.[143] The government used an accommodational strategy that extended existing polices but when this proved insufficient complemented this with an international strategy. The success of the international strategy meant a more problematic restructural

---

140. *Congressional Record: Proceedings and Debates of the 108th Congress First Session April 30, 2003 to May 13, 2003 Volume 149 Part 8;* Washington DC: United States Government Printing Office, 2003, p. 10080.

141. George W. Bush, *Economic Report of the President*; Washington: United States Government Printing Office, February 2003, pp. 56-57.

142. Marc Labonte and Mindy Levit, *CRS Report for Congress: Financing Issues and Economic Effects of American Wars*; Washington: Congressional Research Service, July 29, 2008, p. CRS-16. Steven Kosiak disputes this in holding that the grand strategy is funded out of the total Federal Government budget and thus it is impossible to say which portion is specifically funded by deficit-financing. If this argument is accepted, it would nevertheless still be correct to state that the GWOT grand strategy would be unaffordable without deficit-financing. See: Steven M. Kosiak, *Cost of the Wars in Iraq and Afghanistan, and Other Military Operations through 2008 and Beyond*; Washington: Center for Strategic and Budgetary Assessments, 2008, p. 67.

143. Kosiak, op.cit., p. 63.

approach was not needed.

The GWOT involved significant military deployments of volunteer professional soldiers however the US Armed Forces could not meet the demands for the required logistic and security functions. Extensive use was made of private military companies to support and supplement deployed US military personnel; many of the contractor staff employed were non-American nationals.[144] The GWOT grand strategy, which grew to include the occupation of Iraq, would have been impossible without this large-scale use of domestic and international private military companies and personnel. Richard Fontaine and John Nagl observed that:

> " By 2007, the Congressional Budget Office estimated that at least 190,000 contractors were working in the Iraqi theatre on U.S.-funded contracts, pushing the ratio of contractors to members of the U.S. military to greater than 1:1."[145]

The use of contractors was mirrored by the extensive use of commercial industry for material. In the main this was provided by American sources, although some specialist equipment and components were sourced internationally.

The motivation of American society to support the grand strategy was initially provided by the 9/11 attacks when authoritative Government leaders and officials determined that Al-Qaeda located in Afghanistan was responsible and posed a continuing danger of catastrophic terrorist attacks. The more difficult task was the securitization of Iraq sufficient to justify invasion. While several explanations were proffered, the claim that Iraq sought Weapons of Mass Destruction and might have ties to Al-Qaeda formed the core of the securitization argument.[146] This was an argument based not on

---

144. David Isenberg, *Private Military Contractors and U.S. Grand Strategy*, PRIO Report 1/2009; Oslo: International Peace Research Institute, 2009, pp. 19-20, 29-30.
145. Richard Fontaine and John Nagl, *Contracting in Conflicts: The Path to Reform*; Washington: Center for a New American Security June 2010, p. 11.
146. Andrew Flibbert, 'The Road to Baghdad: Ideas and Intellectuals in Explanations of the Iraq War', *Security Studies,* Vol. 15, No. 2, 2006, pp. 310-52, p. 316.

any specific Iraqi action, but rather on the potential risks to individual security and prosperity of any US inaction. President Bush in 2002 declared:

"America must not ignore the threat gathering against us. Facing clear evidence of peril, we cannot wait for the final proof - the smoking gun - that could come in the form of a mushroom cloud. ... As Americans, we want peace - we work and sacrifice for peace - and there can be no peace if our security depends on the will and whims of a ruthless and aggressive dictator. I am not willing to stake one American life on trusting Saddam Hussein."[147]

This argument was greatly assisted by engendering a strong sense of urgency through creating a sense of impeding crisis, Steven Metz writes: "This was unusual since the Iraq conflict did not meet the usual requirements for a crisis—a very high threat and limited decision time."[148] Deliberately shifting to a crisis decision mode though noticeably strengthened the authority accorded to high-level Bush administration officials and in setting tight parameters minimized public and elite debate over the given rationale or the alternatives.[149] Input legitimacy was relied upon.

The grand strategic synthesis was appropriate for the grand strategy actually implemented, removing the Ba'athist regime, but would probably have been unsuitable for achieving the desired grand strategic outcome of reforming Iraqi's social rules. The Iraq regime change grand strategy was envisaged as short term, with most reconstruction costs to be met by the Iraq state itself through oil sales on the global market. Those resource costs to the US that arose were seen as being able to be easily met using mainly domestic and international bonds, the extensive use of short-term contract staff in

---

147. President George W. Bush address at the Cincinnati Museum Center, Cincinnati, Ohio, October 7, 2002 in John W. Dietrich (ed.), *The George W. Bush Foreign Policy Reader: Presidential Speeches with Commentary;* Armonk, M.E.Sharpe Inc; 2005, p. 92.
148. Metz, *Decisionmaking in Operation Iraqi Freedom: Removing Saddam Hussein by Force*, p. 48.
149. Ibid., pp. 47-53.

limited duration organizations such as the OHRA, and through accessing material needs from American commercial companies.

The American grand strategy for regime change in Iraq succeeded brilliantly in overthrowing Saddam Hussein but failed to quickly replace the regime. Widespread looting and crime erupted immediately after the regime fell in April 2003. US troop numbers were adequate to overthrow Saddam but were both insufficient to prevent this civil disturbance or arranged in place to undertake protective functions. Accompanying this upheaval, the institutions of the Iraqi state collapsed, the OHRA quickly proved inadequate, and the US decided not to install favoured Iraqi exiles as an interim government. A hastily devised Coalition Provisional Authority was put in place to administer a country seemingly on the verge of falling apart. Clearly, the regime change grand strategy had failed to create a new Iraq " based on moderation, pluralism, and democracy" as it was intended and designed to achieve.[150]

Ambassador Paul Bremer, the head of the new CPA, quickly developed a new grand strategy to address the now well-evident failings of the Iraq regime change grand strategy.[151] He envisaged a seven step, 540-day,'outside-in' approach that would progressively put in place a new Iraqi-led government.[152]

A reform grand strategy is suggested for those circumstances where reform of a state or other entity is sought. While the American Iraq regime change grand strategy had a reformist agenda, policymakers used a denial grand strategy type to frame their diagnosis and analysis. In doing this, there was no consideration about the need to change the social rules of the society, its beliefs, norms or identities. The denial grand strategy type is based on realism, a materialist theory not an ideational one, and thus such aspects were completely outside the policymakers' thinking.

---

150. Gordon and Trainor, *The Endgame: The inside Story of the Struggle for Iraq, from George W. Bush to Barack Obama*, p. 8.
151. Ibid., pp. 8-15.
152. Bremer's 'outside-in' approach was derived from a 2003 RAND study into earlier American experiences of nation-building after wars. See Note 19 in ibid., p. 702.

In the denial grand strategy thinking used by policymakers, American military power was in any relative material power comparison overwhelming and thus would of course dominate post-war Iraq ensuring that the country would be largely stable during the reconstruction phase, allowing US forces to start withdrawing after only a few months. Such assumptions fitted the logic of the denial grand strategy's realist underpinnings but in this case the paradigm was being misapplied. Realism and the grand strategic goal of regime change are inherently mismatched; Steve Yetiv writes that:

> " Regime change policy…aims, in addition to eliminating the regime, to reshape society, to alter the ideological foundations and orientation of the people. [The realist] balance of power does not include these motivations….If realism and the balance of power stand for anything, it is not to meddle in the internal affairs of other states. Regime change, especially when achieved through military invasion, blatantly violates that core notion."[153]

This case study is an important example that the international order sought can best be achieved by using the matched grand strategy type. The US denial grand strategy implemented stopped Iraq from achieving its objective of regime survival but the country's social rules were not transformed as America sought. Lawrence Freedman remarks:

> " There were two distinctive influences on the US conduct of the war in Iraq….the first was about removing the regime, the second about inserting a new regime. If the two concerns had been mutually supportive, together there would have been regime change. Unfortunately, the opposite was the case."[154]

In considering the concept of grand strategy as a policymaking methodology, the Iraq regime change grand strategy is an example of a grand strategy focused on a single state within a broader, overarching global grand strategy as discussed in Chapter 2. In a similar manner to the European Recovery Program regional

---

153. Yetiv, op.cit., p. 114.
154. Freedman, *A Choice of Enemies: America Confronts the Middle East*, p. 423.

grand strategy examined earlier, this nesting occurred retrospectively. The Iraq regime grand strategy was approved for serious development beginning in late September 2001 however, it was another year until the overarching global grand strategy, the 2002 National Security Strategy, was formalized.[155] While the Iraq regime change grand strategy focused solely on a single country and the overarching 2002 National Security Strategy grand strategy took a global perspective, some ideas from the Iraqi grand strategy appeared to have informed the later - particularly democracy promotion as a way to permanently address existing and potential threats.

Conclusions

Considered together the three reform grand strategy case studies bring out important policymaking aspects about grand strategies in general and engagement grand strategies in particular.

In general terms, the US Iraq regime change grand strategy highlighted that trying to achieve an objective through using an inappropriate type of grand strategy is unlikely to lead to success. The three types of grand strategy each have their own limited sets of international orders they are matched with. Trying to cross these boundaries in terms of seeking an international order associated with a particular grand strategy type and then using a different grand strategy type to try to achieve this outcome appears imprudent.

The UK's Malayan Emergency grand strategy further reinforces that grand strategies need continual monitoring and refinement. In this case, two other grand strategy types were first implemented and evaluated before the reform type was finally settled upon. Even then the chosen grand strategy was kept under review and continually improved to enhance its effectiveness and efficiency. To reiterate, a grand strategy is not a set-and-forget approach.

More specifically related to reform grand strategies, the success of this type requires the existing ideas to collapse due to some external shock and for desired new ones to then replace them.

---

155. Brands, op.cit., pp 154-55.

As the ICBL case showed, the initial collapse phase may be achieved fortuitously by some other event but, while this may substantially reduce overall resource and time demands, the replacement ideas and the plan to have them accepted should be already developed. The alternative is to deliberately engineer the shock. The British example in Malaya showed this can be a costly, difficult and time-consuming business. The advantage in this however is that the ideational replacement program can then be accurately timed and accordingly more efficiently implemented. Choosing between these two alternatives may depend on the resources the organization implementing the grand strategy can command and the size of the targeted advocate group that needs persuading. Those organizations with few resources and a large target group may need to be ready to exploit external shocks whereas those with large resources and a small target group may prefer to be proactive.

Some shortcomings in this type of grand strategy are also evident. Deliberately changing the ideas of a selected target audience requires suitable and timely access to them. The British achieved this through resettling several hundred thousand rural Chinese close to Malayan towns. The ICBL achieved a similar outcome by generally being granted regular access to their carefully chosen decision-makers who worked within existing structures and institutions. Given gaining suitable access is crucial to success, not all circumstances will lend themselves to the use of reform grand strategies. For example, access to authoritarian states' decision-makers may be particularly difficult.

A related matter is that the target audience at least initially may not be large. In the early stages the focus is principally on influencing potential advocates within the broad target group who are prominent and authoritative in terms of the idea being advanced and who are able to use their organizational platform to give the new ideas credence and clout. This will probably be in most cases a relatively small number of people. While this makes a reform grand strategy more practical then may at first be thought, determining who these key potential advocates are requires deep insight into the broader target group, and this may be hard to obtain in some situations.

In considering the three grand strategy types, a reform grand strategy is the most dependent on the other party to succeed. While a denial grand strategy can simply use force to coerce others, and an engagement grand strategy can make use of another's pre-existing ambitions, it is more difficult to change people's minds. For this, there needs to be a degree of acceptance of the need for change and agreement with the new ideas. As discussed, this issue becomes more complex when issues of adequate and timely access and the need for deep knowledge of the broad target group are considered. The success of a reform grand strategy very much depends on adequate interaction between the parties involved and on the receptiveness of the target group.

8

When To Use Grand Strategies to Solve A Problem (And When Not)

Grand strategy remains in play. No one considers that today's big challenges including the rise of China, Islamic State terrorism or Russian revisionism can be solved with a simple one dimensional strategy approach be it diplomacy, information, military or economics. Instead, a carefully calibrated blend of a diverse array of instruments of national power is considered necessary. Moreover in dealing with the global financial crisis's onset, the importance of the development and sustainment of the various diverse instruments was reemphasised.

Realising that the times and its demands both suit and call for grand strategy approaches, many nations have formally embraced it issuing an array of policy documents explaining how they will make a better future for themselves. In its own way, China exemplifies this. The Chinese Communist Party's constitution has for several years set out the country's goals: by 2021 becoming a moderately prosperous society and by 2049 becoming a modernized socialist country that is rich, strong, democratic, culturally advanced and harmonious.[1] To help advance this its leadership has embraced the 'China Dream', a grand narrative of national rejuvenation that envisages using a diverse array of instruments of national power to return the nation to prominence in the international system.[2] In this, there has long been interest in grand strategies to guide China's development and reforms. To support their development, in 1984 China's paramount leader Deng Xiaoping, requested a method by which to judge the

1. Communist Party Of China, *Full Text of Constitution of Communist Party of China*, viewed 22 August 2016
english.cpc.people.com.cn/206972/206981/8188065.html.
2. Wang Yi, 'Peaceful Development and the Chinese Dream of National Rejuvenation', *China Institute of International Studies*, No. January/ February, 2014, pp. 17-44.

relative capabilities of other states; the answer, the notion of comprehensive national power, remains in use.[3]

Even so, not all problems are suitable for trying to be solved using the grand strategy methodology. There are other alternatives that are better for addressing certain kinds of problems. Before applying grand strategy to any particular problem, these alternatives should be considered, as they may be more effective. Extending this, states generally face multiple problems, some of which might best be solved using the grand strategy methodology and others by the alternative approaches. Most states accordingly use a careful mix of problem-solving methodologies.

In considering the various problem-solving methodologies, as discussed earlier grand strategy tries to shape the future. Grand strategy can then be categorised as an ends-centric approach in that this methodology seeks specific ends thorough using the available means in a certain way. There are however approaches that are the mirror image. These approaches try to be able to respond meaningfully to events that arise; categorised as means-centric, their focus is on having the right means available at the right time as to be able to adequately respond to specific events. Importantly, the two different approaches solve different problems, are animated by distinctly different drivers and provide dissimilar solutions - as comparison reveals.

Ends-Centric Alternatives To Grand Strategy

The grand strategy process developed in this book places emphasis on agency rather than context. The context is examined in terms of the ends sought; environments are scanned to detect if the conditions that will support the use of certain grand strategies to achieve

---

3. Hu Angang and Men Honghua, 'The Rising of Modern China: Comprehensive National Power and Grand Strategy', *"Rising China and the East Asian Economy" International Conference by Korea Institute for International Economic Policy*; March 19-20, Seoul: 2004, pp. 1-36. Wuttikorn Chuwattananurak, 'China's Comprehensive National Power and Its Implications for the Rise of China: Reassessment and Challenges', *CEEISA-ISA 2016 Joint International Conference*; 23-25 June, University of Ljubljana: 2016, pp. 1-39.

particular ends are in place. If not another 'end', and thus grand strategic 'way', is then considered.

Grand strategy *is the art of developing and applying diverse forms of power in an effective and efficient way to try to purposefully change the order existing between two or more intelligent and adaptive entities.* In this, a crucial issue that defines strategy is that it involves interacting with intelligent and adaptive others, whether friends, neutrals or adversaries, in an interdependent manner. If the problem does not involve such social interaction then it is not 'strategic' in this sense but is instead a plan. An example of a plan might be building a very-fast railway between two cities. This would be a complicated problem involving high costs and long-term construction and it might be assumed not everything will go according to the original plan; continual changes will almost certainly be necessary as circumstances change. Such a project though does not consider the plan's object - the new railway - as a sentient being working against or even with the plan; the railway is not in itself *'intelligent and adaptive'* albeit the planning will be complicated and long-term. Similarly, in countering global warming, the problem of excessive CO_2 in the atmosphere is one addressed by a plan not a strategy as CO_2 gas is not an *'intelligent and adaptive'* entity.

In such planning there is a further division into those plans based on existing circumstances and those on imaginary future contexts. National defence forces often devise these later types of plans that feature complicated future scenarios, sometimes set decades into the future, to assist with force structure development and devising future warfighting concepts. A particularly well-known example is War Plan Orange about how America might fight Japan and which was initially developed at the request of President Theodore Roosevelt in 1905. The plan was kept progressively updated and when the Japanese attacked Pearl Harbour and South East Asia in late 1941 became the basis for the Allied Pacific theatre strategy and helped shape American World War Two grand strategy.[4]

The future is of course uncertain and this is overcome in plans by assuming one or more possible tomorrows. In Chapter 3 the various levels of uncertainty were discussed. Level 1 uncertainty formed the basis of War Plan Orange in that only a single future was envisaged. For those situations where Level 2 uncertainty is assumed (two possible worlds) or Level 3 uncertainty (a bounded range of possibilities) the methodology of alternative futures is particularly useful.[5] This methodology is well-suited for long-term planning but may also be useful when developing strategies. It can give an appreciation of how the context in which the strategy is being implemented might develop.

A major early player in the field of alternative futures, the Shell oil company, is credited with foreseeing in the early 1980s that a seismic change in the political structure was coming in the Soviet Union. The alternative futures method gave Shell an indication a major shift was developing that the large intelligence agencies of Western states missed.[6] These agencies dealt in what was expected to happen not what might happen; they focused on Level 1 uncertainty as the basis of their planning rather than Level 2 or 3 uncertainty.

The most extreme type of uncertainty is Level 4, which envisages a limitless range of possible futures where even the variables cannot be identified. In such circumstances, policy ends are often very difficult to define, generally ruling out the use of ends-centric approaches like grand strategy. These conditions might be better addressed using means-centric approaches.

---

4. Edward Miller, *War Plan Orange: The U.S. Strategy to Defeat Japan, 1897-1945*; Annapolis: United States Naval Insititute 1991, pp. 1-8.
5 Hugh Courtney, 20/20 Foresight: Crafting Strategy in an Uncertain World; Boston: Harvard Business School Press, 2001.
6. Peter Schartz, *The Art of the Long View*; Hew York: Doubleday, 1991, pp. 57-58.

Means-Centric Alternatives To Grand Strategy

The two broad means-centric approaches are risk management and opportunism. Both await events: risk management dealing with windows of vulnerability and opportunism dealing with windows of opportunity. Risk management is discussed first.

The intent of a risk management approach is to lessen the impact of any of the identified risks that actually eventuate. Risk management is all about loss control. If risks eventuate there will be losses and associated costs but with careful risk management this can be limited to tolerable levels albeit the acceptable damage levels are rarely elaborated upon.[7] States, societies and organisations will always be sensitive to certain stressors but risk management aims to reduce their vulnerability to the external shocks that do occur.

While there are several types of risk management culture, that examined here derives from an economic culture that weighs the vulnerability, the consequences and the likelihood of a risk eventuating against the cost-benefits.[8] The risk management approach of the economic culture has an investment logic, although this is not an end-means relationship in a resources prioritisation or allocation sense as risk management assumes no likely future or desired end.

Indeed under this risk management approach, the contemporary international and domestic environment is seen as being so complex in its multiple interdependences and cross-linkages that the future is considered non-linear and unpredictable. Given that this complexity is deepening more unexpected consequences will arise from the

---

7. Paul Hopkin, *Fundamentals of Risk Management: Understanding Evaluating and Implementing Effective Risk Management*; (London: Kogan Page, 2010), pp. 148-52, 253-76.
8. An alternative actuarial culture based on the historical analysis of previous calamities and the spreading of costs across many underpins insurance calculations, but it is inappropriate for national security where risk events are unique, relatively rare and hard to predict. Karen Lund Petersen, *Corporate Risk and National Security Redefined*; (Abingdon: Routledge, 2012), pp. 16-22.

actions taken by society.[9] This reflexive nature of risks means problems need to be managed as they become apparent, rather than solved. Knowing new unexpected risks will arise, and that there is always a certain level of residual risk from known factors, governments must retain the flexibility and the resources to deal with a succession of unforeseen events. Accordingly, " ...politics is no longer about initiating a social, economic or political process and bringing an end to a particular problem... Governments no longer master ends, only means. Politics is about managing the process. ...to keep the ship of state afloat." [10]

Risk management incorporates some levels of uncertainty but assumes that many present risks will continue indefinitely. The future will be just like the past albeit with probably simply more risks being progressively added. The assertion that there have always been interstate wars, therefore there always will be, is an example.

The discussion on risk management being about damage limitation appears contrary to some views that hold the approach can include actions taken to ensure anticipated risks do not occur. In going in such a direction though, risk management moves into a grand strategy that has the objective of changing the international order in a particular way that means the identified risk cannot happen. The recent wars in Iraq and Afghanistan can be viewed as risk management conflicts in that the use of Western military force aimed to ensure that any future terrorist attacks on Western countries arising from these countries were small scale and, in Iraq's case, did not involve atomic weapons.[11] The intent arguably was damage limitation rather than to prevent any forms of terrorism occurring again.

---

9. Ulrich Beck and Translated by Mark Ritter, *Risk Society: Towards a New Modernity* (London: Sage Publications Ltd, 1992), p. 21.
10. Mikkel Vedby Rasmussen, *The Risk Society at War: Terror, Technology and Strategy in the Twenty-First Century* (Cambridge: Cambridge University Press, 2006), p. 37.
11. Timothy Edmunds, 'British Civil–Military Relations and the Problem of Risk', *International Affairs,* Vol. 88, No. 2, 2012, pp. 265-82, p. 267.

This focus on means is conceptually quite different to governments using grand strategies to achieve defined and specific ends, as the Dutch National Safety and Security Strategy reveals. The Dutch risk management strategy is an instrument used by the Netherlands government to prepare the country to manage internal and external threats that could cause serious social disruption. Wide-ranging human security threats are considered including climate change, transnational crime, Muslim radicalization, societal polarization, cyber-disruption, economic crises and terrorism.[12] These threats are assessed in terms of risks to vital interests, prioritized in terms of possible consequences and assessed likelihood, and incorporated into a national risk assessment. The Netherlands' Government then determines which particular risks will be addressed through building and sustaining the necessary national capabilities to manage these risks should they eventuate.[13] The overall intent is to reduce the impact of the selected risks down to a level considered both acceptable and controllable if they eventuate.

Recent Australian defence policies have also adopted risk management approaches as a way of selecting specific Australian Defence Force investment options. The 2000 Defence White Paper handled uncertainty in the strategic environment by employing a strategic risk management concept that determined that the risks that Australian Defence Force capabilities would be developed for were a direct armed attack on the country and internal "lower-level" conflicts in Australia's immediate neighbourhood.[14] The 2009

---

12. 'Dutch National Safety and Security Strategy', viewed 10 June 2010 http://www.minbzk.nl/english/subjects/public-safety/national-security/@114278/factsheet-national_0. Dr. Hans Bergmans et al., 'Working with Scenarios, Risk Assessment and Capabilities: In the National Safety and Security Strategy of the Netherlands'; The Hague: Ministry of the Interior and Kingdom Relations, October 2009, pp. 11-12.
13. Programme National Security, 'National Security: Strategy and Work Programme 2007-2008', in *Ministry of the Interior and Kingdom Relations* (ed.); The Hague: May 2007, p. 10.
14. The White Paper noted that the military forces developed to meet these two chosen risks could be used selectively and carefully for other tasks but force structure decisions where to be driven by these two risks. For the rationale behind adopting a Strategic Risk Management approach see: *Defence 2000: Our Future Defence Force* (Canberra: Defence Publishing Service October 2000), pp. 6-7.

Defence White Paper continued this approach explicitly noting that given uncertainty "the key problem in defence planning is strategic risk."[15] In implementing risk management, this later White Paper chose to concentrate available resources on addressing only one risk: a direct armed attack on the country.[16] These two White Papers focussed on building means and did not actively seek to develop a future order in which the nominated risks would not eventuate. Instead the risks were seen as enduring, and against which the only option was to be able to limit the damage inflicted to a manageable level should they occur. What the acceptable damage levels were was not elaborated upon, rather the stress was on developing military means.

The major outcome of risk management is consequently resilience.[17] Foucault's 'ship of state' at some time will hit the rocks but taking specific actions before this could help the passengers, cargo, crew or ship function post-shock. From an organisational perspective, resilience objectives can vary from: building capabilities and capacities to survive shocks; continuing operation in the presence of shocks; recovering from shocks to the original form; or absorbing shocks and evolving in response.[18] Countries will always be sensitive to some stresses. Resilience seeks to reduce states' vulnerability in terms of ongoing costs and affects to the shocks that do occur.[19] Away from state applications though risk management

15. Department of Defence Australian Government, *Defending Australia in the Asia Pacific Century: Force 2030* (Canberra, 2009), p. 27, para 3.7.
16. Ibid., p. 41, para 5.1 to 5.6. There were though some occasional glimpses of a grand strategy approach in brief discussions of preferred future international orders e.g. Ibid., p. 96, para 11.20.
17. Resilience methodologies generally advocate an all-hazard, comprehensive, whole-of-society approach that acts across the spectrum of prevention, preparedness, response and recovery. Athol Yates and Anthony Bergin, *Hardening Australia: Climate Change and National Disaster Resilience*, ASPI Special Report Issue 24; (Canberra, Australia: Australian Strategic Policy Institute Limited, 2009). Jennifer Cole, 'Securing Our Future: Resilience in the Twenty-First Century', *The RUSI Journal,* Vol. 155, No. 2, May 2010, pp. 46-51.
18. Brenton Prosser and Colin Peters, 'Directions in Disaster Resilience Policy', *The Australian Journal of Emergency Management,* Vol. 25, No. 3, July 2010, pp. 8-11, p. 8.
19. Keohane and Nye usefully conceived as sensitivity being the liability to costly effects imposed by external events, while vulnerability was the ability to make

approaches have also been applied to broadly-conceived, human security matters.

In the 1990s, with the Cold War concluded, attention shifted away from national security, epitomised by state sovereignty, military might and territorial boundaries, to human security with individuals the referent object. Human security today encompasses freedom from fear, freedom from want and freedom to live in dignity. Drawing on considerable debate and field experience, the UN applies a risk management approach to human security based on several principles: being people-centred, that is focused on the individual and community level; comprehensive in addressing the full range of insecurities; multi-sectoral in involving state and non-state actors operating at the local, national and international levels; tailoring for the specific context; and focusing on prevention, that is developing people and societal resilience to both mitigate and be adequately prepared to respond to future disasters and emerging crises.[20]

The principal alternative means-centric approach is opportunism where a state's policies and actions change, shift and evolve as circumstances require. Used here, it is considered a technique that states may use and does not have a normative dimension that implies some moral judgement. The intent of opportunism is to seize opportunities and address challenges as they arise rather than work towards some defined objective. To use the well known ship-of-state metaphor, the ship is not heading towards a desired landfall but rather the captain – the government – is simply seeking to take advantage of any favourable winds. Echoing this, Lord Salisbury, then Secretary of State for India, observed near the highpoint of the British Empire that: "English policy is to float lazily downstream,

---

timely changes that reduced the impact of these shocks when they occurred.
Robert O. Keohane and Joseph S. Nye, *Power and Interdependence* 2nd edn.; (Glenview: Scott, Foresman and Company, 1989), pp. 12-16.
20. Human Security Unit, *Human Security Handbook*; New York: United Nations, 2016, pp. 8-10.

occasionally putting out a diplomatic boathook to avoid collisions."[21]

Opportunism focuses on the upside to a situation in seeking significant returns through exploiting unexpected new situations that emerge or the mistakes of others. This is the converse to risk management that seeks to protect on the downside by limiting losses if bad situations arise. Opportunism can be adopted at any time but is well suited to highly dynamic or complex circumstances characterised by a very large range of possible alternative futures that make planning truly impractical.[22] Even so, using the full range of opportunistic possibilities may be constrained depending on the international environment, systemic sanctions and accepted norms. In reality, unbridled opportunism such as that advocated in Machiavelli's *The Prince* is more improbable than may at first be thought.

Crucial to using this approach is being sufficiently prepared and flexible enough to seize new opportunities as they emerge. The broader the capabilities available and the deeper the capacities at hand the wider the range of opportunities that may be taken advantage of. Intellectually, political leaders and bureaucracies need to be sufficiently agile to adapt to the new circumstances and exploit the new opportunities presented before they close. The window of opportunity to act may be brief.

Given time constraints, the recognition of exploitable opportunities early enough to react to them may be difficult. A sophisticated intelligence system with a high degree of analytical skills may be necessary. Moreover, the most gain for the least expenditure is likely to be obtained early in an emerging situation when detection and recognition is at its most challenging.

Opportunism implies moving not just effectively but also quickly and so there is a premium placed on speed rather than methodical preparation and planning. Actions may need to be taken before fully

---

21. Lord Salisbury, 'Letter to Earl of Lytton, 9 March 1877', in Lady Gwendolen Cecil, *Life of Robert, Marquis of Salisbury Vol. 2*, (London: Hodder and Stoughton Ltd, 1921), p. 130
22. Chapter 3 discussed such Level Four type uncertainty

understanding the likely consequences. The actions taken and the situation may then interact in novel and unexpected ways. This inherent uncertainty may make using an opportunist approach something of rollercoaster ride as the situation develops. In contrast, the grand strategy approach suggests steady if unspectacular progress towards a well-defined objective. Opportunism accordingly tends to be criticized for being short-sighted but this is implicit in its operation.

The opportunist approach in operation is well illustrated in John Darwin's examination of the development of the British Empire from around 1830 until the start of the Boer War in 1899. British expansion had no master plan devised and run in Whitehall instead expansion was driven erratically and episodically by jostling domestic interest groups and their "men on the spot." Rather than grand designs imposed from the top, the Empire was expanded from the bottom-up. Darwin writes that:

> "Even to official agents in the field it often seemed that the best plan was to act first and wait for public opinion to rally behind. It was no good asking the Foreign Office for permission to advance, advised [lord] Milner in 1895. 'The people on the spot must take things into their own hands, when, if the occasion of the decisive move is well-chosen, public opinion here will surely approve.'"[23]

In embracing opportunism the Empire expanded dramatically and rapidly. The focus was on the upside and that seemed unlimited but left unconsidered the longer-term implications of over-extension and the political, military and financial difficulties that could arise in maintaining such a sprawling domain.

There are many other examples. Napoleonic France is held to have embraced opportunism rather than a grand strategy and accordingly was guided "...by the needs of the moment and

---

23. John Darwin, *The Empire Project: The Rise and Fall of the British World-System 1830-1970*; Cambridge: Cambridge University Press, 2009, p. 91.

swayed…by circumstance."[24] In analysing the US grand strategy in the Persian Gulf since 1975, Steve Yetiv determined that there actually was no grand strategy simply a continuing reaction to unexpected events and surprises.[25] The opportunism approach can also be embraced in much smaller two-state systems. Successive Australian Governments have had a high-level policy of seeking a deeper security alliance with the US. America though has generally been more concerned about more distant regions and so less interested. Opportunities arising from the deepening American involvement in Vietnam and intense concerns over Iraq post the 9/11 attacks were deliberately exploited by Australia to achieve its broader and unconnected goal: making the alliance with the US more dependable.[26] Australia had the capabilities at hand to take advantage of the opportunities presented but these capabilities were not developed or employed in accordance with some over-arching plan. The capabilities awaited events. Others note opportunist approaches in Denmark's involvement in the 1991 Gulf War, Australia's intervention in the Solomon Islands in 2003 and in Russia's actions in South Ossetia in August 2008.[27]

Evaluating the Competing Approaches

The means-centred approaches comprised grand strategy and planning while the ends centred approaches comprised risk management and opportunism. Given the focus of this book and the considerable literature on the topic, planning will not be discussed further. In this the three remaining approaches have distinct differences that become significant when considered in terms of problem solving.

---

24. Charles J. Esdaile, 'De-Constructing the French Wars: Napoleon as Anti-Strategist', *Journal of Strategic Studies,* Vol. 31, No. 4, 2008, pp. 515-52, p. 515, 50.

25. Yetiv, op.cit., pp. 192-97.

26. Lloyd Cox and Brendon O'connor, 'Australia, the US, and the Vietnam and Iraq Wars: 'Hound Dog, Not Lapdog'', *Australian Journal of Political Science,* Vol. 47, No. 2, June 2012, pp. 173-87.

27. Fredrik Doeser and Joakim Eidenfalk, 'The Importance of Windows of Opportunity for Foreign Policy Change', *International Area Studies Review,* Vol. 16, No. 4, 2013, pp. 390-406.

Firstly and most importantly, the grand strategy approach tries to take you where you wish to go. The grand strategy embraced may not succeed but the intention in using this approach is to reach a particular desired objective. By comparison, with risk management the state awaits expected events. All countries at some time suffer misfortunes but making preparations can moderate their impact. A political advantage of the risk management approach though may be that if the feared risk never eventuates, no action will be needed and thus being held accountable for the approach's success in any qualitative or quantitative sense is impossible. Opportunism is different again. The approach is inherently reactive to events and the actions of others. As noted earlier Salisbury described British policy as "floating lazily downstream" but this immediately raises questions of whose stream, taking the nation where and how fast? Although seeking to exploit others, the state using opportunism does not initiate events and must accept the boundaries set by others.

In the modern world, there are no undiscovered, vacant areas in which unconstrained opportunistic expansion can be undertaken. Instead contemporary opportunism is more like that practised by Denmark and Australia taking advantage of the unexpected events of the 1991 Iraq War and the 9/11 attacks to deepen their alliance with America. In such circumstances, the opportunist state becomes a part of another state's project and is responsive to that. The other more activist state sets the agenda and determines the framework of the debates cognizant of its own goals and capabilities. The opportunist state can only be ready to react as circumstances dictate; the ship of state in this approach is actually captained by another.

Secondly, with a grand strategy approach some form of tentative resource prioritization is possible. There are defined ends so an attempt can be made to rationally develop, distribute and allocate the means in a coherent manner. This is not just for the tangible resources such as manpower, money and material but also for the intangibles like legitimacy and a state's related soft power. A grand strategy can moreover shape means beyond the state in the wider society, in non-governmental organisations, in commercial businesses and practices, and internationally. Over time a state can have the most useful and appropriate means available and mobilised to support its chosen goals. A further resource prioritization benefit in having defined ends is that a benchmark exists against which to judge progress. Over time the efficiency and effectiveness of the grand strategy can be evaluated, unlike the other two approaches.

With opportunism being means-centred, but with the future utility of these means being unclear, resource prioritization is inherently problematic. There are two potential options: either develop the means in a manner that gives the most flexibility of who to join at some future time as events evolve, or determine early whose specific grand strategy will be taken advantage of and develop the means appropriate to that.

In the first option the means developed would stress diversity and variety to give the greatest flexibility; a broad set of capabilities would be sought but each means would not need to be quantitatively large. When the moment arrived these means could be further developed in terms of scale as proved necessary. This is similar to Australia's core force structure approach of the 1970s where a diverse but small Defence force was maintained with the intention that those parts that actually proved useful in some future contingency would be expanded as needed at some future time.[28] The 1975 Strategic Basis of Australian Defence Policy declared that: " The core force should be a force...with relevant skills and equipment capable of timely expansion to ...meet a developing situation."[29] Such an approach allows considerable flexibility in choosing whose grand strategy to join, allowing decisions to be delayed until events necessitated and the circumstances are clear.

In the second option of an early decision being made on the foreign grand strategy to be embraced, the means could be developed

---

28. The concept was criticized at the time on the grounds that in applying its logic the future, fully expanded, force structure was inherently unknowable and so the concept was unusable for determining resource priorities. Paul Dibb, 'The Self-Reliant Defence of Australia: The History of an Idea', in Ron Huisken and Meredith Thatcher (eds.), *History as Policy : Framing the Debate on the Future of Australia's Defence Policy* (Canberra: ANU E Press, 2007), p. 16.
29. Stephan Frühling, *A History of Australian Strategic Policy since 1945* (Canberra: Defence Publishing Service, 2009), p. 537.

and optimised for inclusion in the chosen over-arching design. The precise time of when to formally and materially join the other's grand strategy would be the key remaining judgment and be determined by assessments of when the greatest opportunities presented themselves. The means in this model while qualitatively narrow and selective could become numerically larger if necessary.

Resource prioritization is also problematic in the risk management approach. A risk management table that guides the development of national means can simply be a long list of possible threats that could occur at some future, indefinite time. The likelihood of any particular event occurring is a matter of judgment and subject assessment. Moreover, when assessing the impact of a disaster the tendency is for a 'worse case' analysis to be recommended. As Lord Salisbury further observed: "If you believe the doctors, nothing is wholesome; if you believe the theologians, nothing is innocent; if you believe the military, nothing is safe."[30] The selection of risk is accordingly a political decision, it is inherently a matter for judgment not quantitative assessment.[31] This is fertile ground for debate, disagreement and bureaucratic manoeuvring. Less likely risks that all can agree on may be selected almost by default.

There also remain inherent problems in resource prioritization that arise from organisational arrangements and bureaucratic imperatives that the risk management approach concept intrinsically does not address. In the Netherlands, the National Safety and Security Strategy based on the risk management approach has improved inter-departmental awareness but translating this into coordinated funding decisions that develop new capabilities has proven problematic:

"The [risk] assessment itself is broadly accepted, but translating priorities into capability requirements remains difficult – for

30. Lord Salisbury quoted in Lady Gwendolen Cecil, *Life of Robert, Marquis of Salisbury Vol. 2, op cit,* p 153.
31. Edmunds, p. 272-75. Jonas Hagmann and Myriam Dunn Cavelty, 'National Risk Registers: Security Scientism and the Propagation of Permanent Insecurity', *Security Dialogue,* Vol. 43, No. 1, 2012, pp. 79-96, pp. 90-92.

reasons of methodology and bureaucratic politics. ... The Netherlands ministries are independent, but security requires their interdependent action, even though they may secure national security funding for their issue areas. An overall need is for each ministry to trust the other as the *Work Programme* is implemented and be able to see the connections they all have to security instead of stove-piped responses to their own responsibilities."[32]

The 2010 British National Security Strategy used a particularly sophisticated methodology to prioritising risks but has encountered similar implementation problems in the setting of resource priorities.[33] With only limited Ministerial buy-in to the National Security Strategy and budgets held by individual ministries, a major "...debate is how to relate resources to the strategy."[34] It seems that in prioritizing risks simply a new arena has been created "...in which the traditional struggles and rivalries of defence politics can be fought out and regulated." Edmunds further continues that "...the question of who gets to define what the risks are and how they should be prioritized has [now] become a defining issue for contemporary civil–military relations.[35]

Inertia may be the easiest option. The balance between the various risks is difficult to determine in any quantitative way and for many states it may be politically, economically and socially easier to simply retain the *status quo* resource allocation. The extant resource distribution reflects past difficulties and bureaucratic battles and thus

---

32. Caudle and Spiegeleire, *op.cit.,* p. 11.

33. Mark Phillips, 'Policy-Making in Defence and Security', *The RUSI Journal,* Vol. 157 No.1 (February/ March 2012), pp 32-33. Note that this discussion here relates to prioritizing scarce resources not to the size a budget should be. The UK Government's assessment that the principal threat to national well-being was economic led to a decision that the British Defence budget would be reduced by 7.5% in real terms from the previous year. This guideline shaped the 2010 National Security Strategy but did not in itself determine the priorities for the reduced funding. Paul Cornish and Andrew M. Dorman, 'Smart Muddling Through: Rethinking Uk National Strategy Beyond Afghanistan', *International Affairs,* Vol. 88, No. 2, 2012, pp. 213-22, p. 215.

34. Ibid., p. 17.

35. Edmunds, p. 273.

the onus of proof is on those who would propose that new risks are more likely and more terrible than the old agreed harms. Disrupting an old order can lead to bureaucratic dissension and inside experts marshalling domestic constituents. Moreover being by its nature scenario-based, a risk management approach can be bureaucratically gamed with the probability and impacts of a risk eventuating adjusted to give the departmentally desired resource allocation. In a risk management approach staying with the current prioritization may be the easiest and - given no one knows if a risk may eventuate or not - the most appropriate of all.

Thirdly, the three approaches have different implications for the overall quantum of resourcing. The concept of grand strategy is built around the assumption that a state has limited resources that need to be focused on specific and articulated needs. This suggests it is most appropriate for states with constrained resources including, some have suggested, for states with declining resources.[36]

Risk management on the other hand implicitly assumes a well-resourced state. The conventional approach is to make a list of threats, rank them and then fund the mitigation of those risks for which there is sufficient resources. All risks inherently cannot be addressed as US Defence Secretary Bob Gates in addressing how large the American Defense budget would need to be to mitigate every risk observed: "Nobody lives in that world ... you are never going to get to zero threat. You could spend $2 trillion and you'd never get to zero threat."[37] At the other extreme though without significant resource availability most risks will go unaddressed making the logic of this approach tenuous. In this, risk management does not actively seek a better future order where these risks are eliminated and so they will reoccur, or at least reappear on the risk list indefinitely. The approach of not taking positive action to eradicate the identified risks – continually treating the symptom not the cause - is inherently resource intensive. In the matter of how

---

36. Hew Strachan, 'Strategy and Contingency', *International Affairs*, Vol. 87, No. 6 (2011), pp. 1283-1284.
37. Gates quoted in Philip Ewing, 'Standing alone', *DoD Buzz*, Friday, 17 February 2012, http://www.dodbuzz.com/2012/02/17/standing-alone/ [accessed 22 April 2012].

much resources are enough, in risk management there is almost by design never enough.

Opportunism though can have the least resource requirements. The state can leverage off another's efforts and contribute only what it wishes to from what it has available. Opportunism is inherently a matter of choice – not of necessity - so an opportunistic state can do as much or as little as it wishes in some particular situation depending on the outcomes it seeks. An intrinsic problem though is states usually find it difficult to disengage from a situation they have entered and instead generally prefer for political reasons to continue with their commitment even if this is becoming steadily more expensive. A danger in exploiting a window of opportunity that another's grand strategy offers is that the full resource costs of becoming involved may be very ill-defined and poorly estimated.

Fourthly, there are differences in the degree of coherence across a government or a society that the three conceptual approaches can bring, with grand strategy inherently offering more than opportunism and risk management can. A grand strategy is purposefully constructed as "the overall mosaic...[that] provides the key ingredients of clarity, coherence, consistency over time."[38] As a grand strategic concept cascades downwards though a governmental hierarchy, objectives and goals become progressively more narrowly and more precisely defined as a way of directing and controlling the subordinate levels.

In a grand strategy the ways and the ends are elaborated upon; opportunism and risk management though have no ''ways' and no defined 'ends' they simply address the means. This is not to say that given a national security approach of opportunism or risk management that coordination between the various Departments of State in terms of how they manage their respective means is not possible. Such coordination though being bottom-up and based around pre-determined resource allocations is at the more tactical level of administration and may be relatively ineffective.

---

38. Gregory D. Foster, 'Missing and Wanted', *Strategic Review,* Vol. 13 (Fall, 1985), p. 14.

Lastly, there is a marked difference in intellectual requirements. Grand strategy is intellectually taxing, not just in the formulation stage but also in the on-going implementation as this is continuously reviewed and adjusted to keep 'the ship of state' tacking towards the desired landfall. In putting grand strategies into practice the initial thinking needs to continually evolve as circumstances change. Few states however, have the educated and skilled staff readily available for such a protracted intellectual effort.

By comparison opportunism is simpler in relying upon other states to provide the intellect although the opportunist state needs to be mentally and politically agile when the time comes to both be in synch with the other state's grand strategy and to try to achieve some of its own desires as well. Risk management is easier again needing only the periodic compilation of possible risks, no need for continual strategic adjustment to keep on-course and a simple focus on means almost independent of external factors.

The three different national security conceptual approaches have different purposes, assumptions and implications. The choice of which to apply depends on the context and the judgment of the policymakers involved however this is a real choice with real consequences. The three distinct organizing constructs each have differing objectives, utility in prioritising resources, resource demands, ability to impose coherence across government and society, and required levels of skilled people to formulate and implement.

Stepping away from problem solving methodologies though to the demand for them, states generally have many different problems occurring simultaneously. There may be a need for multiple solutions to be employed concurrently to address multiple problems. If so, coherence is of particular concern. The method embraced to solve one problem should work with, not against, another method being used to solve another different problem. In this regard, nesting grand strategies within each other was discussed earlier and similar issues apply in cases where risk management and/or opportunism approaches nest within grand strategies.

An example of this was found in the American Cold War containment grand strategy. While actions were taken across the globe, it consistently focused on the single bi-lateral relationship between the US and the USSR, with the rest of the world markedly less important in themselves. In discussing the Nixon Administration's policies towards Africa and numerous third world states, US National Security Council staff member Marshall Wright advised that: "We deal with them because they are there, not because we hope to get great things out of our participation. We aim at minimizing the attention and resources which must be addressed to them. What we really want from both is no trouble. Our policy is therefore directed at damage limiting, rather than at accomplishing anything in particular."[39] For these states the US used risk management aiming to constrain any losses that might transpire if some unfortunate event occurred.[40] In more recent times the Obama Administration has adopted a similar approach albeit to different issues in a different international system. A grand strategy has been embraced to manage the rise of China but the threat of terrorism, for which no conclusive solution seems possible, is being handled using risk management.

The discussion so far about grand strategy has revolved around what might be termed technocratic issues: how to use the method practically. A more critical examination however might be useful in highlighting some additional matters that need to be

---

39 Marshall Wright, 'Memorandum to the President's Assistant for National Security Affairs (Kissinger), Washington, January 10 1970 ', in Louis J. Smith and David H. Herschler (eds.), *Foundations of Foreign Policy, 1969–1972*, Foreign Relations of the United States, 1969–1976: Volume I; Washington: Department of State, 2003, p. 163.

40. Such thinking is again illustrated in a Department of State report written in 1950 by George Kennan, the originator of containment. He observed that: "It is important for us to keep before ourselves and the Latin American peoples at all times the reality…that we are a great power; that we are by and large much less in need of them than they are in need of us; that we are entirely prepared to leave to themselves those who evince no particular desire for the forms of collaboration that we have to offer; …and that we are more concerned to be respected than to be liked or understood." Quoted in Gabriel Marcella, *American Grand Strategy for Latin America in the Age of Resentment*; Carlisle: Strategic Studies Institute, September 2007, pp. 2-3.

appreciated before making a choice to use grand strategy to solve some particular problem. There are some non-technocratic downsides to consider.

Problems With Grand Strategy

Implicit in the idea of grand strategy as a problem-solving methodology is that it is an instrument of a strong activist state or organization with a rationalist foundation and an effective and efficient bureaucracy. Examining this hidden assumption however, reveals several concerns.

The archetypal grand strategist of the late 20th Century, Henry Kissinger likened making grand strategy to a journey through space and time with his most favorite metaphor being Plato's ship of state.[41] Gerard Toal writes that for Kissinger: "Nixon is the helmsman of the good ship 'United States' and Kissinger is his principal navigator. Together they, with a small hand-picked crew, navigate the ship of state through dangerous times and stormy seas, all the while striving for balance and equilibrium (against the dangers of wild fluctuations and oscillations). Crises, both domestic and international, are experienced as stormy weather."[42] Grand strategy is then a form of governance, being all about guiding the whole-of-the-nation towards a particular goal. In this, Plato's ship of state metaphor relates to the best manner to govern, to stay afloat and on course. His ideal was rule by philosopher steersmen; a form of elite technocratic management with considerable expertise, knowledge and foresight that ruled for the good not of themselves but of the ship and its sailors, who were the citizens of the city.[43] Instead, Plato saw his contemporaneous city-states as being ships with an unruly crew commanded by ineffectual and intoxicated

---

41. Plato, *Plato: Republic, Volume II: Books 6-10*, ed. Edited and Translated by Christopher Emlyn-Jones and William Preddy, Loeb Classical Library; Harvard: Harvard University Press, 2013, pp. 2-105.

42. Gerard Toal, 'Problematizing Geopolitics: Survey, Statesmanship and Strategy', *Transactions of the Institute of British Geographers, New Series,* Vol. 19, No. 3, 1994, pp. 259-72, p. 265.

43. David Keyt, 'Plato and the Ship of State', in Gerasimos Santas (ed.), *The Blackwell Guide to Plato's Republic*; Oxford: Blackwell Publishing Ltd, 2008, pp. 189-213, p. 201.

captains unfavorably influenced by shrewd, ambitious men who sought power over the ship's wealth and material goods through rhetorical skills that incited and exploited factional conflict.[44]

Plato's distinction between the two alternatives is considered as representative of his opinions about the shortcomings of democracy compared to the benefits of elite governance. There are dangers in such an approach as Toal further observed about Kissinger's policymaking: "The metaphor of the ship of state ascribes an absolute power to the President and represents any political challenge to that power as hazardous weather not legitimate dissent (thus the preoccupation with 'damage control'; megalomania and paranoia soon developed in the Nixon White House)."[45]

The metaphor can go deeper than just one American administration, being also extended to other forms of government. In the first half of the 20th Century the concept of grand strategy became intertwined with notions of total war that required total mobilization of the society. Totalitarian states, fascist or communist, were seen as well suited to this new era compared to the internally fractious democratic states that struggled throughout the 1920s and then almost collapsed with the economic travails of the Great Depression. The concept of grand strategy steadily became implicitly linked with totalitarianism.

J.F.C. Fuller, a noted early grand strategic thinker, become attracted to fascism in the 1930s but before this in his 1923 book *The Reformation of War* he wrestled with how counties with a Westminster parliamentary system could undertake grand strategies.[46] He saw a fundamental tension between elected politicians as amateur Government Ministers making high-level grand strategic decisions and the deep knowledge and specialist skills necessary to develop effective grand strategies. His solution was to suggest a retired General – a "generalissimo' - being a

---

44. Zena Hitz, 'Degenerate Regimes in Plato's Republic', in *Plato's 'Republic': A Critical Guide* (ed.); Cambridge: Cambridge University Press, 2010, pp. 103-31, p. 107.
45. Toal, p. 265.
46. Fuller, pp. 220-28.

Cabinet member, not as an elected representative as conventionally but as an appointed, long-term professional grand strategy adviser and confidant. This tension between elected representatives and professional officials continues to perplex those who seek to make grand strategy in a Westminster system. In the UK a 'community of strategists' has been suggested to better support Cabinet grand strategic decision-making but this concept, as in the similar Australian governmental structure, clashes with the prerogatives of the elected Ministers.[47]

There are some counters though to the arguments that grand strategy has anti-democratic connotations. Grand strategy clearly sets out the ends, ways and means. With such a benchmark, leaders and governments can be assessed, critiqued and called to account by parliament or the public today, and later by historians. In writing the Official History of British relations with the Western Europe, Alan Milward found that being able to compare outcomes against the grand strategy governments followed was invaluable in allowing him to make reasoned judgments concerning the policies, politicians and civil servants of the time.[48] By comparison the alternative problem solving methodology of risk management inherently does not have a suitable benchmark for accountability purposes.[49] The nature of risk management even more than grand strategy, is to rely on the judgements of technocratic experts unable to be called to account for their performance.

Addressing the concerns over latent authoritarianism in the grand strategy methodology though does need the grand strategy to be made public in some manner so accountability is possible. Gaddis thinks that between the time of Pericles advocating a grand strategy for Athens during the Peloponnesian War and recent times,

---

47. Public Administration Select House of Commons and Committee, *Strategic Thinking in Government: Without National Strategy, Can Viable Government Strategy Emerge? Vol.1*; London: The Stationery Office Limited, 24 April 2012, pp. 21-36. Peter Layton, 'A Better Way to Make National Security Decisions', *The Drum*; Canberra: Australian Broadcasting Commission, 26 April 2013.
48. Milward, *The Rise and Fall of a National Strategy 1945-1963: The United Kingdom and the European Community Volume 1*, pp. 6-7.
49. Edmunds, pp. 268-72.

most grand strategies have been kept secret and away from the public gaze or debate. He sees a change in 1947 when George Kennan revealed in an article in a public journal the rationale for the containment grand strategy.[50] Such disclosures have sometimes caused some discomfort but are the basis of accountability in democratic states. While many may disagree with the grand strategies of President George W. Bush 2001-2008, they were available for all to ponder and represent a new benchmark in the area of grand strategy accountability.

If Plato fretted over the best forms of government, Michel Foucault discussed how governments used techniques – of which grand strategy was potentially one – to dominate civil society at the most fundamental level. For Foucault, governmentality involves the "way in which one conducts the conduct of men" and this is achieved through individuals becoming self-regulating in that their ideas are structured and shaped to consider matters only from a particular perspective.[51] Such social domination though may be an effect of the "technologies of government" not necessarily just an outcome of particular actions.[52] Foucault wrote of the captaining, or governance, of a ship that having left a safe harbor with cargo bound for a distant port: " It means clearly to take charge of the sailors, but also the boat and the cargo; to take care of a ship means also to reckon with winds, rocks and storms; and it consists in that activity of establishing a relation between the sailors who are taken care of and the ship which is to be taken care of, and the cargo which is to be brought safely to port, and all those eventualities like winds,

50. John Lewis Gaddis, 'A Grand Strategy of Transformation', *Foreign Policy*, No. 133, Nov. - Dec. 2002, pp. 50-57, p. 50.
51. Michel Foucault, *The Birth of Biopolitics: Lectures at the Collège De France, 1978--1979* Basingstoke: Palgrave Macmillan, 2008, p. 186. Danica Dupont and Frank Pearce, 'Foucault Contra Foucault: Rereading the 'Governmentality' Papers', *Theoretical Criminology,* Vol. 5, No. 2, 2001, pp. 123-58.
52. Thomas Lemke, 'Foucault, Governmentality, and Critique', *Rethinking Marxism: A Journal of Economics, Culture & Society,* Vol. 14, No. 3, 2002, pp. 49-64.

rocks, storms and so on; this is what characterizes the government of a ship."[53]

The operation of a grand strategy in sailing towards a specific objective – its rationality - could have much deeper impacts that that deliberately sought. A grand strategy in itself may seek to systematize, stabilize and regulate the power relationships between those governing and those being governed. Foucault's use of the ship of state metaphor warns that in so doing a grand strategy may have unintended consequences – both positive and negative – that are far-reaching and extend deep inside ones' own society.

Foucault's use of the ship-of-state metaphor further suggests that government involves the "more or less rational application of the appropriate technical means."[54] This assumption that techniques such as grand strategy are rational designs however, may be flawed. The seeming ends-means rationality of grand strategic plans has some logical shortcomings. Historical cases of the ends-means rationality of grand strategies can be examined with the benefit of hindsight, but policy-makers must choose grand strategic alternatives looking forward in time. The real outcomes from their grand strategic choices are obviously unknown, but the very large number of variables involved in a grand strategy suggests that estimated outcomes are more likely to be incorrect than right. However, without a good understanding of the outcomes, the ends-means cost relationship cannot be sensibly comprehended. If it is unknown if the ultimate outcomes will be worth the costs, it is intrinsically impossible to weigh costs in any objective fashion. There is no agreed unit of 'currency', no market value that can be placed on the actual, and the opportunity, costs that implementing a grand strategy imposes. Grand strategy inherently is more than just materially based, as there are issues of values, of fears, of hopes, of honour and of credibility that defy translation into quantitative measures. Ends

53. Michel Foucault, 'Governmentality', in Graham Burchell, Colin Gordon, and Peter Miller (eds.), *The Foucault Effect: Studies in Governmentality: With Two Lectures by and an Interview with Michael Foucault* Chicago: The University of Chicago Press, 1991, pp. 87-104, pp. 93-94.
54. Barry Hindess, *Discourses of Power: From Hobbes to Foucault*; Oxford: Wiley-Blackwell, 1996, p. 106.

and means cannot be readily reconciled in the microeconomic-like manner that the rationalist approach of grand strategy suggests. Indeed, the value of grand strategies in terms of effectiveness and efficiency can only be known in retrospect. In the conception stage, grand strategic alternatives can only be assessed using qualitative measures.

In considering ends there are doubts that the policy-makers and the organizations that implement the grand strategies can have a correct understanding of the desired ends or that this understanding is not distorted by personal or bureaucratic imperatives. Writing about the individual shortcomings of leaders, Richard Betts observes "unconscious emotions and unclear motives, cognitive problems, and cultural biases [can all] prevent strategy from integrating means and ends."[55] Combined with these issues, the necessity of implementing grand strategies through large, complex bureaucracies brings further difficulties. Organizations can distort grand strategic ends and means, making use of these to further their own bureaucratic objectives of growth in power, importance, size, budgets and control of their environment.[56] Moreover, organizations can consciously or unconsciously implement grand strategies using their standard and desired repertoire of actions, even if these have little linkage to the ends sought in a particular circumstance.[57] The means an organization employs can become its own ends, allowing any task the organization can perform to be considered as meeting the policy-maker's grand strategic goals. The instruments and priorities of the bureaucracy can become perceived as the ends of the grand strategy itself.

These problems extend into the policymakers themselves. In some political systems they are assumed to be apolitical while in others they may be political appointees but the differences may have only limited impact on grand strategy development. The technocratic nature of grand strategy formulation should not obscure the reality

---

55. Richard K. Betts, 'Is Strategy an Illusion? ', *International Security*, Vol. 25, No. 2, 2000, pp. 5-50, p. 22.
56. Allison, p. 144-84. Morton H. Halperin, *Bureaucratic Politics and Foreign Policy*; Washington Brookings Institution Press, 1974, pp. 26-62.
57. Allison, pp. 67-100.

that all policymakers as the term suggests are influenced at some level by political considerations. Grand strategy being an interactive social activity is at its core deeply political and the development of grand strategies should be seen in this light. An inherent problem in formulating grand strategy is that there may be bias introduced through the people involved holding particular political positions. Grand strategy as a methodology may seem a technocratic, politically neutral approach but is instead subject, as other methodologies are, to value judgments.

And this brings us to the end of this book. A process has been developed to assist people both *how* to think, and *what* to think about grand strategy. Importantly, and to reiterate, the grand strategy process is only to help people structure their initial thinking. Context and judgment must still be applied to determine sensible, practical grand strategic options. In this, it must be borne in mind that grand strategy is just a problem-solving methodology. Hal Brands in asking what good is grand strategy ends with a warning: "Too often, grand strategy is thought of as a grandiose, transformative project to remake global order, or as a panacea that will wipe away the complexity of world affairs. Both of these aspirations are simply begging for disappointment."[58] Grand strategy as an idea has much to offer but has some real shortcomings and is not suitable for all problems. There are other problem-solving alternatives to also consider.

People use grand strategies to try to go where they wish to. The grand strategies adopted might or might not succeed, but the intention is clear. A grand strategy may fail but if you don't attempt it, events or someone else might choose your destination for you. Grand strategy tries to make the future how we would like it. It's a big, hairy, audacious idea well suited for our complex times.

---

58. Brands, p. 206.

Bibliography

Acharya, Amitav and Buzan, Barry, 'On the Possibility of a non-Western International Relations Theory', in Amitav Acharya and Barry Buzan (eds.), *Non-Western International Relations Theory: Perspectives On and Beyond Asia*; Routledgel, Abingdonl, 2010a, pp. 221-39.

---, 'Why is there no non-Western International Relations Theory? An Introduction', in Amitav Acharya and Barry Buzan (eds.), *Non-Western International Relations Theory: Perspectives On and Beyond Asia*; Routledgel, Abingdonl, 2010b, pp. 1-25.

Allen, Robert C., 'The Rise and Decline of the Soviet Economy', *Canadian Journal of Economics*, Vol. 34, No. 4, November, 2001, pp.

Allison, Graham T., *Essence of Decision: Explaining the Cuban Missile Crisis*; Little Brown and Company, Boston 1971.

Alterman, Jon B., *Iraq and the Gulf States: The Balance of Fear*; United States Institute of Peace Washington August 2007.

---, 'Not in My Backyard: Iraq's Neighbors' Interests', *The Washington Quarterly*, Vol. 26, No. 3, Summer 2003, pp. 149-60.

Angang, Hu and Honghua, Men, 'The rising of modern China: Comprehensive national power and grand strategy', *"Rising China and the East Asian Economy" International Conference by Korea Institute for International Economic Policy*; (March 19-20, Seoul, 2004), 1-36.

'Appeasement reconsidered: Some Neglected Factors', *The Round Table*, Vol. 53, No. 212, 1963, pp. 358-71.

Art, Robert J., *A Grand Strategy for America*; Cornell University Press, Ithaca 2003.

Arthur F. Lykke, Jr., *Military Strategy: Theory and Application*; U.S. Army War College, Carlisle 1989.

Azani, Eitan, *Hezbollah: The Story of the Party of God: From Revolution to Institutionalization*; Palgrave Macmillan, New York 2009.

Bank, World, 'Country Brief - Iran'; (go.worldbank.org/ME0HZPWIB0: World Bank, September 2010).

Barnett, Michael and Duvall, Raymond, 'Power in International Politics', *International Organization*, Vol. 59, No. 1, Winter 2005, pp. 39-75.

Barnett, Michael N., *Confronting the Costs of War: Military Power, State, and Society in Egypt and Israel*; Princeton University Press, Princeton 1992.

Battle, Stephen L., 'Lessons In Legitimacy: The LTTE End-Game Of 2007–2009 ', Naval Postgraduate School, June 2010.

Beier, J. Marshal and Crosby, Ann Denholm, 'Harnessing Change for Continuity: The Play of Political and Economic Forces behind the Ottawa Process', in Maxwell A. Cameron, Brian W. Tomlin, and Robert J. Lawson (eds.), *To Walk without Fear: The Global Movement to Ban Landmines*; Oxford University Pressl, Don MIllsl, 1998, pp. 269-92.

Bensahel, Nora, et al., *After Saddam: Prewar Planning and the Occupation of Iraq*; RAND Corporation, Santa Monica 2008.

Berenskoetter, Felix, 'Thinking about Power', in Felix Berenskoetter and Michael J. Williams (eds.), *Power in World Politics* Routledgel, Abingdonl, 2007, pp. 1-22.

Bergmans, Dr. Hans, et al., 'Working with Scenarios, Risk Assessment and Capabilities: in the National Safety and Security Strategy of the Netherlands'; (The Hague: Ministry of the Interior and Kingdom Relations, October 2009).

Betts, Richard K., 'Is Strategy an Illusion? ', *International Security,* Vol. 25, No. 2, 2000, pp. 5-50.

Bond, Brian, *The Pursuit of Victory: From Napoleon to Saddam Hussein*; Oxford University Press, Oxford 1996.

Brands, H. W., 'George Bush and the Gulf War of 1991', *Presidential Studies Quarterly,* Vol. 34, No. 1, March 2004, pp. 113-31.

Brands, Hal, *What Good is Grand Strategy? Power and Purpose in American Statecraft from Harry S. Truman to George W. Bush*; Cornell University Press, Ithaca 2014.

Brawley, Mark R., *Political Economy and Grand Strategy: A Neoclassical Realist View*; Routledge, Abingdon 2010.

Brooks, Stephen G., *Producing Security: Multinational Corporations, Globalization, and the Changing Calculus of Conflict*; Princeton University Press, Princeton 2005.

Brown, Michael E., et al. (eds.), *America's Strategic Choices: Revised Edition* The MIT Press; Cambridge 2000.

Bukovansky, Mlada, 'Liberal States, International Order, and Legitimacy: An Appeal for Persuasion over Prescription', *International Politics,* Vol. 44, No. 2-3, 2007, pp. 175-93.

Bull, Hedley, *The Anarchical Society: A Study of Order in World Politics*, 2nd Edition edn.; Columbia University Press New York 1995.

Bunce, Valerie, 'The Political Economy of the Brezhnev Era: The Rise and Fall of Corporatism', *British Journal of Political Science* Vol. 13, No. 2, April 1983, pp. 129-58

Bush, George, 'National Security Directive 26 '; (Washington The White House, 2 October 1989).

---, 'National Security Directive 45 '; (Washington: The White House, 20 August 1990).

---, *The Public Papers of the President, 1990. Vol. 2*; Government Printing Office, Washington 1991.

Bush, George H.W. and Scowcroft, Brent, *A World Transformed*; Knopf, New York 1998.

---, *A World Transformed*; Vintage Books, New York 1999.

Bush, George W., *Economic Report of the President*; United States Government Printing Office, Washington February 2003.

Buzan, Barry, Jones, Charles, and Little, Richard, *The Logic of Anarchy: Neorealism to Structural Realism*; Columbia University Press, New York 1993.

Byman, Daniel, *Deadly Connections: States that Sponsor Terrorism* Cambridge University Press, Cambridge 2005.

Byman, Daniel, et al., *Trends in Outside Support for Insurgent Movements*; RAND, Santa Monica 2001.

Cameron, Maxwell A., 'Democratization of Foreign Policy: The Ottawa Process as a Model', in Maxwell A. Cameron, Brian W. Tomlin, and Robert J. Lawson (eds.), *To Walk without Fear: The Global Movement to Ban Landmines*; Oxford University Pressl, Don MIllsl, 1998, pp. 424-47.

Cameron, Maxwell A., Lawson, Robert J., and Tomlin, Brian W., 'To Walk Without Fear', in Maxwell A. Cameron, Brian W. Tomlin, and Robert J. Lawson (eds.), *To Walk without Fear: The Global Movement to Ban Landmines*; Oxford University Pressl, Don MIllsl, 1998, pp. 1-19.

Carr, Edward Hallett, *The Twenty Years' Crisis, 1919-1939: An Introduction to the Study of International Relations*, 2nd edn.; Harper & Row, New York 1939.

Casey, Terence, 'Of Power and Plenty? Europe, Soft Power, and 'Genteel Stagnation'', *Comparative European Politics,* Vol. 4, No. 4, 2006, pp. 399-422.

Centre, Tamil Information, 'Exodus Of Tamils From Jaffna: The Displacement Crisis'; (www. tamilcanadian.com/article/469: TamilCanadian: Tamils True Voice, December 1995).

Checkel, Jeffrey T., 'Social Constructivisms in Global and European Politics (A Review Essay)'; (Oslo, Norway: ARENA Working Papers 15, University of Oslo, 2003).

'Child Soldiers of The Liberation Tiger of Tamil Eelam (LTTE)'; (www. satp.org/satporgtp/countries/shrilanka/terroristoutfits/child_solders.htm [accessed 1 December 2010]: South Asia Terrorism Portal, Institute for Conflict Management, Delhi, India, 2001).

China, Communist Party of, 'Full text of constitution of Communist Party of China', 2012 <english.cpc.people.com.cn/206972/206981/8188065.html>, accessed 22 August 2016.

Chuwattananurak, Wuttikorn, 'China's Comprehensive National Power and Its Implications for the Rise of China: Reassessment and Challenges', *CEEISA-ISA 2016 Joint International Conference*; (23-25 June, University of Ljubljana, 2016), 1-39.

Clark, Tom and Dilnot, Andrew, *Long-Term Trends in British Taxation and Spending* Institute for Fiscal Studies, London 2002a.

---, *Measuring the UK Fiscal Stance since the Second World War* Institute for Fiscal Studies, London 2002b.

Clausewitz, Carl von, *On War: Edited and Translated by Michael Howard and Peter Paret*; Princeton University Press, Princeton 1984.

Clutterbuck, Richard L., *The Long. Long War: Counterinsurgency in Malaya and Vietnam*; Frederick A Praeger, New York 1966.

Coghlan, F., 'Armaments, Economic Policy And Appeasement. Background To British Foreign Policy, 1931-7', *History* Vol. 57, No. 190, June 1972, pp. 205-16.

Colin Powell, with Joseph E. Persico, *My American Journey* Ballantine Books, New York 1995.

Congressional Record: Proceedings and Debates of the 108th Congress First Session April 30, 2003 to May 13, 2003 Volume 149 Part 8 United States Government Printing Office, Washington DC 2003.

Connelly, Matthew, 'Rethinking the Cold War and Decolonization: The Grand Strategy of the Algerian War of Independence', *International Journal of Middle East Studies,* Vol., No. 33, 2001, pp. 221-45.

Corbett, Julian S., *Some Principles of Maritime Strategy* Classics of Sea Power Series; United States Naval Institute, Annapolis 1911 (reprinted 1988).

Cornish, Paul and Dorman, Andrew M., 'Smart muddling through: rethinking UK national strategy beyond Afghanistan', *International Affairs,* Vol. 88, No. 2, 2012, pp. 213-22.

Courtney, Hugh, *20/20 Foresight: Crafting Strategy in an Uncertain World*; Harvard Business School Press, Boston 2001.

Courtney, Hugh, Kirkland, Jane, and Viguerie, Patrick, 'Strategy Under Uncertainty', *Harvard Business Review,* Vol. 75, No. 6, November-December 1997, pp. 66-79.

Cox, Lloyd and O'Connor, Brendon, 'Australia, the US, and the Vietnam and Iraq Wars: 'Hound Dog, not Lapdog'', *Australian Journal of Political Science,* Vol. 47, No. 2, June 2012, pp. 173-87.

Darwin, John, *The Empire Project: The Rise and Fall of the British World-System 1830-1970*; Cambridge University Press, Cambridge 2009.

Davies, Norman, *Europe: A History*; Pimlico, London 1997.

Deery, Phillip, 'The Terminology of Terrorism: Malaya, 1948-52', *Journal of Southeast Asian Studies,* Vol. 34, No. 2, 2003, pp. 231-47.

Defense, US Department of, 'Report on Military Power of Iran '; (Washington, DC US Department of Defense, April 2010).

DeSilva-Ranasinghe, Sergei, 'Land Warfare Lessons from Sri Lanka', *Asian Defence & Diplomacy,* Vol. 16, No. 6, December 2009/January 2010, pp. 29-37.

Dietrich, John W. (ed.), *The George W. Bush Foreign Policy Reader: Presidential Speeches With Commentary*M.E.Sharpe Inc; Armonk 2005.

Divine, Robert A., 'The Persian Gulf War Revisited: Tactical Victory, Strategic Failure', *Diplomatic History,* Vol. 24, No. 1, Winter 2000, pp. 129-38.

Doeser, Fredrik and Eidenfalk, Joakim, 'The importance of windows of opportunity for foreign policy change', *International Area Studies Review,* Vol. 16, No. 4, 2013, pp. 390-406.

Drezner, Daniel W., 'The Grandest Strategy Of Them All', *The Washington Post,* 17 December 2006, pp. B03.

Dueck, Colin, *Reluctant Crusaders: Power, Culture, and Change in American Grand Strategy*; Princeton University Press, Princeton 2006.

Dupont, Danica and Pearce, Frank, 'Foucault contra Foucault: Rereading the 'Governmentality' papers', *Theoretical Criminology,* Vol. 5, No. 2, 2001, pp. 123-58.

'Dutch National Safety and Security Strategy', 2009 <http://www.minbzk.nl/english/subjects/public-safety/national-security/@114278/factsheet-national_0>, accessed 10 June 2010.

Edgerton, David, *Warfare State: Britain 1920-1970*; Cambridge University Press, Cambridge 2006.

Edmunds, Timothy, 'British civil–military relations and the problem of risk', *International Affairs,* Vol. 88, No. 2, 2012, pp. 265-82.

Edrisinha, Rohan, 'Trying Times: Constitutional attempts to resolve armed conflict in Sri Lanka', in Liz Philipson (ed.), *Accord: an International Review of Peace Initiatives - Demanding Sacrifice: War and Negotiation in Sri Lanka*, 4; Conciliation Resourcesl, Londonl, 1998, pp. 28-36.

Esdaile, Charles J., 'De-Constructing the French Wars: Napoleon as Anti-Strategist', *Journal of Strategic Studies,* Vol. 31, No. 4, 2008, pp. 515-52.

F. Gregory Gause, III, 'Iraq's Decisions to Go to War, 1980 and 1990', *The Middle East Journal,* Vol. 56, No. 1, 2002, pp. 47-70.

Fair, C. Christine, *Urban Battle Fields of South Asia: Lessons Learned from Sri Lanka, India, and Pakistan*; RAND, Santa Monica 2004.

Fater, David H., *Essentials of Corporate and Capital Formation*; John Wiley & Sons, Inc, Hoboken 2010.

Feith, Douglas J., *War and Decision: Inside the Pentagon at the Dawn of the War on Terrorism*; Harper, New York 2008.

Feyerabend, Paul, 'Explanation, Reduction, and Empiricism', in Yuri Balashov and Alex Rosenberg (eds.), *Philosophy of Science: Contemporary Readings*; Routledgel, London, UKl, 2002, pp. 141-63.

Fiske, S. T. and Taylor, S. E., *Social Cognition*; Addison-Wesley, Reading 1984.

Flanigan, Shawn Teresa, 'Nonprofit Service Provision by Insurgent Organizations: The Cases of Hizballah and the Tamil Tigers', *Studies in Conflict and Terrorism,* Vol. 31, No. 6, 2008, pp. 499-519.

Flibbert, Andrew, 'The Road to Baghdad: Ideas and Intellectuals in Explanations of the Iraq War', *Security Studies,* Vol. 15, No. 2, 2006, pp. 310-52.

Flournoy, Michèle A., et al., 'Making America Grand Again', in Michèle A. Flournoy and Shawn Brimley (eds.), *Finding Our Way: Debating American Grand Strategy*; Center for a New American Securityl, Washingtonl, 2008, pp. 123-50.

Fontaine, Richard and Lord, Kristin M., 'Debating America's Future', in Richard Fontaine and Kristin M. Lord (eds.), *America's Path: Grand Strategy for the Next Administration*; Center for a New American Securityl, Washingtonl, May 2012, pp. 3-12.

Fontaine, Richard and Nagl, John, *Contracting in Conflicts: The Path to Reform*; Center for a New American Security Washington June 2010.

Forgang, William G., *Strategy-Specific Decision Making: A Guide for Executing Competitive Strategy*; M.E.Sharpe, Inc, Armonk 2004.

Foucault, Michel, 'Governmentality', in Graham Burchell, Colin Gordon, and Peter Miller (eds.), *The Foucault Effect: Studies in Governmentality: with two lectures by and an interview with Michael Foucault* The University of Chicago Pressl, Chicagol, 1991, pp. 87-104.

---, *The Birth of Biopolitics: Lectures at the Collège de France, 1978--1979* Palgrave Macmillan, Basingstoke 2008.

Freedman, Lawrence, *A Choice of Enemies: America Confronts the Middle East*; PublicAffairs, New York 2008.

---, *Strategy: A History* Oxford University Press, Oxford 2013.

---, 'On War and Choice', *The National Interest,* Vol., No. 107, May-June, 2010 pp. 9-16.

Friedberg, Aaron L., *In the Shadow of the Garrison State: America's Anti-Statism and Its Cold War Grand Strategy*; Princeton University Press, Princeton 2000.

Fuller, Col. J.F.C., *The Reformation of War (2nd Edition)*; Hutchinson and Co, London 1923

Fuller, Graham E., 'The Hizballah-Iran Connection: Model for Sunni Resistance', in Alexander T. J. Lennon (ed.), *The Epicenter of Crisis: The New Middle East*; The MIT Pressl, Cambridgel, 2008, pp. 207-20.

Gaddis, John Lewis, 'What is Grand Strategy? Karl Von Der Heyden Distinguished Lecture ', *American Grand Strategy after War*; (Triangle Institute for Security Studies and the Duke University Program in American Grand Strategy: Duke University 26 February 2009).

---, *The Cold War: A New History*; The Penguin Press, New York 2005.

---, 'A Grand Strategy of Transformation', *Foreign Policy,* Vol., No. 133, Nov. - Dec. 2002, pp. 50-57.

Gambill, Gary C. and Abdelnour, Ziad K., 'Hezbollah between Tehran and Damascus', *Middle East Intelligence Bulletin,* Vol. 4, No. 2, February 2002, pp. meforum.org/meib/articles/0202_ll.htm.

Gathoff, Raymond L., *Detente and Confrontation: American-Soviet Relations from Nixon to Reagan*; Brookings Institution Press, Washington Revised Edition 1994.

George, Alexander L., 'The "Operational Code": A Neglected Approach to the Study of Political Leaders and Decision-Making', *International Studies Quarterly,* Vol. 13, No. 2, 1969, pp. 190-222.

---, *Presidential Decisionmaking in Foreign Policy: The Effective Use of Information and Advice* Westview Press, Boulder 1980.

---, *Bridging the Gap: Theory and Practice in Foreign Policy*; United States Institute of Peace, Washington 1993.

George, Alexander L. and Bennett, Andrew, *Case Studies and Theory development in the Social Sciences*, BCSIA Studies in International Security; MIT Press, Cambridge 2005.

Gilbert, Martin and Gott, Richard, *The Appeasers*, 2nd edn.; Weidenfield and Nicholson, London 2nd Edn 1967.

Gillard, David, *Appeasement in Crisis: From Munich to Prague, October 1938- March 1939* Palgrave Macmillan, Basingstoke 2007.

Gilpin, Robert, *The Political Economy of International Relations*; Princeton University Press International, Princeton 1987.

---, *Global Political Economy: Understanding the International Economic Order*; Princeton University Press, Princeton 2001.

Goldstein, Erik, 'Neville Chamberlain, the British official mind and the Munich crisis,' *Diplomacy & Statecraft,* Vol. 10, No. 2-3, 1999, pp. 276-92.

Goodhand, Jonathan, *Aid, conflict and peace building in Sri Lanka*, Conflict Assessments; Conflict, Security and Development Group, King's College, University of London, London July 2001.

Goose, Stephen and Williams, Jody, 'The Campaign to Ban Antipersonnel Landmines', in Richard Anthony Matthew, Bryan McDonald, and Kenneth R. Rutherford (eds.), *Landmines And Human Security: International Politics And War's Hidden Legacy*; State University of New York Pressl, Albanyl, 2006, pp. 239-50.

Gorbachev, Mikhail, 'Speech to the 43rd U.N. General Assembly Session'; (New York, 7 December 1988).

Gordon, Michael R. and Trainor, Bernard E., *Cobra II: The Inside Story of the Invasion and Occupation of Iraq*; Pantheon Books, New York 2006.

---, *The Endgame: The Inside Story of the Struggle for Iraq, from George W. Bush to Barack Obama*; Vintage Books, New York 2013.

Grant, Robert M., 'Strategic Planning in a Turbulent Environment: Evidence from the Oil Majors', *Strategic Management Journal,* Vol. 24, 2003, pp. 491-517.

Gray, Colin S., *The Strategy Bridge: Theory for Practice*; Oxford University Press, Oxford 2010.

Grob-Fitzgibbon, Benjamin, *Imperial Endgame: Britain's Dirty Wars and the End of Empire*; Palgrave Macmillan, Basingstoke 2011.

---, 'Securing the Colonies for the Commonwealth: Counterinsurgency, Decolonization, and the Development of British Imperial Strategy in the Postwar Empire', *British Scholar,* Vol. II, No. 1, September 2009, pp. 12-39.

Grosser, Alfred, *The Western Alliance: European-American Relations Since 1945* The MacMillan Press, London 1980.

Gunaratna, Rohan, 'Sri Lanka: Feeding the Tamil Tigers', in Karen Ballentine and Jake Sherman (eds.), *The Political Economy of Armed Conflict: Beyond Greed and Grievance*; Lynne Rienner Publishersl, Boulderl, 2003, pp. 197-224.

Haass, Richard N, *War of Necessity, War of Choice: A Memoir of Two Iraq Wars*; Simon & Schuste, New York 2009.

Habeck, Mary, 'Attacking America: Al-Qaida's Grand Strategy in its War with the World', *Templeton Lecture on Religion and World Affairs* (Philadelphia: Foreign Policy Research Institute 3 October 2013).

Hack, Karl, 'British intelligence and counter-insurgency in the era of decolonisation: The example of Malaya', *Intelligence and National Security,* Vol. 14, No. 2, Summer 1999, pp. 124-55.

Hagmann, Jonas and Cavelty, Myriam Dunn, 'National risk registers: Security scientism and the propagation of permanent insecurity', *Security Dialogue,* Vol. 43, No. 1, 2012, pp. 79-96.

Halperin, Morton H., *Bureaucratic Politics and Foreign Policy*; Brookings Institution Press, Washington 1974.

Hamby, Joel E., 'Civil-Military Operations: Joint Doctrine and the Malayan Emergency ', *JFQ: Joint Force Quarterly,* Vol., No. 32, 2002, pp. 54-61.

Hamieh, Christine Sylva and Ginty, Roger Mac, 'A very political reconstruction: governance and reconstruction in Lebanon after the 2006 war', *Disasters,* Vol., No. 34(S1), 2010, pp. S103–S23.

Hamzeh, Nizar, 'Lebanon's Hizbullah: From Islamic Revolution to Parliamentary Accommodation', *Third World Quarterly,* Vol. 14, No. 2, 1993, pp. 321-37.

Harper, T. N., *The End of Empire and the Making of Malaya*; Cambridge University Press, Cambridge 2001.

Hattendorf, John B., *England in the War of the Spanish Succession: A Study of the English View and Conduct of Grand Strategy, 1702-1712*; Garland, New York 1987.

Heerkens, Gary R., *The Business-Savvy Project Manager: Indispensable Knowledge and Skills for Success* McGraw-Hill, New York 2006.

Hindess, Barry, *Discourses of power: From Hobbes to Foucault*; Wiley-Blackwell, Oxford 1996.

Hitz, Zena, 'Degenerate Regimes in Plato's Republic', in Plato's 'Republic': A Critical Guide (ed.); Cambridge University Pressl, Cambridgel, 2010, pp. 103-31.

Hobson, John M., *The State and International Relations*; Cambridge University Press, Cambridge 2000.

Hoffman, Paul, 'The Marshall Plan: Peace Building-Its Price and Its Profits', *Foreign Service Journal* Vol. 44, No. June, 1967, pp. 19-21.

Hoffman, Stanley, 'An American Social Science: International Relations', *Daedalus,* Vol. 106, No. 3, Summer 1977, pp. 41-60.

Hogan, Michael J., *The Marshall Plan: America, Britain and the Reconstruction of Western Europe, 1947-1952*; Cambridge University Press, Cambridge 1987.

Hopf, Ted, 'The Promise of Constructivism in International Relations Theory', *International Security,* Vol. 23, No. 1, 1998, pp. 171-200.

Hormats, Robert D., *The Price of Liberty: Paying for America's Wars*; Times Books, New York 2007.

House of Commons, Public Administration Select and Committee, *Strategic thinking in Government: without National Strategy, can viable Government strategy emerge? Vol.I*; The Stationery Office Limited, London 24 April 2012.

Howard, Michael, *Continental Commitment: The Dilemma of British Defence Policy in the Era of the Two World Wars*; Temple Smith, London 1972.

Hurrell, Andrew, 'Legitimacy and the use of force: can the circle be squared?', *Review of International Studies,* Vol. 31, No. Supplement S1, 2005, pp. 15-31.

Husseini, Rola El, 'Hezbollah and the Axis of Refusal: Hamas, Iran and Syria', *Third World Quarterly,* Vol. 31, No. 5, 2010, pp. 803-15.

Ikenberry, G. John, *After Victory: Institutions, Strategic Restraint, and the Rebuilding of Order after Major Wars*; Princeton University Press, Princeton 2001.

---, 'An Agenda for Liberal International Renewal', in Michèle A. Flournoy and Shawn Brimley (eds.), *Finding Our Way: Debating American Grand Strategy*; Center for a New American Securityl, Washingtonl, 2008, pp. 43-60.

---, *Liberal Leviathan: The Origins, Crisis, and Transformation of the American World Order*; Princeton University Press, Princeton 2011.

Isenberg, David, *Private Military Contractors and U.S. Grand Strategy*, PRIO Report 1/2009; International Peace Research Institute, Oslo 2009.

Jackson, Ian, 'The Geopolitics of President George W. Bush's Foreign Economic Policy', *International Politics*, Vol. 44, No. 5, 2007, pp. 572-95.

Jackson, Patrick Thaddeus, *The Conduct of Inquiry in International Relations: Philosophy of Science and Its Implications for the Study of World Politics*; Routledge, Abingdon 2011.

Jackson, Robert, *The Malayan Emergency: the Commonwealth's Wars 1948-1960*; Routledge, London 1991.

Jackson, Robert and Sorensen, Georg, *Introduction to International Relations: Theories and Approaches: 4th Edition*; Oxford University Press, Oxford 2010.

James A. Baker, III with Thomas M.DeFrank, *The Politics of Diplomacy: Revolution, War and Peace, 1989-1992*; G.P.Putnam's Sons, New York 1995.

Jervis, Robert, *Systems Effects: Complexity in Political and Social Life*; Princeton University Press, Princeton 1997.

Jeyaraj, D.B.S., 'Ramifications of crackdown on LTTE in Switzerland'; (Toronto, Canada: dbsjeyaraj.com/dbsj/archives/1952, 28 January 2011).

Jiangli, Wang and Buzan, Barry, 'The English and Chinese Schools of International Relations: Comparisons and Lessons', *The Chinese Journal of International Politics*, Vol. 7, No. 1, 2014, pp. 1-46.

Johnston, Alastair Iain, *Cultural Realism: Strategic Culture and Grand Strategy in Chinese History*; Princeton University Press, Princeton 1995.

Judt, Tony, *Postwar: A History of Europe Since 1945*; The Penguin Press, New York 2005.

Kagan, Donald, *On the Origins of War: And the Preservation of Peace*; Anchor Books, New York 1996.

Kagan, Frederick W., 'Grand Strategy for the United States', in Michèle A. Flournoy and Shawn Brimley (eds.), *Finding Our Way: Debating American Grand Strategy*; Center for a New American Securityl, Washingtonl, 2008, pp. 61-80.

Kagan, Kimberly, 'Redefining Roman Grand Strategy', *The Journal of Military History,* Vol. 70, No. 2, April 2006, pp. 333-62.

Kahneman, Daniel and Tversky, Amos, 'Prospect Theory: An Analysis of Decision under Risk', *Econometrica,* Vol. 47, No. 2, March 1979, pp. 263-91.

Kaldor, Mary, *New and Old Wars: Organized Violence in a Global Era, 3rd Edition*; Stanford University Press, Stanford 2012.

Karabell, Zachary, 'Backfire: US Policy toward Iraq, 1988 - 2 August 1990 ', *Middle East Journal,* Vol. 49, No. 1, Winter 1995, pp. 28-47.

Katzenstein, Peter J. and Sil, Rudra, 'Rethinking Asian Security: A Case for Analytical Eclecticism', in Peter J. Katzenstein (ed.), *Rethinking Japanese Security: Internal and External Dimensions*; Routledgel, Oxonl, 2008, pp. 249-85.

Katzman, Kenneth, 'Hizbollah: Narrowing Options in Lebanon', in Stephen C. Pelletiere (ed.), *Terrorism: National Security Policy and the Home Front*; Strategic Studies Institute, U.S. Army War Collegel, Carlisle Barracksl, 1995, pp. 5-27.

Keller, Bill, 'The Sunshine Warrior', *The New York Times Magazine,* 22 September 2002, pp. 50-54, 88.

Kennedy, Paul, *Strategy and Diplomacy 1870-1945: Eight Studies*; Fontana Paperbacks, Aylesbury 1984.

---, *The Rise and Fall of the Great Powers: Economic Change and Military Conflict from 1500 to 2000*; Vintage Books, New York 1989.

---, 'Grand Strategy in War and Peace: Toward a Broader Definition', in Paul Kennedy (ed.), *Grand Strategies in War and Peace*; Yale University Pressl, New Havenl, 1991, pp. 1-7.

Keohane, Robert O., 'The old IPE and the new', *Review of International Political Economy,* Vol. 16, No. 1, February 2009, pp. 34-46.

Keyt, David, 'Plato and the Ship of State', in Gerasimos Santas (ed.), *The Blackwell Guide to Plato's Republic*; Blackwell Publishing Ltdl, Oxfordl, 2008, pp. 189-213.

Kheng, Cheah Boon, 'The Communist Insurgency In Malaysia, 1948-90: Contesting The Nation-State And Social Change', *New Zealand Journal of Asian Studies,* Vol. 11, No. 1, June 2009, pp. 132-52.

Khong, Yuen Foong, *Analogies at War: Korea, Munich, Dien Bien Phu, and the Vietnam Decisions of 1965* Princeton University Press, Princeton 1992.

Kirshner, Jonathan, 'Political Economy in Security Studies After the Cold War', *Peace Studies Program*; (Ithaca, NY: Cornell University, April 1997).

Komer, R. W., 'The Malayan Emergency in Retrospect: Organization of A Successful Counterinsurgency Effort'; (Santa Monica, CA: RAND, 1972).

Kontorovicha, Vladimir and Weinb, Alexander, 'What did the Soviet Rulers Maximise?', *Europe-Asia Studies,* Vol. 61, No. 9, 2009, pp. 1579-601.

Kosiak, Steven M., *Cost of the Wars in Iraq and Afghanistan, and Other Military Operations Through 2008 and Beyond*; Center for Strategic and Budgetary Assessments, Washington 2008.

Krieger, David, 'The war in Iraq as illegal and illegitimate', in Ramesh Chandra Thakur and Waheguru Pal Singh Sidhu (eds.), *Iraq Crisis and World Order: Structural, Institutional and Normative Challenges*; United Nations University Pressl, Tokyol, 2006, pp. 381-96.

Kristensen, Peter M. and Nielsen, Ras T., 'Constructing a Chinese International Relations Theory: A Sociological Approach to Intellectual Innovation', *International Political Sociology,* Vol. 7, No. 1, 2013, pp. 19-40.

Ku, Charlotte, 'Legitimacy as an assessment of existing legal standards: The case of the 2003 Iraq war', in Ramesh Chandra Thakur and Waheguru Pal Singh Sidhu (eds.), *Iraq Crisis and World Order: Structural, Institutional and Normative Challenges*; United Nations University Pressl, Tokyol, 2006, pp. 397-412.

Kuisong, Yang, 'The Sino-Soviet Border Clash of 1969: From Zhenbao Island to Sino-American Rapprochement', *Cold War History*, Vol. 1, No. 1, August 2000, pp. 21-52.

Kunz, Diane B., 'The Marshall Plan Reconsidered: A Complex of Motives', *Foreign Affairs*, Vol. 76, No. 3, May-June 1997, pp. 162-70.

Kuppusamy, Chellamuthu, *Prabhakaran: The Story of his struggle for Eelam* [online text], Kindle Edition, Amazon Digital Services, 2013,

Labonte, Marc and Levit, Mindy, *CRS Report for Congress: Financing Issues and Economic Effects of American Wars*; Congressional Research Service, Washington July 29, 2008.

Larrinaga, Miguel de and Sjolander, Claire Turenne, '(Re)Presenting Landmines from the Protector to Enemy: The Discursive Framing of a New Multilateralism ', in Maxwell A. Cameron, Brian W. Tomlin, and Robert J. Lawson (eds.), *To Walk without Fear: The Global Movement to Ban Landmines*; Oxford University Pressl, Don MIllsl, 1998, pp. 364-91.

Larson, Deborah Welch, 'The Role of Belief Systems and Schemas in Foreign Policy Decision-Making', Political Psychology', *Political Psychology*, Vol. 15, No. 1, 1994, pp. 17-33.

Lasswell, Harold D., *Politics: Who Gets What, When, How*; McGraw-Hill, New York 1958.

Lawson, Alastair, 'The enigma of Prabhakaran', *BBC News*, 2 May 2000. <news.bbc.co.uk/2/hi/south_asia/212361.stm>, accessed 24 October 2013.

Lawson, Fred H., 'Rethinking the Iraqi Invasion of Kuwait', *The Review of International Affairs*, Vol. 1, No. 1, 2001, pp. 1-20.

Layne, Christopher, *The Peace of Illusions: American Grand Strategy from 1940 to the Present*; Cornell University Press, Ithaca 2006.

---, 'Security Studies and the Use of History: Neville Chamberlain's Grand Strategy Revisited', *Security Studies*, Vol. 17, No. 3, 2008, pp. 397-437.

---, 'The Influence of Theory on Grand Strategy: The United States and a Rising China', in Annette Freyberg-Inan, Ewan Harrison, and Patrick James (eds.), *Rethinking Realism in International Relations*; The Johns Hopkins University Pressl, Baltimorel, 2009, pp. 103-35.

---, 'Rethinking American Grand Strategy: Hegemony or Balance of Power in the Twenty-First Century?', *World Policy Journal*, Vol. 15, No. 2, Summer 1998, pp. 8-28.

Layton, Peter, (26 April 2013), 'A better way to make national security decisions'. Australian Broadcasting Commission <www.abc.net.au/unleashed/4651120.html>

LeDonne, John P., *The Grand Strategy of the Russian Empire, 1650-1831*; Oxford University Press, Oxford 2004.

Leffler, Melvyn P., *For the Soul of Mankind: The United States, the Soviet Union and the Cold War*; Hill and Wang New York 2007.

---, '9/11 in Retrospect: George W. Bush's Grand Strategy, Reconsidered', *Foreign Affairs*, Vol. 90, No. 5, September/ October 2011, pp. 33-44.

Leibsohn, Seth, et al., 'TRANSCRIPT: America, Iraq and the War on Terrorism, UCLA (April 2, 2003)'; (http://www.claremont.org/projects/pageID.2499/default.asp: The Claremont Institute

Lemke, Thomas, 'Foucault, Governmentality, and Critique', *Rethinking Marxism: A Journal of Economics, Culture & Society*, Vol. 14, No. 3, 2002, pp. 49-64.

Lichbach, Mark I., *Is Rational Choice All of Social Science?*; University of Michigan Press, Ann Arbor 2003.

Liddell-Hart, B.H., *The decisive wars of history: a study in strategy*; G.Bell & Sons, London 1929.

---, *Strategy*, 2nd Revised edn.; Penguin, New York 1991.

Lieber, Robert J., *The American Era: Power and Strategy for the 21st Century*; Cambridge University Press, New York 2005.

Lilja, Jannie, 'Trapping Constituents or Winning Hearts and Minds? Rebel Strategies to Attain Constituent Support in Sri Lanka', *Terrorism and Political Violence*, Vol. 21, No. 2, 2009, pp. 306-26.

Lipschutz, Ronnie D., 'On the transformational potential of global civil society', in Felix Berenskoetter and Michael J. Williams (eds.), *Power in World Politics* Routledgel, Abingdonl, 2007, pp. 225-43.

Lobell, Steven E., 'The grand strategy of hegemonic decline: Dilemmas of strategy and finance', *Security Studies*, Vol. 10, No. 1, 2000, pp. 86-111.

---, 'The second face of security: Britain's 'Smart' appeasement policy towards Japan and Germany', *International Relations of the Asia-Pacific*, Vol. 7, No. 1, 2007, pp. 73-98.

Lock, Edward, 'Soft power and strategy: Developing a 'strategic' concept of power', in Inderjeet Parmar and Michael Cox (eds.), *Soft Power and US Foreign Policy: Theoretical, Historical and Contemporary Perspectives* Routledgel, Abingdonl, 2010, pp. 32-50.

Luttwak, Edward N., *Strategy: The Logic of War and Peace*; Belknap Press, Cambridge 1987.

Luvaas, Jay, 'Clausewitz, Fuller and Liddell Hart', *Journal of Strategic Studies*, Vol. 9, No. 2-3, 1986, pp. 197-212.

MacDonald, C. A., 'Economic Appeasement and the German "Moderates" 1937-1939: An Introductory Essay', *Past & Present* Vol., No. 56, August 1972, pp. 105-35.

MacDonald, David, 'The Power of Ideas in International Relations', in Nadine Godehardt and Dirk Nabers (eds.), *Regional Powers and Regional Orders*; Routledgel, Abingdonl, 2011, pp. 33-48.

MacDonald, David B., *Thinking History, Fighting Evil: Neoconservatives and the Perils of Analogy in American Politics*; Rowman & Littlefield Publishers, Lanham 2009.

Macdonald, Scot, 'Hitler's Shadow: Historical Analogies and the Iraqi Invasion of Kuwait', *Diplomacy & Statecraft,* Vol. 13, No. 4, December 2002, pp. 29-59.

Machado, Barry, *In Search of a Usable Past: The Marshall Plan and Postwar Reconstruction Today*; George C. Marshall Foundation, Lexington 2007.

Malone, David M, *The International Struggle Over Iraq: Politics in the UN Security Council 1980-2005*; Oxford University Press, Oxford 2006.

Mandelbaum, Michael, *The Fate of Nations: The Search for National Security in the Nineteenth and Twentieth Centuries* Cambridge University Press, Cambridge 1988.

Marcella, Gabriel, *American Grand Strategy For Latin America In The Age Of Resentment*; Strategic Studies Institute, Carlisle September 2007.

The "Marshall Plan" speech at Harvard University, 5 June 1947 (Organisation for Economic Co-operation and Development 1947), Marshall, George C. (dir.).

Mastanduno, Michael, Lake, David A., and Ikenberry, G. John, 'Toward a Realist Theory of State Action ', *International Studies Quarterly* Vol. 33, No. 4, December 1989, pp. 457-74.

Matthew, Richard A., 'Human Security and the MIne Ban Movement 1: Introduction', in Richard Anthony Matthew, Bryan McDonald, and Kenneth R. Rutherford (eds.), *Landmines And Human Security: International Politics And War's Hidden Legacy*; State University of New York Pressl, Albanyl, 2006, pp. 3-20.

Maurice, Sir Frederick, *British Strategy: a study of the application of the principles of war*; Constable and Co, London 1929.

McDermott, Rose, *Political Psychology in International Relations*; The University of Michigan Press, Ann Arbor 2004.

McDonough, Frank, *Neville Chamberlain, appeasement and the British road to war*; Manchester University Press, Manchester 1998.

Mearsheimer, John J., *The Tragedy of Great Power Politics*; W.W. Norton and Company, Inc New York 2001.

Mehta, Ashok, *Sri Lanka's Ethnic Conflict: How Eelam War IV was Won*, Manekshaw Paper No.22; Centre for Land Warfare Studies, New Delhi 2010.

Metz, Steven, *Iraq and the Evolution of American Strategy*; Potomac Books, Inc., Washington 2008.

---, *Decisionmaking In Operation Iraqi Freedom: Removing Saddam Hussein By Force*, ed. John R. Martin, Operation IRAQI FREEDOM Key Decisions Monograph Series; Strategic Studies Institute, U.S. Army War College, Carlisle 2010.

Middlemas, Keith, *The Strategy of Appeasement: The British Government and Germany, 1937-39*; Quadrangle Books, Chicago 1972.

Milevski, Lukas, *The Modern Evolution of Grand Strategic Thought*; Oxford University Press, Oxford 2016.

Miller, Edward, *War Plan Orange: The U.S. Strategy to Defeat Japan, 1897-1945*; United States Naval Insititute Annapolis 1991.

Miller, Eric A. and Yetiv, Steve A., 'The New World Order in Theory and Practice: The Bush Administration's Worldview in Transition', *Presidential Studies Quarterly*, Vol. 31, No. 1, March 2001, pp. 56-68.

Mills, Nicolaus, *Winning the Peace: The Marshall Plan and America's Coming of Age as a Superpower*; John Wiley & Sons, Hoboken 2008.

Milward, Alan S., *War, Economy and Society 1939-1945*; University of California Press, Berkeley 1979.

---, *The Reconstruction of Western Europe, 1945-51*; Routledge, London 1987.

---, *The Rise and Fall of a National Strategy 1945-1963: The United Kingdom and The European Community Volume 1*; Routledge, Abingdon 2012.

Mintz, Alex, 'How Do Leaders Make Decisions? A Poliheuristic Perspective', *The Journal of Conflict Resolution*, Vol. 48, No. 1, 2004, pp. 3-13.

Mintz, Alex and DeRouen, Karl, *Understanding Foreign Policy Decision Making*; Cambridge University Press New York 2010.

Mintzberg, Henry and Waters, James A., 'Of Strategies, Deliberate and Emergent', *Strategic Management Journal*, Vol. 6, 1985, pp. 257-72.

Monroe, Kristen Renwick, 'Paradigm Shift: From Rational Choice to Perspective', *International Political Science Review*, Vol. 22, No. 2, 2001, pp. 151-72.

Monteiro, Nuno P. and Ruby, Keven G., 'IR and the false promise of philosophical foundations', *International Theory*, Vol. 1, No. 1, 2009, pp. 15-48.

Moran, Michael, Rein, Martin, and Goodin, Robert E., 'The Public and its Policies', in Michael Moran, Martin Rein, and Robert E. Goodin (eds.), *The Oxford Handbook of Public Policy*; Oxford University Pressl, New Yorkl, 2006, pp. 3-35.

Moravcsik, Andrew, 'Liberal International Relations Theory: A Social Scientific Assessment', *Weatherhead Center for International Affairs Working Papers*; (Cambridge, MA: Harvard University, 2001).

---, 'Theory Synthesis in International Relations: Real Not Metaphysical', *International Studies Review*, Vol. 5, No. 1, 2003, pp. 131-36.

Murdock, Graham, 'Notes From The Number One Country: Herbert Schiller on culture, commerce and American power', *International Journal of Cultural Policy*, Vol. 12, No. 2, 2006, pp. 209-27.

Nagal, John A., *Learning to Eat Soup with a Knife: Counterinsurgency Lessons from Malaya and Vietnam*; The University of Chicago Press, Chicago 2005.

Narizny, Kevin, *The Political Economy of Grand Strategy*; Cornell University Press, Ithaca 2007.

Nation, R. Craig, *Black Earth, Red Star: A History of Soviet Security Policy, 1917-1991*; Cornell University, Ithaca 1992.

Neustadt, Richard E. and May, Ernest R., *Thinking in Time: The Uses of History for Decisionmakers* The Free Press, New York 1986.

Newnham, Randall, '"Coalition of the Bribed and Bullied?" U.S. Economic Linkage and the Iraq War Coalition', *International Studies Perspectives*, Vol. 9, No. 2, 2008, pp. 183-200.

Newton, Scott, 'The 'Anglo-German connection' and the political economy of appeasement', *Diplomacy & Statecraft*, Vol. 2, No. 3, 1991, pp. 178-207.

Nichols, George Ward, *The Story of the Great March: From the Diary of a Staff Officer*; Harper & Brothers New York 1865.

Norton, Augustus Richard, 'Hizballah and the Israeli Withdrawal from Southern Lebanon', *Journal of Palestine Studies* Vol. 30, No. 1, 2000, pp. 22-35.

---, *Hezbollah: A Short History*; Princeton University Press, Princeton 2007.

Nye, Joseph S., *The Future of Power*; PublicAffairs New York 2011.

O'Ballance, Edgar, *Malaya: The Communist Insurgent War: 1948-1960*; Faber and Faber, London 1966.

'Obituary: Prabhakaran', *The Economist*, 21 May 2009. <economist.com/node/13687889>, accessed 24 October 2013.

Ouimet, Matthew J., *The Rise and Fall of the Brezhnev Doctrine in Soviet Foreign Policy*; The University of North Carolina Press, Chapel Hill 2003.

Pape, Robert A., *Dying to Win: The Strategic Logic of Suicide Terrorism*; Random House New York 2005.

Parasiliti, Andrew T., 'The Causes and Timing of Iraq's Wars: A Power Cycle Assessment', *International Political Science Review*, Vol. 24, No. 1, 2003, pp. 151-65.

Parker, Geoffrey, *The Grand Strategy of Philip II*; Yale University Press, New Haven 2000.

Parker, R.A.C., *Chamberlain and Appeasement: British Policy and the Coming of the Second World War*; Palgrave Macmillan, Basingstoke 1993.

'Patterns of Global Terrorism 2001'; (Washington: United States Department of State, May 2002).

Pearton, Maurice, *The Knowledgeable State: Diplomacy, War and Technology since 1830*; Burnett Books, London 1982.

Peden, G.C., *British Rearmament and the Treasury, 1932–1939*; Scottish Academic Press, Edinburgh 1979.

---, *Arms, Economics and British Strategy: From Dreadnoughts to Hydrogen Bombs*; Cambridge University Press, Cambridge 2007.

Philipson, Liz and Thangarajah, Yuvi, *The Politics of the North-East: Part of the Sri Lanka Strategic Conflict Assessment 2005*; The Asia Foundation, Colombo 2005.

Plato, *Plato: Republic, Volume II: Books 6-10*, ed. Edited and Translated by Christopher Emlyn-Jones and William Preddy, Loeb Classical Library; Harvard University Press, Harvard 2013.

Porter, Wayne and Mykleby, Mark, *A National Strategic Narrative by Mr.Y*; Woodrow Wilson Center, Washington 2011.

Posen, Barry R., *The Sources of Military Doctrine: France, Britain, and Germany Between the World Wars*; Cornell University Press, Ithaca 1984.

---, 'A Grand Strategy of Restraint', in Michèle A Flournoy and Shawn Brimley (eds.), *Finding our Way: Debating American Grand Strategy*; Center for a New American Securityl, Washingtonl, June 2008, pp. 81-102.

Posen, Barry R. and Ross, Andrew L., 'Competing Visions of U.S. Grand Strategy', *International Security*, Vol. 21, No. 3, Winter 1996/97, pp. 3-51.

Prabhakaran, V., 'LTTE Leader Calls Upon Sri Lanka To End Military Oppression For Peace Talks', [accessed 26 November 2010] edn.; (London, UK: International Secretariat of LTTE, 1999).

Price, Richard, 'Reversing the Gun Sights: Transnational Civil Society Targets Land Mines', *International Organization,* Vol. 52, No. 3, Summer 1998, pp. 613-44.

Quiggin, John, 'Economic Constraints on Public Policy', in Michael Moran, Martin Rein, and Robert E. Goodin (eds.), *The Oxford Handbook of Public Policy*; Oxford University Pressl, New Yorkl, 2006, pp. 529-42.

Ramakrishna, Kumar, *Emergency Propaganda: The Winning of Malayan Hearts and Minds 1948-1958*; Curzon Press, Richmond 2002.

Ranstorp, Magnus, *Hizb'Allah in Lebanon: The Politics of the Western Hostage Crisis*; MacMillan Press, Basingstoke 1997.

Rathbun, Brian, 'A Rose by Any Other Name: Neoclassical Realism as the Logical and Necessary Extension of Structural Realism', *Security Studies,* Vol. 17, No. 2, 2008, pp. 294-321.

'Remarks and Exchange with Reporters, August 5, 1990 ', *Public Papers of the Presidents: George Bush*; (College Station: George Bush Library, 1990).

Renshon, Jonathan and Renshon, Standley A., 'The Theory and Practice of Foreign Policy Decision Making', *Political Psychology,* Vol. 29, No. 2, 2008, pp. 509-36.

Reus-Smit, Christian, 'International Crises of Legitimacy', *International Politics,* Vol. 44, No. 2-3, 2007, pp. 157-74.

Ricks, Thomas E., 'War Plans Target Hussein Power Base: Scenarios Feature A Smaller Force, Narrower Strikes ', *Washington Post* 22 September 2002, pp. A01.

Ripsman, Norrin M. and Levy, Jack S., 'Wishful Thinking or Buying Time?: The Logic of British Appeasement in the 1930s', *International Security,* Vol. 33, No. 2, Fall 2008, pp. 148-81.

Roberts, Geoffrey, *The Soviet Union in World Politics: Coexistence, Revolution and Cold War, 1945-1991*; Routledge, London 1999.

Roi, Michael L., *Alternative to Appeasement: Sir Robert Vansittart and Alliance Diplomacy, 1934-1937*; Praeger Publishers, Westport 1997.

Rothberg, Robert I., 'Sri Lanka's Civil War: From Mayhem toward Diplomatic Resolution', in Robert I. Rothberg (ed.), *Creating Peace in Sri Lanka: Civil War and Reconciliation*; (Washington: Brookings Institution Press; , 1999), 1-16.

Rubin, Michael, *Deciphering Iranian Decision Making and Strategy Today*, Middle Eastern Outlook; American Enterprise Institute Washington January 2013.

Rudner, Martin, 'Hizbullah: An Organizational and Operational Profile', *International Journal of Intelligence and CounterIntelligence,* Vol. 23, No. 2, 2010, pp. 226-46.

Rutherford, Kenneth, 'Post-Cold War Superpower? Mid-size State and NGO Collaboration in Banning Landmines', in Kenneth Rutherford, Stefan Brem, and Richard Matthew (eds.), *Reframing the Agenda: The Impact of*

NGO and Middle Power Cooperation in International Security Policy; Praegerl, Westport l, 2003, pp. 23-38Collaboration.

Rutherford, Kenneth R., 'Nongovernmental Organisations and the Landmine Ban', in Richard Anthony Matthew, Bryan McDonald, and Kenneth R. Rutherford (eds.), *Landmines And Human Security: International Politics And War's Hidden Legacy*; State University of New York Pressl, Albanyl, 2006, pp. 51-66.

---, 'The Evolving Arms Control Agenda: Implications of the Role of NGOs in Banning Antipersonnel Landmines', *World Politics,* Vol. 53, No. 1, October 2000, pp. 74-114.

Saad-Ghorayeb, Amal, *Hizbu'llah: Politics and Religion*; Pluto Press, London 2002.

Sahadevan, P., 'Sri Lanka's War for Peace and the LTTE's Commitment to Armed Struggle', in Omprakash Mishra and Sucheta Ghosh (eds.), *Terrorism and Low Intensity Conflict in South Asian Region*; Manak Publicationsl, New Delhil, 2003, pp. 284-315.

Samaranayakea, Gamini, 'Political Terrorism of the Liberation Tigers of Tamil Eelam (LTTE) in Sri Lanka', *South Asia: Journal of South Asian Studies,* Vol. 30, No. 1, 2007, pp. 171-83.

Samii, Abbas William, 'A Stable Structure on Shifting Sands: Assessing the Hizbullah-Iran-Syria Relationship', *Middle East Journal,* Vol. 62, No. 1, Winter 2008, pp. 32-53.

Schartz, Peter, *The Art of the Long View*; Doubleday, Hew York 1991.

Schelling, Thomas C., *The Strategy of Conflict*; A Galaxy Book, Oxford University Press New York 1963.

Schmidt, Gustav, *The Politics and Economics of Appeasement: British Foreign Policy in the 1930s*; St Martin's Press, New York 1986.

Schwartz, Barry, et al., 'Maximizing Versus Satisficing: Happiness Is a Matter of Choice', *Journal of Personality and Social Psychology,* Vol. 83, No. 5, 2002, pp. 1178-97.

Schwenninger, Sherle R., 'Revamping American Grand Strategy', *World Policy Journal,* Vol. 20, No. 3, Fall 2003, pp. 25-44.

Security, Programme National, 'National Security: Strategy and Work Programme 2007-2008', in Ministry of the Interior and Kingdom Relations (ed.); (The Hague, May 2007).

Short, Anthony, *The Communist insurrection in Malaya, 1948-1960*; Frederick Muller Limited, London 1975.

Short, Nicola, 'The Role of NGOs in the Ottawa Process to Ban Landmines', *International Negotiation,* Vol. 4, No. 3, 1999, pp. 481-502.

Sil, Rudra and Katzenstein, Peter J., 'Analytic Eclecticism in the Study of World Politics: Reconfiguring Problems and Mechanisms across Research Traditions', *Perspectives on Politics,* Vol. 8, No. 2, June 2010, pp. 411-31.

Simon, Herbert A., 'Human Nature in Politics: The Dialogue of Psychology with Political Science', *The American Political Review,* Vol. 79, No. 2, 1985, pp. 293-304.

Slaughter, Anne-Marie, 'America's Path: Grand Strategy for the Next Administration', in Richard Fontaine and Kristin M. Lord (eds.), *America's Path: Grand Strategy for the Next Administration*; Center for a New American Securityl, Washingtonl, May 2012, pp. 43-56.

Smith, Steve, 'Dialogue and the Reinforcement of Orthodoxy in International Relations', *International Studies Review,* Vol. 5, No. 1, 2003, pp. 141-43.

Snider, Lewis W., 'Identifying the Elements of State Power: "Where Do We Begin"?', *Comparative Political Studies,* Vol. 20, No. 3, October 1987 pp. 314-56.

Snyder, Jack, 'One World, Rival Theories', *Foreign Policy,* Vol., No. 145, November/ December 2004 pp. 52-62.

Spear, Joanna and Williams, Phil, 'Belief Systems and Foreign Policy: The Cases of Carter and Reagan', in Richard Little and Steve Smith (eds.), *Belief Systems and the Study of International Relations*; Basil Blackwelll, New Yorkl, 1988, pp. 190-208.

Spellman, Barbara A. and Holyoak, Keith J., 'If Saddam is Hitler Then Who Is George Bush? Analogical Mapping Btween Systems of Social Roles', *Journal of Personality and Social Psychology,* Vol. 62, No. 6, 1991, pp. 913-33.

Stein, Janice Gross, 'Foreign Policy Decision Making: Rational, Psychological, and Neurological Models', in Steve Smith (ed.), *Foreign Policy: Theories, Actors and Cases* Oxford University Pressl, Oxfordl, 2007, pp. 101-16.

Sterling-Folker, Jennifer, 'Constructivist Approaches', in Jennifer Sterling-Folker (ed.), *Making Sense of International Relations Theory*; Lynne Rienner Publishersl, Boulderl, 2006, pp. 115-22.

Steuerle, C. Eugene, *Contemporary U.S. Tax Policy: 2nd edition*; Urban Institute Press, Washington 2008.

Stoker, Gerry, 'Blockages on the Road to Relevance: Why has Political Science Failed to Deliver?', *European Political Science,* Vol. 9, No. 1, 2010, pp. S72-S84.

Stubbs, Richard, *Hearts And Minds In Guerrilla Warfare: The Malayan Emergency 1948-1960*; Oxford University Press, Oxford 1989.

Suri, Jeremi, *Power and Protest: Global Revolution and the Rise of Detente*; Harvard University Press, Cambridge 2003.

Tago, Atsushi, 'Is there an aid-for-participation deal?: US economic and military aid policy to coalition forces (non)participants', *International Relations of the Asia-Pacific,* Vol. 8, No. 3, 2008, pp. 379-98.

Tammita-Delgoda, SinhaRaja, *Review Essay: Sri Lanka's Ethnic Conflict* Manekshaw Paper 22A; Centre for Land Warfare Studies, New Delhi 2010.

Tarling, Nicholas, "Ah-Ah': Britain and the Bandung Conference of 1955', *Journal of Southeast Asian Studies,* Vol. 23, No. 1, 1992, pp. 74-111.

Tarnoff, Curt, *The Marshall Plan: Design, Accomplishments, and Relevance to the Present*, Report 97-62; Congressional Research Service, The Library of Congress, Washington 1997.

Tata, Juan Carlos Di, et al., 'IMF Country Report No. 07/101: Islamic Republic of Iran: Statistical Appendix'; (Washington, D.C.: International Monetary Fund, 9 February 2007).

Thomas, Daniel C., *The Helsinki Effect: International Norms, Human Rights, and the Demise of Communism*; Princeton University Press Princeton 2001.

Tilly, Charles, *Coercion, Capital, and European States, AD 990-1990*; Basil Blackwell, Cambridge 1990.

Toal, Gerard, 'Problematizing Geopolitics: Survey, Statesmanship and Strategy', *Transactions of the Institute of British Geographers, New Series*, Vol. 19, No. 3, 1994, pp. 259-72.

Tooze, Adam, *The Wages of Destruction: The Making and the Breaking of the Nazi Economy*; Viking, New York 2007.

Trachtenberg, Marc, *A Constructed Peace: The Making of the European Settlement 1945-1963* Princeton University Press, Princeton 1999.

Ubayasiri, Kasun, 'An illusive leader's annual speech ', *Ejournalist: a refereed media journal,* Vol. 6, No. 1, 2006, pp. 1-27.

'UNESCO Constitution', 1945 <portal.unesco.org/en/ev.php-URL_ID=15244&URL_DO=DO_TOPIC&URL_SECTION=201.html>, accessed 24 June 2013.

Unit, Human Security, *Human Security Handbook* United Nations, New York 2016.

Van-Ham, Peter, *Social Power in International Politics*; Routledge, Abingdon 2010.

Vance, Cyrus, *Hard Choices: Critical Years in America's Foreign Policy*; Simon and Shuster, New York 1983.

Vatahov, Ivan, 'US recognises 'functioning' economy', *The Sofia Echo: http://sofiaecho.com/2003/03/06/630528_us-recognises-functioning-economy,* 6 March 2003.

Vennesson, Pascal, 'Competing Visions for the European Union Grand Strategy ', *European Foreign Affairs Review,* Vol. 15, No. 1, 2010, pp. 57-75.

Vertzberger, Yaacov Y. I., *The World In Their Minds: Information Processing, Cognition and Perception in Foreign Decision-Making* Stanford University Press, Stanford 1990.

---, 'Foreign Policy Decisionmakers As Practical-Intuitive Historians: Applied History and Its Shortcomings ', *International Studies Quarterly* Vol. 30, No. 2, June 1986, pp. 223-47.

Vivekanandan, Jayashree, *Interrogating International Relations: India's Strategic Practice and the Return of History* Routledge, New Delhi 2011.

Voorde, Cécile Van de, 'Sri Lankan Terrorism: Assessing and Responding to the Threat of the Liberation Tigers of Tamil Eelam (LTTE)', *Police Practice and Research,* Vol. 6, No. 2, May 2005, pp. 181-99.

Vuori, Juha A., 'Illocutionary Logic and Strands of Securitization: Applying the Theory of Securitization to the Study of Non-Democratic Political Orders', *European Journal of International Relations,* Vol. 14, No. 1, 2008, pp. 65-99.

W.T.Sherman, 'The Grand Strategy of the War of the Rebellion', *The Century Illustrated Monthly Magazine*, Vol. 36, 1888, pp. 597-98.

Walsh, James P., 'Managerial and Organizational Cognition: Notes from a Trip Down Memory Lane', *Organization Science*, Vol. 6, No. 3, May-June 1995, pp. 280-321.

Waltz, Kenneth N., *Theory of International Politics*, First Edition edn.; McGraw-Hill, Inc, New York 1979.

Wapner, Paul, 'The Campaign to Ban Antipersonnel Landmines and Global Civil Society', in Richard Anthony Matthew, Bryan McDonald, and Kenneth R. Rutherford (eds.), *Landmines And Human Security: International Politics And War's Hidden Legacy*; State University of New York Pressl, Albanyl, 2006, pp. 251-68.

Ward, James H., *A Manual of Naval Tactics: Together with a Brief Critical Analysis of the Principal Modern Naval battles*; D. Appleton & Company, New York 1859.

Ward, Michael J., et al., *Driving Your Company's Value: Strategic Benchmarking for Value* John Wiley & Sons, Inc., Hoboken 2004.

Watteville, H. de, 'The Conduct of Modern War', *The RUSI Journal*, Vol. 75, No. 497, 1930, pp. 70-81.

Wehrey, Frederic, et al., *Dangerous But Not Omnipotent: Exploring the Reach and Limitations of Iranian Power in the Middle East*; RAND Corporation, Santa Monica 2009.

Weigley, Russell F., *The Age of Battles: The Quest for Decisive Warfare from Breitenfeld to Waterloo*; Pimlico, London 1991.

Westad, Odd Arne, *The Global Cold War: Third World Interventions and the Making of Our Times*; Cambridge University Press, Cambridge 2007.

Wexler, Lesley, 'The International Deployment Of Shame, Second-Best Responses, And Norm Entrepreneurship: The Campaign To Ban Landmines And The Landmine Ban Treaty ', *Arizona Journal of International and Comparative Law*, Vol. 20, No. 3, 2003, pp. 561-606.

White, Nicholas J., 'Capitalism and Counter-Insurgency? Business and Government in the Malayan Emergency, 1948 57 ', *Modern Asian Studies* Vol. 32, No. 1, Feburary, 1998, pp. 149-77.

---, 'The Frustrations of Development: British Business and the Late Colonial State in Malaya, 1945 -57 ', *Journal of Southeast Asian Studies* Vol. 28, No. 1, March, 1997, pp. 103-19.

Wiegand, Krista E., 'Reformation of a Terrorist Group: Hezbollah as a Lebanese Political Party', *Studies in Conflict & Terrorism*, Vol. 32, No. 8, 2009, pp. 669-80.

Williams, Jody and Goose, Stephen, 'The International Campaign to Ban Landmines', in Maxwell A. Cameron, Brian W. Tomlin, and Robert J. Lawson (eds.), *To Walk without Fear: The Global Movement to Ban Landmines*; Oxford University Pressl, Don MIllsl, 1998, pp. 20-47.

'Winning the shooting war in Malaya', *Observer*, 4 January 1953.

Winslow, Deborah and Woost, Michael D., 'Articulations of Economy and Ethnic Conflict in Sri Lanka', in Deborah Winslow and Michael D. Woost (eds.),

Economy, Culture, and Civil War in Sri Lanka; Indiana University Pressl, Bloomingtonl, 2004, pp. 1-30.

Wivel, Anders and Oest, Kajsa Ji Noe, 'Security, profit or shadow of the past? Explaining the security strategies of microstates', *Cambridge Review of International Affairs,* Vol. 23, No. 3, September 2010, pp. 429-.

Wohlforth, William Curti, *The Elusive Balance: Power and Perceptions during the Cold War* Cornell University Press, Ithaca 1993.

Wolfers, Arnold, '"National Security" as an Ambiguous Symbol', *Political Science Quarterly,* Vol. 67, No. 4, December 1952, pp. 481-502.

Wright, Donald P. and Reese, Timothy R., *On Point II: Transition to the New Campaign: The United States Army in Operation Iraqi Freedom, May 2003-January 2005*; Combat Studies Institute Press, US Army Combined Arms Center, Fort Leavenworth 2008.

Wright, Marshall, 'Memorandum to the President's Assistant for National Security Affairs (Kissinger), Washington, January 10 1970 ', in Louis J. Smith and David H. Herschler (eds.), *Foundations of Foreign Policy, 1969–1972,* Foreign Relations Of The United States, 1969–1976: Volume I; Department of Statel, Washingtonl, 2003, pp. 163.

Yarger, Harry R., 'Toward a Theory of Strategy: Art Lykke and the Army War College Strategy Model', in Jr. J. Boone Bartholomees (ed.), *U.S. Army War College Guide To National Security Policy And Strategy*; Strategic Studies Institutel, Carlisle Barracks, June 2006.

Yetiv, Steve A., *The Absence of Grand Strategy: The United States in the Persian Gulf, 1972-2005*; John Hopkins University Press, Baltimore 2008.

Yi, Wang, 'Peaceful Development and the Chinese Dream of National Rejuvenation', *China Institute of International Studies,* Vol., No. January/ February, 2014, pp. 17-44.

Zacher, Mark W. and Matthew, Richard A., 'Liberal International Theory: Common Threads, Divergent Strands ', in Charles W. Kegley (ed.), *Controversies in International Relations Theory: Realism and the Neoliberal Challenge*; St Martin's Pressl, New Yorkl, 1995, pp. 107-50.

Zubok, Vladislav, 'The Soviet Union and détente of the 1970s', *Cold War History,* Vol. 8, No. 4, November 2008, pp. 427-47.

---, 'The Soviet Union and Détente of the 1970s', *Cold War History,* Vol. 8, No. 4, November, 2008, pp. 427-47.

Zubok, Vladislav M., *A Failed Empire: The Soviet Union in the Cold War from Stalin to Gorbachev*; The University of North Carolina Press, Chapel Hill 2009

Index

Made in the USA
Monee, IL
02 January 2022

87783949R00163